Boom and Bust
in St. Louis

Boom and Bust in St. Louis
A Cardinals History, 1885 to the Present

JON DAVID CASH

Foreword by JEFFREY KITTEL

McFarland & Company, Inc., Publishers
Jefferson, North Carolina

LIBRARY OF CONGRESS CATALOGUING-IN-PUBLICATION DATA

Names: Cash, Jon David, author.
Title: Boom and bust in St. Louis : a Cardinals history,
    1885 to the present / Jon David Cash ; Foreword by Jeffrey Kittel.
Description: Jefferson, North Carolina : McFarland & Company, Inc.,
    Publishers, 2020 | Includes bibliographical references and index.
Identifiers: LCCN 2020027729 | ISBN 9781476680835 (paperback :
    acid free paper) ∞
    ISBN 9781476638966 (ebook)
Subjects: LCSH: St. Louis Cardinals (Baseball team)—History. |
    Baseball—Economic aspects—Missouri—St. Louis.
Classification: LCC GV875.S3 C39 2020 | DDC 796.357/640977866—dc23
LC record available at https://lccn.loc.gov/2020027729

BRITISH LIBRARY CATALOGUING DATA ARE AVAILABLE

ISBN (print) 978-1-4766-8083-5
ISBN (ebook) 978-1-4766-3896-6

© 2020 Jon David Cash. All rights reserved

*No part of this book may be reproduced or transmitted in any form
or by any means, electronic or mechanical, including photocopying
or recording, or by any information storage and retrieval system,
without permission in writing from the publisher.*

Front cover: (top) 1909 baseball card of player/manager Roger Bresnahan,
(middle) the 1911 St. Louis Cardinals team (both Library of Congress),
(bottom, left to right) first baseman Albert Pujols at bat in 2009 (Leoraúl Torres),
Senator Harry S. Truman of Missouri shakes hands with opposing managers,
Billy Southworth of the St. Louis Cardinals and Luke Sewell of the St. Louis
Browns at the 1944 World Series (S.L. Scott, Harry S. Truman Library)

Printed in the United States of America

McFarland & Company, Inc., Publishers
  Box 611, Jefferson, North Carolina 28640
  www.mcfarlandpub.com

To my two older sisters,
Becky and Marilyn,
as well as our parents
whom we still miss,
David K. Cash (1924–1997) and
Hazel Hancock Cash (1929–2009)

Table of Contents

Acknowledgments — ix

Foreword by Jeffrey Kittel: Roots of Early St. Louis Ball-Playing — 1

Preface — 15

Introduction: St. Louis and the Midwest and the Frontier of MLB — 23

1. The Cardinals' Family Robison — 45
2. Branch Rickey, Sam Breadon and Creation of the Farm System — 52
3. The Rajah's Redbirds of 1926 — 60
4. Managerial Merry-Go-Round — 69
5. Rise and Decline of the Gas House Gang — 81
6. St Louis Swifties — 92
7. Slicing the Baloney Too Thin — 107
8. Bing Devine Ends a Pennant Drought — 118
9. El Birdos — 129
10. Vern Rapp, Ken Boyer and Whitey Herzog — 135
11. Exit Anheuser-Busch, Enter Tony La Russa — 141

Epilogue: St. Louis Cardinals Baseball, 2012–2019 — 155

Appendix A: St. Louis Cardinals Baseball Franchise Records, 1882–2019 — 157

Appendix B: Single-Season and Career Leaders for Cardinal Franchise, 1882–2019 — 165

Table of Contents

Appendix C: Noteworthy Achievements — 166
Chapter Notes — 171
Bibliography — 177
Index — 191

Acknowledgments

Along my journey to becoming a historian of the St. Louis Cardinals discussed in detail in the Preface to this book, I have met many helpful people. Some of them are still living and some of them are not, but they all assisted me in understanding the significance of St. Louis baseball. I want to thank my entire dissertation committee at the University of Oregon (chair Daniel Pope, Richard Maxwell Brown, Jack Maddex, Larry Singell, and Kelly Eakin); Paul MacFarlane of *The Sporting News*; Ralph Horton of Horton Publishing; Paula Homan, manager and curator of the St. Louis Cardinals Hall of Fame and Museum; Jeffrey Kittel, who was kind enough to contribute the foreword of this book; Jim Rygelski, who authored an influential journal article on Chris Von der Ahe and, with Robert Tiemann, wrote *10 Rings: Stories of the St. Louis Cardinals World Championships*; Steve Pona, president of the Saint Louis Baseball Historical Society; John Brenner, whom I first met when he was an editor at the University of Missouri Press, but who now works as the managing editor of the State Historical Society of Missouri and its first-class historical journal, *Missouri Historical Review*; everybody else from the staff of the University of Missouri Press who helped me with the publication of my previous book, *Before They Were Cardinals: Major League Baseball in Nineteenth-Century St. Louis* (Mr. Clair Willcox, Jane Lago, Karen Caplinger, and Beth Chandler); and, as always, all of my friends from my time spent in Arkansas and Oregon and my family scattered across the United States from coast to coast.

I would like to extend special thanks to Gary Mitchem, acquisitions editor of McFarland, the large publisher in the small mountain town of Jefferson in western North Carolina, for all of his help in publishing this book; John Horne, rights and reproduction coordinator at the National Baseball Hall of Fame in Cooperstown, New York, for all of his help in providing photographs; Laura R. Jolley, assistant director of manuscripts

Acknowledgments

with the State Historical Society of Missouri in Columbia, for her help in securing photographic prints, particularly the Daniel Fitzpatrick cartoon of Pepper Martin for Chapter 4; and Laurie Austin, from Audiovisual Archives at the Harry S. Truman Library in Independence, Missouri, for helping me obtain our front cover photo. Finally, I am extremely appreciative for four former Cardinals from North Carolina, who either talked or corresponded with me, or in some cases did both: Pat Crawford, Burgess Whitehead, Stu Martin, and Enos "Country" Slaughter.

Foreword
by Jeffrey Kittel
Roots of Early St. Louis Ball-Playing

"Here stands baseball's perfect warrior. Here stands baseball's perfect knight."

Those words, spoken by baseball commissioner Ford Frick upon the retirement of Stan Musial, are inscribed on the base of a statue honoring the greatest Cardinal of all time. The Musial statue, which now stands at the main entrance of Busch Stadium, home of the team for which Stan the Man played for 22 years, was originally located near the corner of Walnut and Broadway, outside of what was the right-field entrance to old Busch Memorial Stadium.

Opening in 1966, Busch Memorial Stadium was built as part of an effort to revitalize the downtown business district in St. Louis, an area which had fallen on hard times in the years after the Second World War. The Jefferson National Expansion Memorial, which includes the Gateway Arch, had opened a year earlier and was part of the same effort to bring people, tourists, and dollars to the downtown area. These two great monuments captured the essence of what St. Louis was: a baseball town with a frontier past. Sitting in the grandstands at old Busch or the new park, looking across the infield and the spacious green of the outfield, one could glimpse the Arch towering over the city and capture, in one image, what St. Louis was and what it is.

However, to make room for the new downtown ballpark and the Arch grounds, the city tore down blocks of its history. A great deal of the architectural history of St. Louis has been lost, only to be caught in glimpses around Cupples Station, just west of the ballpark, or on La-

Foreword by Jeffrey Kittel

The Stan Musial statue at its original site of Walnut and Broadway, outside of old Busch Stadium (David K. Cash, July 1986).

clede's Landing, a bar and restaurant district just north of the Arch. The St. Louis that once existed was swept away in hopes of building a new and better city.

Two buildings that survived the revitalization efforts and afford a visitor a glimpse into the old St. Louis are the Old Cathedral and the Old Courthouse. The Basilica of St. Louis, King of France, built in the 1830s, was the first Catholic cathedral west of the Mississippi, and the site was used as a place of Catholic worship going back to the founding of the city. The Old St. Louis County Courthouse, best known as the site where Dred Scott sued for his freedom, was built in the 1820s. Both of these buildings, which are located just west of the Arch, were constructed on land donated by prominent men in St. Louis history. The Old Cathedral is located on a plot that was given to the city by Auguste Choteau, just west of the Choteau/Laclede family home, while the Old Courthouse stands on land donated by Choteau and Jean Baptiste Charles Lucas. By the beginning of the 19th century, these two men were the wealthiest men in the city, as well as the two largest landowners, and their progeny would play important roles not only in the history of St. Louis but also in the history of 19th century baseball.

Roots of Early St. Louis Ball-Playing

The Old Cathedral, the first Catholic cathedral west of the Mississippi, built in the 1830s on land given to St. Louis by Auguste Choteau, with the Gateway Arch looming in the background (David K. Cash, July 1986).

The St. Louis of Choteau and Lucas no longer exists and has been replaced by a modern city. Their St. Louis, the St. Louis that existed at the beginning of the 19th century, was a fur-trading village that hugged the Mississippi River. It was a small town with only a few dirt streets, mostly wood buildings, and around a thousand people. Walking the modern, paved streets of St. Louis today and visiting the downtown landmarks such as the Arch, Laclede's Landing, the Old Cathedral, the Old Courthouse, and the ballpark, you trace the outlines of the old colonial French trading village, an area where the city was born and where baseball in St. Louis has its origins.

Auguste Choteau first came to what would become St. Louis in December of 1763, arriving on the west bank of the Mississippi, just south of where the Missouri River flowed into the Father of Waters, along with Pierre Laclede Liquest, the common-law husband of the 14-year-old Choteau's mother, Marie-Therese Bourgeois. Laclede's company had gained the rights to "the exclusive trade with the savages of the Missouri, and all

Foreword by Jeffrey Kittel

the nations residing west of the Mississippi,"[1] and he and his step-son had traveled upriver from New Orleans to find a suitable site to establish a center for the new company's fur-trading enterprises. As Shirley Christian wrote in *Before Lewis and Clark*, "[the] founders of St. Louis were not fleeing injustice, nor were they driven by religious sentiments or political ideals. Neither did they aspire to become gentleman farmers overseeing vast plantations worked by slaves. They simply wanted to make money and provide well for themselves and their families. The business of St. Louis, and of Laclede and the Choteaus, was to be the fur trade."[2]

The two men had traveled as far north as the confluence of the Mississippi and Missouri rivers, "studying topography and the quality of land extending inland from the river,"[3] before Laclede found the perfect spot a few miles south of the confluence. Historian James Neal Primm described what Laclede and Choteau had found. "A gently sloping plateau," he wrote, "terminating in a rocky bluff safely above the river's flood presented an ideal site for his headquarters. A break in the bluff afforded easy acess to the river; and there was plenty of timber for firewood and lumber, outcroppings of stone for building, flowing springs, good drainage, and no deep ravines to hinder the laying out of streets."[4]

"He was delighted to see the situation," Choteau later remembered, "[and] he did not hesitate a moment to form there the establishment that he proposed. Besides the beauty of the site, he found there all the advantages that one could desire to found a settlement which might become very considerable hereafter."[5] Marking the site, Laclede notched several trees before returning with the young Choteau to the French colonial settlement of Fort de Chartres, 50 miles downriver, where Laclede spent the winter "procuring all things necessary for the settlement—men, provisions, tools, &c."[6]

Busy with the planning and organization of the new enterprise, Laclede placed Choteau in charge of the construction of the new trading village. "You will proceed and land at the place where we marked the trees," he instructed his teenage step-son, "[and you] will commence to have the place cleared, and build a large shed to contain the provisions and the tools, and some small cabins, to lodge the men."[7] The boy headed north, up the cold river, in February of 1764, along with 30 men, and arrived at what would become St. Louis on March 14. "[On] the morning of the next day," Choteau wrote, "I put the men to work."[8] Quickly the small group began clearing away trees on land that would one day become the grounds of the Gateway Arch, constructing the buildings that Laclede, who would join the men in April, had ordered, and laying the foundation of a future great city.

Over the next 40 years, the small village would prosper, adding over 1,000 people to the population, as Laclede's fur-trading enterprise grew in profitability. Physically, Laclede laid out the new town in a gridiron pattern, with three streets running parallel to the river, from the modern Laclede's Landing in the north to just south of where Busch Stadium stands today, intersected by shorter streets running east to west. To the west of the village lay the Commons, a wide stretch of prairie that was used for farming and pasturage. Among the new buildings of the village was a public Market house on First Street, the large, stone Choteau/Laclede home on Second Street, which originally served as a governmental office, and a stone fort tower, on Walnut Street, just west of Third Street. While the rest of the village was dominated by individual dwellings, a new structure erected in the 1780s would play a prominent role in the history of baseball in St. Louis.

A French soldier, cartographer, and engineer named Nicolas de Finiels arrived in St. Louis in 1797, at a time when the city was under Spanish governance. Finiels, traveling from Philadelphia with his wife and mother-in-law, had come to St. Louis to oversee improvements to the city's defenses. While his appointment would, in 1798, be rejected by the Spanish government in Madrid, Finiels's time in the area produced "two of the most valuable source documents pertaining to Upper Louisiana in colonial times: a lengthy memoir titled *An Account of Upper Louisiana* and a meticulously drawn map of the central Mississippi River valley."[9] In Finiels's memoir, he mentions a windmill "[built] of wood in St. Louis on the slope of the plateau where the fort is located."[10] The wooden windmill that Finiels had seen in St. Louis in the late 1790s and that had fallen into disrepair and disuse by the time he had arrived in the city was locally referred to as Motard's Mill. It was at Motard's Mill that the history of St. Louis baseball began.

Born in Avignon, France, around 1722, Joseph Motard immigrated to St. Louis within the first decade of the founding of the city, seeking his fortune, like Laclede and others, in the fur trade. Described as "one of the principle merchants"[11] of the city, "a major St. Louis fur merchant for twenty years,"[12] and as a "goldsmith,"[13] Motard, in the late 1780s, received a grant of a lot measuring 200 square feet just south of the fort tower. Through the lot flowed a creek that ran from a large pond down into the Mississippi, and Motard was granted the land by Don Manuel Perez, the

Foreword by Jeffrey Kittel

Spanish lieutenant-governor, under the stipulation that he develop a mill on the property, in order to process the grain grown by the community on the Commons.

When, specifically, Motard built his mill and what, exactly, the mill looked like is a subject of debate. It's clear that the mill was built in the mid to late 1780s, and it is possible that it was built as early as 1784[14] or as late as 1789.[15] It is known that a gentleman named Francois Cotard was living on what was by then known as Mill Creek in 1788 and working for Motard, cultivating an orchard of apple trees.[16] Based on this account, it appears that Motard was already in possession of the land on Mill Creek before 1788, had already taken steps to develop it, and, therefore, the mill most likely had already been built by the time Cotard was living there. The mill itself was described by Finiels as having been built of wood, and Charles Peterson, in his history of colonial St. Louis, agrees that it was a wooden structure.[17] However, there is at least one source that describes Motard's Mill as having been built of stone.[18] To complicate the matter even more, it is entirely possible that the base of the mill was built of stone and the upper structure of wood.

While it is difficult to pinpoint the date of the construction of the mill and what materials were used to build it, all sources agree on its location. Motard built his windmill just south of what became known as Fort San Carlos, the old fort tower that once stood near the modern intersection of Walnut and Fourth Street. Just one block west of that is the intersection of Walnut and Broadway, where Stan Musial's statue once stood, and one block south of that is the modern site of Busch Stadium. Motard's Mill most likely stood on the grounds now occupied by the St. Louis Cardinals and where millions of baseball fans come to watch their favorite team play the game they all love. In an interesting display of convergence, the present history of St. Louis baseball takes place at the site of the earliest known instance of ball-playing in the city. The modern Cardinals play ball at the same location where the young Henry Gratiot and his friends played ball in St. Louis over 200 years earlier.

The first reference to ball-playing in St. Louis is found in the papers of Theodore Hunt, who was the recorder of land titles in Missouri for the United States government,[19] and, in the early part of the 19th century, played an important role in settling complicated and muddled colonial land claims in St. Louis, a city that had been governed by France, Spain, and United States. Hunt also happened to be married to Anne Lucas, the daughter of J. B. C. Lucas, one of the two largest landowners in St. Louis, and one can imagine that, given the nature of his job, he was a rather influential figure in a city where wealth and power were tied closely to land ownership.[20]

In 1825, Henry Gratiot was desposed by Theodore Hunt regarding a disputed land claim and, in the course of the desposition Gratiot was asked if he was familiar with Motard's Mill. He answered that he had "a perfect knowledge of the situation of Motard's windmill, for when a Boy he has frequently played Ball against this same mill."[21] Gratiot's testimony is significant because it is the earliest known reference to ball-playing in St. Louis and Missouri and is also one of the earliest references to ball-playing west of the Appalachian Mountains. Louis Houck, in the second volume of his history of Missouri, mentions Gratiot's testimony, adding that Gratiot considered the mill as "a sort of resort"[22] for the boys and girls of the village, a place where they often congregated and played.

The young ball-playing Henry Gratiot was a member of one of the most prominent families in St. Louis. His mother, Victoire, was the daughter of Pierre Laclede and the half-sister of Auguste Choteau, while his father, Charles Gratiot, was a member of a wealthy Swiss Huguenot family. The elder Gratiot came to the New World around 1764 and, like his father-in-law, made his fortune in the fur-trading business.[23] During the American Revolution, he was living in Cahokia, across the river from St. Louis, and provided George Rogers Clark with $8,000 worth of supplies, support that insured the success of Clark's expedition and helped gain the Illinois Country for the new American nation.[24] In 1781, after his marriage, the successful merchant moved to St. Louis, where he lived the rest of his life, serving at various times as a judge and accumulating large landholdings in the city.

His son, Henry, who was born in St. Louis on April 12, 1789, inherited Charles Gratiot's entrepreneurial and adventurous spirit. At the time of Henry's birth, George Washington had not yet been inaugurated as President of the United States, the British still held forts in the newly organized Northwest Territory, the French Revolution was about to break out, and St. Louis was part of the Spanish Empire, after the French ceded their territories in Louisiana following the French and Indian War. While the young Gratiot may have been born under Spanish rule, St. Louis and her citizens "were thoroughly and completely French, in language, habits, and thought."[25] A Frenchman by culture, a subject of imperial Spain, and, after March 10, 1804, a citizen of the United States, he grew up in a cosmopolitan, frontier environment that was unique in American history.

Foreword by Jeffrey Kittel

Gratiot must be remembered as one of the most significant pioneer-era, St. Louis ball-players, whose deposition before Theodore Hunt gives us the earliest references to ball-playing in the city's history and one of the earliest references to ball-playing in the American West. Because of this testimony, we know that the children of St. Louis engaged in ball games in the 18th century, a hundred years before the St. Louis Cardinals ever took the field. But Gratiot's testimony raises one rather important question: What kind of ball-game were the young Henry Gratiot and his friends playing?

While it's an impossible question to answer with any certainty, there are clues in Gratiot's testimony and his circumstances that allow for speculation. What we can say for certain is that he was not playing baseball. The New York game of baseball, as defined by rules codified in 1857, obviously did not exist during Gratiot's lifetime and, therefore, he had to have played a different type of ball-game. However, a series of bat and ball games, roughly defined as the American family of baseball games, had developed in North America over the course of several centuries. These games, from which the New York game of baseball evolved, came over to the New World with the first colonists and spread across the continent, as Americans settled the Trans-Appalachian West. Since this form of proto-baseball did not reach St. Louis and the Illinois Country until around 1810, at the earliest, it's unlikely that Gratiot was playing any of the variants of American baseball in existence at the time. Since he wasn't playing baseball or early American baseball variants such as town-ball, trap-ball or cat, what kind of ball-game was Gratiot playing?

An important clue comes from an address that Elihu Washburne, a former congressman from Illinois, minister to France, and the shortest-serving Secretary of State in United States history, gave to the State Historical Society of Wisconsin in 1884. Washburne, who was also Henry Gratiot's son-in-law, stated that the people of St. Louis, when Gratiot was a young boy, "were thoroughly and completely French, in language, habits, and thought."[26] St. Louis, in the 18th century, was culturally a French city, and Gratiot, being a St. Louisan, was a Frenchman, regardless of whether he was a subject of the French or Spanish empires. As someone who was French in habit and living in a town that was thoroughly and completely French, it seems likely that Gratiot would have been playing a French ball-game.

It's important to note the influence that culture had on the spread of baseball across the United States. When the first colonists arrived in the United States, they brought their culture with them, and ball-playing was part of that culture. In 1609, a group of Polish laborers at the Jamestown colony are known to have played a type of bat and ball game called pilka palantowa that was popular in central Europe.[27] William Bradford, the governor of Plymouth Colony, noted that, in 1621, some members of the colony were playing stool-ball, a bat and ball game that had been popular in England for over 100 years.[28] The European settlers of the New World were ball-players and came from a culture that embraced ball-playing. That culture of ball-playing flourished in the new colonies, evolving into a unique family of American baseball games that would spread across the continent. This is specifically true of the English colonies but is most likely also true of the French colonies in America.

While an abundance of sources support the idea that the English settlers brought their ball-playing culture to America in the 17th century, there is much less evidence of ball-playing among the French settlers, and Gratiot's testimony is particularly unique in that respect. Almost all of the references to ball-playing that appear in the earliest histories of New France involve Native American ball-games but, while the history of Native American ball-playing is fascinating and worthy of study, it does not appear to have had much of an impact on the development of the American family of baseball games. There were also numerous references to the way in which the French settlers of the Illinois Country spent what little leisure time they had, but they do not mention ball-playing, instead stressing the French love of card-playing, horse-racing and gambling. So the evidence of French ball-playing in the Illinois Country is scant, but it does exist.

The new American Territory of Illinois was created in 1809, with the old French town of Kaskaskia as its capital. That summer, the new territorial legislature, under the guidance of Governor Ninian Edwards, met in the capital to create a new law code for the territory, relying heavily on the law codes of Indiana, Kentucky, and Virginia.[29] One of the new laws passed was "An Act to prevent unlawful gaming" and outlawed gambling on "cards, dice, tables, tennis, bowles or any other game or games whatsoever, or at any horse race, cock fighting, or any other sport or pastime."[30] This law gives a rather interesting look at what the people in the Illinois Territory liked to do with their free time and specifically mentions two ball-games: tennis and boules. Both were popular French games, and the implication is that these games were played in Illinois at the beginning of the 19th century, which shows the influence of French culture in the old Illinois Country.

Tennis developed from a French game called jeu de paume, whose origins may date to the 14th century, and variants could be played indoors or outdoors and with or without a racket.[31] Boules was another French game, known as jeu de boules, that was played as early as the 15th century and developed from an earlier game known as jeu de mail. The modern games of bocce, petanque, and billiards are all descendants of jeu de boule.[32] If tennis and boules were played in the old French towns of Illinois in 1809, it's quite likely that they were being played in the old French town of St. Louis during Henry Gratiot's youth, and it's possible that Gratiot and his friends played some variant of jeu de paume or jeu de boules in St. Louis during the late 18th century.

Within two 19th century French children's books are other possibilities. The fourth edition of *Les Jeux des Jeunes Garcons*, which in English translates to *Games for Young Boys*, was published in Paris in 1815, included a description of a game called la balle empoisonee, or poisoned ball. David Block, in *Baseball Before We Knew It*, describes:

> Eight or ten children divide themselves into two teams. In a courtyard or in a large square area, four corners are marked, one as the home base and the others as bases which the runners must touch in succession. Straws are drawn; the team that wins occupies the home base. The players of the other team place themselves among the other bases at suitable distances. One of their team serves the ball to one of the players at home base. This one repels the ball, and runs to first base, to the second and to others if he has time.
>
> Players from the team on the field must pick up the ball as promptly as possible in order to touch or hit one of the runners before he reaches base. In that case, the player who has been hit by "the poisoned ball" suspends his running, and his team has lost the home base. His team then becomes the serving team."[33]

Add a bat and poisoned ball seems rather familiar. Robert Henderson, in *Ball, Bat, and Bishop*, implies that there actually was a bat used in the game and states that poisoned ball "is clearly a fore-runner of baseball."[34]

However, there are problems with implying that poisoned ball was played in St. Louis in the late 18th century. For Henry Gratiot to play poisoned ball at Motard's Mill, the game would have to be a popular, traditional bat and ball game played in France in the 18th century and transported to the New World with French settlers. This is possible, but there is no evidence supporting the idea. It's also possible, according to both Block and Henderson, that this was not a French game at all but rather an

Roots of Early St. Louis Ball-Playing

English game that crossed the Channel sometime in the 18th century.[35] So, while one must entertain the possibility that this clear fore-runner of baseball was being played in St. Louis in the late 1790s, it appears unlikely.

Another book that gives clues as to what kind of ball-games a young French boy may have been playing in the late 18th century is *Jeux des Adolescents*, or *Games for Youths*, published in 1856. This wonderful book contains descriptions of numerous French ball-games, along with illustrations of the games being played. Block finds the book significant for its description of la balle au baton, or stick-ball, a game similar to theque, which he believed was a possible direct ancestor of American baseball games.[36] But another game, which is mentioned in the book, was la balle au mur, or wall ball:

> You draw a horizontal line along the length of the wall, a meter or a meter and a half above the ground.... The simplest version is for two players. One will serve the ball, that is, throw it against the wall. The other one sends it back against the wall, either hitting it on the fly or after it has bounced once. The first player hits it back ... and it goes from one to another.
>
> Every ball that is missed, that is to say, every ball that a player cannot return against the wall, is a fault and counts for a certain number of points for his adversary. It is likewise a fault to hit the wall above the line. Finally, it is useless to say that it is not permitted to return the ball on the second bounce, or the third.[37]

La balle au mur sounds like a simple game that a group of young children could play against the wall of a windmill but, again, there is an obvious problem with the implication that one of the ball-games mentioned in *Jeaux des Adolescents* could have been played in late–18th century St. Louis. While Henry Gratiot was playing ball in the 1790s, the book wasn't published until the mid–19th century, when Gratiot was already dead. However, many of the games in the book, such as la balle au mur, appear to be simple, rudimentary and traditional children's games, and there is a good possibility that the popularity of these games go back several generations, if not several centuries, and that they were being played, in some variant, by French children in the 17th and 18th century. But there is no evidence supporting the idea that any of the games in *Jeux des Adolescents* was old enough and popular enough to have made it to the New World by the 18th century.

While it's impossible to say with any certainty whether or not Henry Gratiot played jeu de paume, jeu de boules, la balle empoisonee, la balle au baton, la balle au mur, or any other French ball-game, there is enough evidence to suggest the possibility of a ball-playing culture in the

Foreword by Jeffrey Kittel

French towns of the Illinois Country. There is ample evidence of French ball-games going back centuries that could have been transported to the New World by French settlers. There is the 1809 Illinois law outlawing gambling on ball-games, suggesting that these games were played in the old French towns. And there is Henry Gratiot's testimony that he and his friends played ball in St. Louis when he was a young boy. The references to ball-playing in the old French Illinois Country may be few and far between but, when added together, they present a picture of the first active ball-playing culture in an area that, less than 50 years after Henry Gratiot's death, would go baseball mad.

Joseph Motard's windmill failed to prosper and, by the beginning of the 19th century, it was in ruins—rotted, crumbling, and soon to be torn down. But the beginning of a ball-playing culture that took root at Motard's Mill blossomed over the next 200 years. Today, millions of people come every year to the spot of Henry Gratiot's youthful ball-playing to watch a more modern form of the game. As the fans cheer the Cardinals on at Busch Stadium, they unknowingly pay tribute to the pioneers of baseball in St. Louis. The love of the game so evident among Cardinal fans honors Henry Gratiot and the French pioneers who settled and built St. Louis and who played the first ball-games in the future Best Baseball Town in America.

There are many great baseball cities in the United States and many great baseball fans throughout the country, but the relationship that St. Louis has with the game is unique if not idiosyncratic. It is something that is ingrained in the culture of the city and something that defines that culture. The idea that St. Louis is a baseball town is almost a cliché at this point, but within that cliché exist truths that speak to the nature of who St. Louisans are as a people. It is our love of the game that binds us and it is the St. Louis Cardinals, as an institution that hold us together in the face of the myriad of things that would tear us apart. St. Louisans' love of baseball and, specifically, their love of the Cardinals transcends any economic, racial, religious, or gender differences that tear at us.

It is not possible to understand St. Louis and its history without understanding that. The history of baseball in the city, as evident in the story of Henry Gratiot, begins almost at the same time as the city's founding. Strange variants of the game were played by boys, girls, men, and women throughout the first half of the 19th century in the greater St. Louis area. The history of the Civil War in St. Louis is entwined with the early history of baseball in the area. One can see the history of the game when look-

Roots of Early St. Louis Ball-Playing

ing at the economic and population growth that the city experienced in the 19th century. How does one discuss the Great Depression in St. Louis without talking about the Gas House Gang? How does one talk about the Second World War in the city without discussing Stan Musial and the great war-era clubs he played on? How does one talk about the economic deterioration of downturn St. Louis during the 1960s and 1970s without talking about the impact of Busch Memorial Stadium? One cannot separate the history of baseball in St. Louis from the history of the city itself. Go look at James Neal Primm's *Lion of the Valley*, which is probably the best general history of St. Louis out there. There was no way for Primm to tell that story without writing about baseball and the Cardinals. If one were to write about the history of women in St. Louis, or Irish immigrants, or African Americans, you would have to discuss baseball and their participation in and love of the game. There is simply no way to understand the people of St. Louis, the city of St. Louis, and the history of St. Louis without understanding our love of the game and where that came from.

This book is, in many ways, the story of where St. Louisans' love of baseball came from, how it grew, and how it evolved. It is the story of one of the most important aspects of culture in the city. In my opinion, there is no one better to tell this story than Jon David Cash. His earlier book, *Before They Were Cardinals: Major League Baseball in Nineteenth-Century St. Louis*, is one of the most influential works on the history of 19th century baseball, and there is no better book on the subject of 19th century baseball in St. Louis. While there are numerous books about the history of baseball in St. Louis, most are popular histories written by journalists which contain countless errors in fact and propagate myths and legends which are provably false. It is an extraordinarily rare and wonderful occasion to see the history of baseball in St. Louis taken up and treated seriously by a historian of Cash's talent.

This is a book that is necessary. It is a book that needed to be written. It is not just another book about the Cardinals that spins yarns and tells tales. Cash applies an academic discipline to the subject that has been missing from previous histories of baseball in St. Louis. If one believes, as I do, that the history of St. Louis and the history of baseball in the city are so entwined as to be inseparable and that the defining characteristic of culture in St. Louis is a love of the game, then it is of the utmost significance that the subject matter be taken seriously and treated with respect. There is no one working in the field of baseball history that has done that better than Jon David Cash.

Foreword by Jeffrey Kittel

As a bonus, he happens to be a Cardinal fan. So not only do we have here a respectful and disciplined treatment of the history of baseball in St. Louis, we get it from someone who loves that history and someone who has lived it, breathed it, and experienced it. It has been my pleasure to converse with Jon over the years about 19th century St. Louis history but I don't believe that there has ever been one conversation that we have had that didn't involve some side-talk about the Cardinals and how they were playing. We both are creatures of that strange, idiosyncratic St. Louis baseball culture. This book that he has written is our history and the history of countless millions of people who, through the years, have bound themselves together through a shared love of baseball.

For ten years from 2007 to 2017, Jeffrey Kittel maintained the blog This Game of Games: St. Louis Baseball in the 19th Century. *He also wrote the chapter on St. Louis amateur baseball in* Base Ball Pioneers, 1850–1870 *(McFarland, 2012), edited by Peter Morris, William J. Ryczek, Jan Finkel, and Richard Malatzky, and collaborated with Steve Pona, Edward Achorn, and Jon David Cash on* Chris Von der Ahe: A Case for Hall of Fame Consideration *(St. Louis Baseball Historical Society, 2015). In addition, Kittell contributed to a pair of books compiled and edited by David Nemec:* Major League Baseball Profiles, 1871–1890, *volumes 1 and 2 (University of Nebraska Press, 2011) and* The Rank and File of 19th Century Major League Baseball *(McFarland, 2012).*

Preface

I first became a baseball fan as a seven-year-old boy in 1964 watching the CBS "Game of the Week," broadcast by Dizzy Dean and Pee Wee Reese. The year of 1964 would also be a memorable one for Dizzy's former team, the St. Louis Cardinals, who erased a 6½-game deficit in their last 12 games to clinch the National League pennant on the final day of the regular season and went on to upset the New York Yankees in seven games in the World Series.

When I started playing Little League baseball the next year on Maple Street in my hometown of Crossett, Arkansas, my team was also named the Cardinals, so the St. Louis Cardinals quickly became my favorite major league team. I particularly enjoyed watching their championship clubs of 1967–1968 and agonized when team owner Gussie Busch dismantled his champions. Later, however, when I was a history graduate student at the University of Arkansas in Fayetteville, Gussie Busch redeemed himself by hiring Whitey Herzog, who promptly managed the St. Louis Cardinals to the 1982 World Series championship. By the time I entered the doctoral program at the University of Oregon in Eugene, I was committed to the idea of writing my dissertation about the history of the St. Louis Cardinals baseball team and, fortunately, immediately received encouragement from one of the finest Western historians then practicing the craft, Richard Maxwell Brown.

I originally intended to write about the 1934 World Series champion Cardinals that Dizzy Dean had pitched for, nicknamed "The Gas House Gang," but changed my mind when the Cardinals erroneously celebrated their centennial in 1992, ten years after the centennial should have commemorated the true 1882 founding of the franchise. With the Cardinals implying that major league baseball in St. Louis had started in 1892, I decided to write about the "lost years" of major-league baseball in St. Louis from 1875 to 1891 and did so in my dissertation, "The Spirit of St. Louis

Preface

in Major League Baseball, 1875–1891," and subsequent book, *Before They Were Cardinals: Major League Baseball in Nineteenth-Century St. Louis* (Columbia, MO: University of Missouri Press, 2002).

Steven A. Riess wrote a favorable review of *Before They Were Cardinals* in *Business History Review* and invited me to write the chapter on the Cardinals for a multi-volume work, the *Encyclopedia of Major League Baseball Clubs*, that he was editing for Greenwood Press in Westport, Connecticut. I eagerly accepted the opportunity of moving my writing about the Cardinals beyond the 19th century, through the entire 20th century, and into the 21st century. My chapter on the Cardinals appeared in Volume 1 on the National League in 2006 and covered their history through the opening of their new ballpark in April of that year.

Like the American economy, operating on "boom and bust" cycles which mixed financial growth with the Panics of 1819, 1837, 1857, 1873, 1893, the Great Depression, and more recently, the Great Recession, the fortunes of the St. Louis Cardinals baseball franchise have undergone a series of "boom and bust" cycles. After winning its first pennant in 1885 in its fourth year of existence and through 2011, the franchise enjoyed five distinct periods of success: 1885–1888, 1926–1946, 1964–1968, 1982–1987, and 1996–2011. In between those years, it endured four distinct eras of failure: 1889–1925, 1947–1963, 1969–1981, and 1988–1995. This book seeks to explain the reasons for both their successes and failures.

Chris Von der Ahe, founder of the Cardinals franchise, also established its propensity for boom and bust cycles. Von der Ahe's St. Louis Browns started play in 1882 as a charter member of the American Association (AA), a new major league that catered to the ethnic working classes. The older National League (NL) had shunned support from the working class, doubling ticket prices to 50 cents, banning beer sales, and prohibiting games on Sundays, which were usually the only day off for industrial workers. In contrast, the American Association restored quarter tickets, permitted liquor sales, and supported Sunday games. Within its first five years, the AA established itself as more popular at the box office and competitive on the field than the NL. Von der Ahe, a German immigrant and saloon owner, turned his Browns into the most successful and prosperous AA team. From 1882 to 1891, his Browns led the major leagues in attendance four times, were the only AA team to defeat an NL team in the nineteenth-century version of the World Series, and became one of only four baseball teams prior to the 1950s to win four consecutive pennants.

Preface

After the initial AA season in 1882, Von der Ahe enjoyed nine successive winning seasons, with the Browns finishing either first or second in seven of them. However, in the second half of the ten-year history of the AA, fierce competition between the leagues enabled the NL to overcome the early AA advantages in total attendance, market size, and World Series competition. As early as 1887, Von der Ahe voiced support for a consolidation of the strongest teams from both leagues, but the NL resisted the idea because of its opposition to quarter tickets, beer sales, and Sunday games. By December 1891, when the NL dropped its objections to these AA practices, player raids between the two leagues had deprived Von der Ahe of all remnants of his championship clubs, including first baseman Charles Comiskey, the only manager Von der Ahe ever trusted. If the consolidation had taken place in 1887, Von der Ahe might have thrived in the NL. In putting together his AA champions, Von der Ahe had accepted advice from Comiskey and other trusted scouts, sparing no expense and outbidding rivals for valuable players. But by the time he joined the NL, he could no longer afford free-spending tactics. He was overextended from purchasing property near Sportsman's Park, especially after real estate values plummeted in the late 1880s and left him heavily indebted to the Metropolitan Savings Bank of St. Louis.

Von der Ahe instead entered the NL in financial distress and stocked the Browns with a cheap and ineffective collection of over-the-hill veterans and unproven young players. For seven successive seasons, the Browns suffered losing records while Von der Ahe restlessly changed managers. Eighteen different men, including Von der Ahe himself, tried to reverse the team's fortunes. But their efforts were hindered by the owner, who frequently sold the most promising players for funds that only briefly alleviated his economic woes.

Rather than hiring an experienced manager and following a coherent, long-range rebuilding project, Von der Ahe pursued a misguided plan to build a new ballpark. In April 1893, he opened the new Sportsman's Park at Vandeventer Avenue and Natural Bridge Road, just a few blocks from the original Sportsman's Park on Grand Avenue. A new ballpark did not disguise a losing ballclub, and by 1897, despite Von der Ahe adding amusement park rides and horse racing, the Browns fell to the cellar of the NL standings and outdrew only the Cleveland Spiders.

In 1898, Von der Ahe's finances deteriorated further. During the second home game of the season on April 16, flames engulfed the new Sportsman's Park. Although nobody perished, hundreds of lawsuits were filed

Preface

for injuries from the fire or suffered during the chaos of the fleeing crowd. The ballpark was nearly destroyed, and Von der Ahe's financial problems had prevented him from securing sufficient insurance. Although he managed to rebuild the ballpark, he faced too many debts and too few assets and lost control of the Browns in a foreclosure suit brought by the Mississippi Valley Trust Company. The Browns were subsequently sold at public auction on March 14, 1899. The complete story of Chris Von der Ahe's sensational rise to the peak of major league baseball success and tragic decline to the depths of major league baseball failure is discussed in detail in the Introduction of this book.

The new owners, Frank and Stanley Robison, were brothers who owned a streetcar line and the NL franchise in Cleveland. Since their Spiders had put together seven straight winning seasons but could not outdraw even Von der Ahe's inept Browns, the Robisons reckoned that a winning team would restore St. Louis to the ranks of the best-drawing cities in baseball. Therefore, they transferred their best Spiders to St. Louis and introduced bright red uniforms that quickly led to the team being called the "Cardinals." For two of their first three years under Robison ownership, 1899 and 1901, the plan worked well. The St. Louis Cardinals enjoyed the city's first winning seasons since leaving the AA, and, after trailing only the Philadelphia Phillies in attendance in 1899, capitalized on the inroads made by Connie Mack and the Philadelphia Athletics of the new American League (AL) in 1901 to top all of major league baseball in attendance two years later.

However, the Robisons' revitalization of St. Louis as a baseball market attracted the attention of the operators of the AL, who took over the lease of the original Sportsman's Park and transferred their last-place Milwaukee Brewers to St. Louis to begin play in 1902 under the traditional nickname of the "St. Louis Browns." Furthermore, by raiding seven players on the Cardinals' roster, the Browns decimated their local opposition and rose to second place in the AL. The Browns thereby established themselves as early favorites in the new battle for control of St. Louis, major league baseball's westernmost market. This competition between the Robisons' Cardinals and the AL St. Louis Browns is first discussed near the end of the Introduction and focused upon in Chapter 1 ("The Cardinals' Family Robison").

After the arrival of the AL Browns in St. Louis, the Cardinals under Frank and Stanley Robison never again produced a winning team between 1902 and 1910 and only twice surpassed the Browns in attendance.

Preface

Their successor, Helene Robison Britton, fared better after she inherited the club following the deaths of her father, Frank, in 1908 and Uncle Stanley during spring training of 1911. Mrs. Britton, dubbed "Lady Bee" by the press and the first female owner of a major league ballclub, enjoyed two winning seasons in 1911 and 1914. In 1914, after she fired one future Hall of Fame manager, Roger Bresnahan, and replaced him with another future Hall of Fame manager, Miller Huggins, the Cardinals rose as high as third place, their best finish ever under Robison family ownership. In four of five seasons from 1911 to 1915, Lady Bee's Cardinals outdrew the rival Browns.

However, in 1916 the landscape of St. Louis baseball dramatically changed again. The culmination of the Federal League War of 1914–1915 allowed Phil Ball, owner of the St. Louis Feds, to pay $425,000 to Robert Lee Hedges, the Browns' absentee owner from Cincinnati, for the Browns and Sportsman's Park. Lady Bee now faced a more dangerous adversary. She had moved to St. Louis in 1913 and, as a hometown owner with a better ballclub than the Browns, had swung public opinion toward the Cardinals. Ball, a wealthy St. Louis businessman who earned millions from his ice-manufacturing plants, stalemated her hometown advantage and could draw from deeper reservoirs of capital. Furthermore, he combined his holdovers from the St. Louis Federal League team with the old Browns to finish 79–75, snapping the Browns' seven-year losing skid. The Browns' attendance doubled under Ball and surpassed that of the 1916 Cardinals by 33 percent.

Mrs. Britton also suffered a painful divorce and, as a single mother of two, longed for financial security. Deciding to sell the Cardinals and their ballpark for $375,000, she offered them to her manager, Huggins, and attorney, James Jones. While Huggins hurried to his hometown of Cincinnati in search of investors, Jones stayed in St. Louis and closed the deal.

The syndicate that Jones put together would soon produce a pair of executives, Branch Rickey and Sam Breadon, who would take the Cardinals to the top of the National League. Chapter 2 opens with a brief look at how these two individuals rose to the top of the Cardinals organization and moves onto an analysis of three key moves that they took in tandem in 1920 that laid the groundwork for the Cardinals' ascent. First, Breadon convinced Ball to rent Sportsman's Park to the Cardinals for an annual payment of $35,000 and half of maintenance expenses. Then they sold the site of the Cardinals' old ballpark to the Board of Education, which tore down the ballpark to build Beaumont High School. Finally, rather than

Preface

using the $275,000 proceeds as a nest egg, Breadon invested the money to develop Rickey's notion of a farm system.

The farm system enabled the Cardinals to sign young, unproven players and develop them at various rungs of their farm system, starting off at a low-level classification minor-league team such as Fort Smith (Ark.) of the Western Association and, if a player showed promise, ultimately advancing him to a higher-classification minor-league team like Houston of the Texas League. Previously, the Cardinals had usually been unable to compete against wealthier major league clubs for top minor-leaguers, but after 1920, the Cardinals would harvest their own crop of minor-leaguers from their own farm clubs. Sunny Jim Bottomley, a future Hall of Fame first baseman, was the farm system's first graduate in August 1922, and many other players soon followed the same trail as he had, working their way through the farm system to the Cardinals.

Baseball Commissioner Kenesaw Mountain Landis, always an opponent of the farm system, had refrained from taking action against it because Pittsburgh Pirates owner Barney Dreyfuss and Detroit Tigers owner Frank Navin had both advised him that the farm system would collapse from its own weight. Instead, the farm system not only brought the Cardinals a pennant in 1926 after a 38-year drought, but proved to be a sustainable and renewable system of player development that enabled the Cardinals to win nine pennants and six World Series between 1926 and 1946, the longest sustained boom period in team history.

Chapters 3–7 look at this second boom period of Cardinals history. Chapter 8 begins by analyzing why the Cardinals' 1926–1946 boom era gave way to another bust cycle that lasted from 1947 to 1963, starting with Breadon's last year as owner, a season of combined ownership with Robert Hannegan and Fred Saigh (1948), four years of sole ownership by Saigh (1949–1952), and the early years of ownership by Gussie Busch and Anheuser-Busch (1953–1963). It ends with a discussion of the moves made by Bing Devine, hired by Busch as general manager after the 1957 season, that led to the Cardinals winning the NL pennant on the final day of the 1964 regular season and subsequently upsetting the New York Yankees in seven games in the World Series. Unfortunately, Busch had impatiently fired Devine on August 17 and considered replacing manager Johnny Keane at the end of what did not look like a championship season until the last two weeks of the regular season. Keane resigned after the World Series victory and took over the managerial reins of the Yankees, the team he had just defeated in the World Series.

Preface

Although Keane's replacement, Red Schoendienst, was accepted immediately because he had been a coach on Keane's staff and a former star player for the Cardinals, Devine's replacement, Bob Howsam, was viewed as an intruder who claimed inordinate credit for the 1964 championship and antagonized Cardinals players with petty memorandums directing them to keep their hair trimmed, wear the legs of their pants high, and avoid slouching on the bench. Only when Howsam departed to take over as general manager of the Cincinnati Reds and was succeeded by the affable Stan Musial in 1967, did the Cardinals win another NL pennant and World Series. When Musial resigned after the 1967 World Series to devote more time to his business interests, Busch brought back Bing Devine to replace him in a goodwill gesture. The Cardinals repeated as NL champions in 1968, but lost the World Series in seven games to the Detroit Tigers.

This 1964–1968 boom period of the Cardinals was shattered on March 22, 1969, at their St. Petersburg spring training site, when Busch gathered together the Cardinals, sportswriters, and Anheuser-Busch executives and berated his team, accusing them of being more concerned with money than about their fans or the image of the game. Over the next three years, all of the champion Cardinals either retired or were auctioned away, except for Hall of Famers Lou Brock and Bob Gibson. In the spring of 1972, Busch traded away a future Hall of Fame pitcher, Steve Carlton, for having the audacity to ask for a raise after winning 20 games for the first time. He also traded a 22-year-old hometown product, Jerry Reuss, for requesting a raise after establishing himself with 14 wins in 1971. Those two trades would haunt the Cardinals. Carlton pitched the Philadelphia Phillies to five divisional titles and became a 300-game winner and Hall of Famer. Reuss won over 200 games in his career and pitched for five divisional champions with the Pittsburgh Pirates and the Los Angeles Dodgers. In every season from 1974 to 1978, the Cardinals lost out in the National League East to a team whose best pitcher was either Reuss or Carlton. During that period, Busch made Schoendienst, his popular manager, the fall guy for his own mistakes, dismissing him as manager after the 1976 season, a move that concludes Chapter 9, which had started on a happier note with Schoendienst winning the consecutive pennants of 1967–1968.

The third bust period that Busch initiated with his tirade of March 22, 1969, did not end until 1982, when after two years of wheeling and dealing like a whirlwind, Whitey Herzog managed the Cardinals to the NL pennant and a World Series championship, as portrayed in Chapter 10.

Preface

Herzog had taken over a last-place team with the second-highest payroll in the league, slashed payroll 30 percent, and won the World Series. He had a close friendship with Gussie Busch and originally only answered to Gussie, but after winning the 1982 World Series in seven games over the Milwaukee Brewers, Anheuser-Busch insisted on governing the Cardinals with a three-man executive committee, comprised of Gussie Busch and two company attorneys. Nevertheless, Herzog managed the Cardinals to NL pennants in 1985 and 1987, despite losing the World Series in seven games both years. However, Herzog blamed the company attorneys for sabotaging salary discussions that resulted in the loss of ace reliever Bruce Sutter and star slugger Jack Clark to free agency after the 1984 and 1987 seasons. As long as Gussie Busch lived, Herzog still had some leverage with the Cardinals' front office, but the team president passed away on September 29, 1989, at the age of 90, leaving Herzog without power at corporate headquarters. Fred Kuhlman, one of the Anheuser-Busch attorneys with whom Herzog feuded, became president of the Cardinals. In July 1990, with ten Cardinals in their option year and Kuhlman refusing to negotiate, Herzog resigned as manager, leaving the Cardinals in last place, where they had been when he took over. Joe Torre could not lift the gloom surrounding the Cardinals, who finished last for the first time since 1918.

This fourth bust period, which had actually started with the loss of Jack Clark to free agency after the 1987 season, continued as long as Anheuser-Busch owned the club. In December 1995, Anheuser-Busch sold the Cardinals for $150 million to a group of investors, including local banker Andrew Bauer and William DeWitt, Jr. The new owners brought in Tony La Russa, who had won three consecutive AL pennants with the Oakland Athletics from 1988 to 1990, as manager and gave him more financial support than Anheuser-Busch had given to Torre. Cardinals baseball entered another boom phase over the next 16 years with La Russa guiding them to nine playoff appearances, three NL pennants, and a pair of World Series championships in 2006 and his last year of 2011 (when he retired shortly after leading the Cardinals to a seventh-game victory over the Texas Rangers). This fifth boom period in Cardinals history is discussed in the book's final chapter, Chapter 11.

A brief epilogue then provides an overlook of the post–La Russa Cardinals from 2012 to 2019.

Introduction
St. Louis and the Midwest and the Frontier of MLB

Part I: The Middle West and Major League Baseball, 1869–1881

Although organized baseball clubs first developed in Eastern cities, they evolved into something very different in the West. In 1869, the Cincinnati Red Stockings dispensed with the under-the-table payments prevalent among Eastern amateurs. They openly proclaimed their professionalism and completed an undefeated season. Another Western team, the Chicago White Stockings, became the first team to copy the Red Stockings' model of success. In 1870, civic boosters and baseball enthusiasts from Chicago raised $20,000 to recruit players and sponsor a professional team which would be able to challenge the Cincinnati club. This Western innovation of professionalism filtered back to the East and led to the 1871 formation of the first major league, the National Association of Professional Baseball Players.

St. Louis amateurs tried to compete against National Association teams, but this undertaking resulted in many humiliating, one-sided losses. Given St. Louis's fierce economic rivalry with Chicago, a series of 20 consecutive losses to the White Stockings proved especially galling. The *St. Louis Dispatch* described the impetus for forming the city's first professional baseball team, the Brown Stockings, as a desire to compete with the city's foremost trade rival. "Chicago could ill brook Cincinnati's success on the diamond field," it explained, "and St. Louis in turn desires to lower the standard of a rival." Joining the National Association in 1875, the St. Louis Brown Stockings faced the White Stockings twice in their opening home stand at Grand Avenue Park—a ballpark on the northwestern out-

Introduction

skirts of town that had been converted from a corn field in 1866 because of its proximity to local streetcar lines. When the Brown Stockings won both games in front of overflow crowds of 9,000 to 10,000, the *St. Louis Republican* rejoiced: "Time was when Chicago had an excellent baseball club, the best in the West, but that was before St. Louis decided to make an appearance on the diamond field and there, as everywhere else, attest the supremacy of the Western city with the greatest popularion, the most flourishing trade, the biggest bridge, and the prettiest women."[1]

After only one year in the National Association, the St. Louis Brown Stockings assisted the Chicago White Stockings in establishing the National League. The two rivals shared a dislike of various National Association policies, particularly the disproportionate numerical balance between Eastern and Western clubs.

Chris Von der Ahe, owner of the St. Louis Browns, enjoyed tremendous success in the American Association from 1882 to 1891 and endured disastrous failure in the National League from 1892 to 1898 (Library of Congress).

Throughout the opening months of the 1875 season, nine Eastern teams played exclusively among themselves, while four Western teams competed solely against each other. This haphazard scheduling meant that, in the early stages of the season, Eastern teams played more than twice as many games as Western teams. Such a disorderly scheduling process prevented cogent comparisons between the records of Eastern and Western clubs.

St. Louis and the Midwest and the Frontier of MLB

In January 1876, baseball representatives from four Western cities—St. Louis, Chicago, Louisville, and Cincinnati—met at a Louisville hotel. The four cities tentatively agreed to create a Western League, but White Stockings president William Hulbert privately emphasized that their real objective was to persuade an equal number of Eastern clubs to join them. Towards this end, Brown Stockings managing director C. Orrick Bishop drew up a constitution for the new organization. The four Western partners approved the document and authorized Hulbert and the Brown Stockings' secretary, Charles Fowle, to act as a special committee in future negotiations with Eastern clubs.

On February 2, 1876, Hulbert and Fowle met with delegates from four Eastern teams—the Boston Red Stockings, Philadelphia Athletics, Hartford Dark Blues, and New York Mutuals—at the Grand Central Hotel in New York City. Hulbert and Fowle skillfully used the projected Western League to achieve their ends, offering the Eastern representatives a choice only of either joining them or competing against them. The two Westerners then presented the constitution that Bishop had drawn up for the proposed National League. Late that night, following a full day of discussion, the Eastern teams accepted an equal partnership with the West.

When play began in the spring of 1876, the National League stood alone as the sole major league in the country. After losing six of its seven survivors from the 1875 season, the National Association simply dissolved. Nevertheless, in its first six seasons, the National League never drew crowds as large as those of the old National Association. While it is true that the National League formed during the midst of the economic depression of 1873–1879, such an explanation alone fails to address why the National Association's attendance in 1875 surpassed the National League's following the return of prosperity. In 1880, only the pennant-winning White Stockings turned a profit; by 1881, six of the National League's eight original franchises had been lost.

Much of the blame can be attributed to the leadership of Hulbert, league president since 1877 and still simultaneously president of the White Stockings. After the New York Mutuals and Philadelphia Athletics refused to take their last Western road trips of the 1876 season, Hulbert, rather than punishing the organizations of the Mutuals and Athletics by replacing them with another club from New York City and Philadelphia, opted instead to punish the two cities by revoking their franchises in the National League. Thus, from 1877 to 1882, he denied his own league access to the two largest cities in the country. Following the 1877 season,

Introduction

besieged by financial deficits and a gambling scandal, Louisville, St. Louis, and Hartford resigned from the National League, which survived only as an organization top-heavy with a succession of small-market northeastern cities such as Providence (RI, 1878–1885); Syracuse (1878), Troy (1879–1882), and Buffalo (NY, 1877–1885); and Worcester (MA, 1880–1882).

Furthermore, in seeking to appeal to the upper and middle classes, Hulbert shunned support from the working classes and almost suffocated the growth of the game. At a time when the wages of an average industrial worker were about a dollar a day, Hulbert and his league had doubled ticket prices from a quarter to 50 cents. While the average industrial worker toiled ten hours a day, six days a week, with only Sundays off, Hulbert's league prohibited Sunday games, effectively banning the working-class from their ballparks except for rare holidays, since ballpark lights and night games did not yet exist.

Finally, the National League banned alcohol sales at its ballparks. Worcester spent much of its debut season of 1880 attacking Cincinnati's "questionable custom" of selling beer in the ballpark and leasing its grounds on Sundays to non–League teams. O. P. Caylor, the sports editor of the *Cincinnati Enquirer*, delivered a ringing denunciation of the New England moralists. "Puritanical Worcester is not liberal Cincinnati by a jugful," he wrote sarcastically, "and what is sauce for Worcester is wind for the Queen City. Beer and Sunday amusements have become a popular necessity in Cincinnati.... We drink beer as freely as you used to drink milk."[2]

Hulbert, a native-born, Republican coal tycoon, sided with Worcester in this dispute. The *Chicago Tribune*, a reliable gauge of his prejudices, described "beer-peddling" as "an unnatural and incompatible adjunct, a disgrace and a curse to baseball." In a similar tirade published two weeks later, the *Tribune* complained that "this association of beer and baseball" was "degrading, offensive, [and] ruinous" to the game and to public morals.[3] On October 4, 1880, the National League convened a special meeting in Rochester, New York. Every club, with the exception of Cincinnati, pledged to support amendments prohibiting the sale of liquor on League grounds and the leasing of League ballparks for Sunday baseball. Two days later, prodded by Hulbert, the National League expelled Cincinnati for refusing to agree to abide by these agreements that the League planned on officially adopting at its winter meeting in December.

Hulbert misunderstood public sentiment. Looking at figures from the 1890 census, historian Frederick Jackson Turner commented on the magnitude of the German presence in the Middle West: "Persons of

St. Louis and the Midwest and the Frontier of MLB

German parentage in the Middle West numbered over four millions out of a total of less than seven millions in the whole country."[4] The Germans' love of beer particularly affected Cincinnati, where 27 breweries were operating in 1879, and St. Louis, where 23 breweries employed 1,335 workers and produced over $4,000,000 worth of beer in 1880.

These two German-influenced Western river cities would soon dramatically alter the world of major league baseball. The Cincinnati Red Stockings, despite finishing last in three of the National League's first five seasons, had averaged an annual income of $3,000 from beer sales and refreshment concessions. In St. Louis, Chris Von der Ahe, a German immigrant and Democrat whose Golden Lion Saloon on the corner of Grand and St. Louis Avenues was just down the block from Grand Avenue Park, stepped up to save the ballpark when it was slated for demolition in October 1880. The St. Louis Brown Stockings, after three seasons as an impoverished independent club, were revitalized when Von der Ahe took over the lease of the ballpark. Al Spink, a local sportswriter, looked upon Von der Ahe as "a plump angel who, [despite] knowing next to nothing about baseball, was still ready to finance any outdoor recreation that promised to bring crowds of people into one place on Sunday, where he might sell them beer."[5] Von der Ahe, also well aware of the correlation between baseball games played at the park and increased beer sales at his saloon, became president of the Sportsman's Park and Club Association and provided most of the funding to renovate the renamed ballpark. Spink, as secretary of the organization, handled most of the day-to-day arrangements for its construction.

When it opened in 1881, Sportsman's Park featured a beer garden in right field and a double-decked grandstand that was the largest in the country. On Sunday, May 29, 1881, Spink and Caylor scheduled a contest between the St. Louis Brown Stockings and the Cincinnati Red Stockings. A crowd of 4,000 overflowed from the stands onto the outfield. Bleachers were added down the first-base line during the course of the season, raising the seating capacity to 6,000, and Sportsman's Park filled to the brim for contests between the Browns and top-notch competitors from Louisville and Philadelphia, two other cities whose clubs had either resigned or been evicted from the National League.

The success of the 1881 season, hailed by the *St. Louis Globe-Democrat* as an "old-time baseball revival," encouraged Von der Ahe to join a campaign to form a new league. On November 2, 1881, the American Association announced its formation at the Hotel Gibson in Cincinnati. Men with

Introduction

brewery interests were the primary investors in four of the six AA clubs (St. Louis, Cincinnati, Louisville, and Baltimore) and owned stock in the other two clubs (Pittsburgh and Philadelphia). These beer barons brought a new series of business practices to the AA. Condemning the National League's restrictions on quarter tickets, liquor sales, and Sunday games as "tyrannical articles," the American Association's owners restored quarter tickets, permitted liquor sales, and supported Sunday games wherever local law permitted (originally the westernmost cities of Cincinnati, Louisville, and St. Louis). For the same price as a 50-cent ticket to a National League game, spectators at American Association games could afford not only the cost of admission, but five nickel beers as well. AA leaders reveled in the working-class appeal of their reforms when they proclaimed allegiance to the Association's slogan: "We Have Brought Baseball To The People!"[6]

The American Association-National League debates over liquor sales, Sunday games, and ticket prices mirrored deeper divisions within the United States. A landmark political study described "the prohibition question" as "the paramount state or local issue, year in and year out, throughout most of the Midwest (and much of the rest of the country) in the 1880s."[7] Democrats such as Von der Ahe were usually staunch opponents of prohibition; Republicans such as Hulbert generally advocated for it. Prohibition received widespread support from large sectors of native-born Americans such as Hulbert; opposition to prohibition proved popular among European immigrants, such as Von der Ahe. Similarly, native-born Protestants tended to prefer an "American Sabbath," believing Sunday should be set aside as a day of worship. On the other hand, European immigrants, whether they were Catholic, Jewish, or German Lutherans, normally championed the "Continental Sabbath," in which Sunday was viewed as a day of rest and recreation. The National League's 50-cent ticket prices had been adopted with the goal of increasing patronage from the upper and middle classes, while the American Association actively courted ethnic working-class support with quarter tickets, Sunday games, and liquor sales.

The Eastern-oriented National League mocked the Western-oriented American Association as a "Beerball League" or a "Beer and Whiskey Circuit." The *Chicago Tribune* predicted that the Association would "degrade and disgrace baseball, to be sure, but only in cities like Cincinnati and St. Louis, where through immoral practices and questionable associations, the game has long ceased to be regarded as fit for the patronage of respectable ladies and gentlemen."[8]

Although Denny McKnight of Pittsburgh became the Association's first president, Von der Ahe, Caylor of Cincinnati, and Lou Simmons of Philadelphia established themselves as influential individuals who ran the new organization in their own self-interest. William Hulbert died on April 10, 1882, of a heart attack at the age of 49. But before his death, he sent a letter to McKnight, urging him not to pursue "the patronage of the degraded" but to strive instead to be "worthy of the patronage, support, and respect of the best class of people."[9] Hulbert did not live long enough to see the working-class American Association, with four of its franchises castoffs from the National League, outdraw its older rival for five successive seasons from 1882 to 1886.

Part II: American Association Versus National League Cultural War

For the next decade, the workingman's American Association waged a cultural war against the high-minded National League. Economic competition proved healthy for major league baseball, as A. G. Spalding, Hulbert's successor as owner of the White Stockings, later conceded: "That 'competition is the life of trade' seldom had a better exemplification, for business ... was immediately improved."[10]

The six charter members of the AA represented the same major cities from the old western river network that had flourished back in the pre-industrial days when St. Louis boasted that commerce always followed natural avenues of trade. In 1882, the first year of the rivalry between the leagues, the six cities with AA teams touched a population of slightly over 2,000,000, while the eight-team NL's market reached slightly over 1.5 million. The AA benefited from its presence in four large cities with franchises that had either resigned from the NL (St. Louis and Louisville) or been evicted from it (Philadelphia and Cincinnati). In contrast, the NL cities included Troy, New York, and Worcester, Massachusetts, neither of which reached even the minimum population of 75,000 supposedly required by the league's constitution.

No city yet possessed teams in both the AA and the NL, so all civic boosters felt that the future of professional baseball in their city would be determined by the success of the league to which they belonged. Despite the AA's population advantage, upper- and middle-class spectators turned out at NL parks in unprecedented numbers. National League attendance

Introduction

rose 26 percent over the previous year and for the first time topped the total attendance drawn by the National Association in 1875. But average crowds at AA games surpassed those of the NL by 30 percent, and all six of the Association's teams turned a profit.

The success of the AA forced the NL to scrap its markets in Troy and Worcester and replace them with New York and Philadelphia, thus returning the league to the nation's two largest markets (the AA also moved into New York in 1883 and then into Brooklyn in 1884). Crowds at AA games in 1883 now exceeded those of the NL by 40 percent, and the AA became the first major league to reach the one million mark in attendance for a single season. According to the *St. Louis Globe-Democrat*, the two most profitable AA ball clubs, the Philadelphia Athletics ($75,000 in profits) and the St. Louis Browns ($50,000), each earned more than the NL's biggest moneymaker, the Boston Red Caps ($48,000). Moreover, the earnings of a third AA team, the Cincinnati Reds ($25,000), exceeded the amount accumulated by the NL's second-most profitable club, the Chicago White Stockings ($20,000).

The American Association continued to lead the NL in attendance through 1886, and in three of those five years Von der Ahe's St. Louis Browns outdrew all other major-league clubs. Von der Ahe displayed a flair for showmanship, and his promotional instincts boosted the Browns' popularity. He built ladies' rooms to encourage female attendance, hired bands as pre-game entertainment, and even scheduled a doubleheader featuring the Browns and Buffalo Bill's Wild West Show. In his heyday of the 1880s, Von der Ahe earned approximately $500,000 from ticket and beer sales at Sportsman's Park. He invested much of his windfall in the working-class neighborhood that surrounded the ballpark on St. Louis's northwestern outskirts. Von der Ahe resided, along with his wife and son, in this primarily German-American community that was slightly more affluent than the working-class German neighborhood in south St. Louis. He built entire city blocks in the area around Sportsman's Park and placed a neighborhood bar on every corner.

His Browns brought St. Louis its first sustained success on the baseball diamond. After firing his manager in midseason and appointing first baseman Charles Comiskey as an interim replacement the two preceding years, Von der Ahe gave Comiskey a chance to manage a full season in 1885. Comiskey responded by leading the team to the first of four consecutive pennants from 1885 to 1888. In each year, the Browns faced the NL champion in the "World Series" (a phrase coined by Al Spink, soon to be founder of *The Sporting News*, in anticipation of the 1885 postseason matchup between the Browns and Chicago White Stockings).[11] The Browns claimed victory in 1885 and 1886 over the White Stockings, but lost to the Detroit Wolverines in 1887 and the New York Giants in 1888.

The Browns' 1885 triumph ended in controversy, with St. Louis boasting of victory while Chicago declared it a tie. The disputed outcome stemmed from the second game of the series. After a darkness-shortened tie in the opening game in Chicago, the next contest in St. Louis concluded in chaos. In the top of the sixth inning, 200 St. Louis fans stormed onto the field and chased NL umpire Dave Sullivan out of Sportsman's Park. Sullivan retreated to the safety of his hotel room and awarded a forfeit to Chicago on the basis that Comiskey had pulled his men from the field. The Browns objected that they did not leave the field prematurely, but had exited when the spectators forced both teams off the field. Furthermore, they insisted that the declaration of a forfeit was invalid, because Sullivan did not issue it on the playing site as required by the rules.

The Browns went on to defeat the White Stockings in the next two games at Sportsman's Park, but then lost in Pittsburgh and Cincinnati. Immediately before the seventh and final game, upon the request of Comiskey and Chicago's player-manager Cap Anson, umpire "Honest John" Kelly issued a public announcement to the crowd in Cincinnati. This well-respected umpire, brought in after the fourth game to curtail carping over officiating, explained that the forfeit no longer counted and the upcoming contest would decide the championship. The Browns prevailed, 13–4, and staked claim to the title of world champions.

The two teams met in a rematch the following year. Anson fueled the flames of the rivalry, bragging in July 1886 that the Browns would finish "fifth or sixth" if they played in the NL. Once the clubs clinched their respective pennants, Von der Ahe formally challenged Spalding to a series of games between their teams that would be known as the "World's Championship Series." When Spalding insisted that the White Stockings would only play the Browns on a winner-take-all basis, Von der Ahe accepted the challenge. This format captured the public's imagination, contributing to a tripling of attendance over the preceding year. Von der Ahe had built bleachers around the outfield fences and down the foul lines before the 1886 season, doubling seating capacity to 12,000, and Sportsman's Park was packed for each World Series game in St. Louis. Local newspapers praised the Browns for bridging divisions between genders, classes, and rural and urban residents.[12]

Introduction

Von der Ahe and Spalding settled on a best-of-seven-game series and a four-man umpiring crew, with two selections made by each owner. The Browns lost two of the first three contests in Chicago, but returned home to sweep the next three games and win the World Series. In the bottom of the tenth inning of the sixth game, Browns center fielder Curt Welch scored the winning run on a wild pitch, giving Von der Ahe the entire $13,920 in gate receipts. He pocketed half of the proceeds and divided the other half among his 12 players, whose winners' share of $580 apiece exceeded the annual income of a typical manufacturing worker.

With the 1886 World Series victory, Chris Von der Ahe, the St. Louis Browns, and the AA had reached their apex. The Browns had validated their claim of superiority over the White Stockings, who had won five of the last seven NL pennants. Even the *Chicago News*, which had claimed at the outset of the series that the Browns were "entirely outclassed," now conceded: "Humiliating as the confession is, we are obliged to admit that the champion baseball players reside in St. Louis.... The fact is, the St. Louis Brown Stockings are, as a team, better players than the Chicago men."[13] For its part, the AA had emerged victorious against the NL in other post-season tests of strength as well, with its second- and third-place teams defeating the second- and third-place teams of the NL in other contests. The AA had drawn larger crowds to its games than the NL for five successive seasons and had won most of its pre-season and post-season games against NL opponents for the previous two years. By the end of its fifth year of existence, the AA had established superiority over its older rival.

Beneath the surface, however, a crack had developed in the American Association's foundation. Denny McKnight, the league's first president and an investor in its Pittsburgh franchise, had overseen most of the early prosperity. On March 20, 1886, however, the AA ousted McKnight from power. The NL, under the unofficial leadership of Spalding, soon capitalized on McKnight's departure, implementing a strategy that ended the AA's dominance.

After retiring as a baseball player, Spalding, once a star pitcher, had gained predominance in the sporting goods industry by buying out his competition. Like his fellow monopolists Andrew Carnegie in the steel industry and John D. Rockefeller in oil, he benefited from the nation's lack of any antitrust laws. Applying his business experience to baseball's interleague rivalry, he adopted the strategy of preying upon the franchises of the AA. His efforts following the 1885 season were unsuccessful: Pittsburgh and Brooklyn both rejected offers to join the NL. But the dissent sown by the Sam Barkley case enabled Spalding to convince Pittsburgh to jump to the NL.

Barkley, the second baseman on the Browns' first pennant-winner in 1885, had become disgruntled in St. Louis and wanted to play elsewhere. Von der Ahe, after verbally accepting Baltimore's offer of $1,000 for Barkley's services over a $750 Pittsburgh offer, changed his mind when Pittsburgh raised its offer to $1,000. He immediately returned Baltimore's payment upon receipt. Barkley, meanwhile, had signed a contract with Baltimore, but he repudiated it and signed instead with Pittsburgh. Baltimore then appealed to the AA's board of directors.

Although McKnight had given up the presidency of the Pittsburgh Alleghenys to devote attention to AA matters, he remained an investor in the Pittsburgh club. Von der Ahe, serving simultaneously as president of the Browns and vice-president of the AA, also held a conflict of interest in the Barkley case. Therefore, in a hearing in which neither the AA's president nor its vice-president could participate, the case was decided by the only two board members without a stake in the controversy. They awarded Barkley to Pittsburgh, claiming his contract with Baltimore was invalid on the grounds that it had been signed before Von der Ahe legally sold the rights to Barkley's services.

During the controversy, McKnight had advised Barkley to honor his contract with Baltimore. Nevertheless, the Barkley decision caused friction between other team owners and McKnight, who was wrongly perceived as giving his own club preferential treatment. Consequently, on March 20, 1886, McKnight was dismissed as president in a 6–2 vote, over the objections of Pittsburgh and St. Louis. By ousting McKnight, the AA outraged his friend William A. Nimick, the majority owner of the Pittsburgh club. Nimick became even angrier when the AA forced Pittsburgh to provide Baltimore with a player as compensation and to pay a $500 fine levied against Barkley for "duplicity" and "dishonorable conduct" in signing multiple contracts.[14]

In the wake of losing the 1886 World Series, A. G. Spalding had retreated to the wilds of the Dakotas on a hunting expedition. He emerged in early November, scarcely stopping in Chicago before traveling to Pittsburgh, where he bagged the AA's Pittsburgh franchise for the NL. Spalding successfully convinced Nimick that the "circus" of the Barkley case would never have occurred in his league, which was guided by "thorough business principles."[15] Furthermore, since Pennsylvania law prevented

Introduction

Pittsburgh or Philadelphia teams from playing on the Sabbath, Nimick derived no benefit from the AA allowing Sunday games.

Pittsburgh's departure had profound consequences. The Pittsburgh Alleghenys, runners-up to the Browns in both the 1886 standings and attendance figures, had been a gate attraction at home and on the road. The NL substituted Pittsburgh for its Kansas City Cowboys, the team with the worst attendance in the two major leagues in 1886. As a replacement for Pittsburgh, the AA turned to the Cleveland Blues, who would have the worst attendance in 1887. In the 1887 season, for the first time ever, the NL outpaced the AA in attendance.

The successful raid of Pittsburgh emboldened Spalding and other NL operators to target more AA clubs, launching successful raids of the new AA franchise in Cleveland following the 1888 season and of both Cincinnati and Brooklyn following the 1889 season. Cincinnati betrayed the founding principles of the AA because Aaron Stern, the new president of the club, as a clothes merchant rather than a brewer, had a smaller stake in beer sales and had professed enthusiasm for 50-cent tickets. Local sabbatarians also had temporarily blocked Sunday games in Cincinnati, prompting Stern to announce: "Now that we are not allowed the privilege of playing Sunday games at Cincinnati, we belong in the League."[16] Frank Robison, owner of the Cleveland franchise, was also a proponent of 50-cent tickets. Charles Byrne, president of the Brooklyn club, preferred 50-cent tickets, had a team that led the majors in attendance in 1887 and 1889, and had grown increasingly tired of fighting Von der Ahe for control of the AA.

Byrne and Ferdinand Abell, his fellow casino magnate and co-owner of the Brooklyn club, were partly responsible for the AA losing their franchise in New York following the 1887 season. After acquiring the New York Metropolitans from Erastus Wiman in order to sign three of the best Metropolitan players to Brooklyn contracts, they failed at efforts to lure another team to New York in place of the Metropolitans. Instead they turned the Metropolitans franchise over to the AA, which chose to relocate the team, abandoning the nation's largest market for Kansas City with its population of only 55,785 and thereby allowing the NL to surpass the AA in market size.

As early as 1887, Von der Ahe had sought a consolidation of the strongest teams from the two leagues. His effort was quickly quashed, however, when Spalding, a native-born Republican who shared the same class biases as Hulbert, sounded alarms over quarter tickets, beer sales, and Sunday games. Spalding supported the Sabbatarian cause so fervently that he once told the *Chicago Tribune* of his intention "to wash his hands of the game" if the NL ever accepted Sunday play. Nick Young, president of the NL, pointed to Sunday games as the largest obstacle to any merger. Von der Ahe, however, remained committed to consolidation, complaining to *The Sporting News* in 1889: "We have to skirmish around each year, in each ball organization to find cities. Some of these don't amount to much ... but you have to take them in."[17]

The tumultuous seasons of 1890 and 1891 would renew interest in Von der Ahe's idea. On November 4, 1889, John Montgomery Ward, star shortstop of the two-time defending world champion New York Giants and president of the Brotherhood of Professional Baseball Players, stood in New York's Fifth Avenue Hotel and announced the formation of a third major league, the Players' League. Ward, an honor graduate of Columbia University Law School who had formed the first local chapter of the Brotherhood while with the Giants, organized its revolt in response to the NL's passage of the Salary Classification Plan in November 1888. John Brush, owner of the NL Indianapolis Hoosiers franchise, had concocted this scheme calling for all player salaries in the NL to be "limited, regulated and determined by the classification and grade to which such players may be assigned by the secretary of the league."[18] Salaries were to range from $1,500 for a Class E player to a maximum of $2,500 for a Class A player, with a $250 incremental increase at each level up the scale for Class D, C, and B players. The NL secretary, in determining a public grade for the value of each NL player, would take into account playing ability and personal conduct.

Despite the presence of a virtually ignored Limit Agreement previously adopted by both the NL and the AA in October 1885, top players of the era received salaries twice as large as the maximum $2,500 permitted under the new Salary Classification Plan. Furthermore, the Brotherhood resented the idea of players being publicly graded on their personal and professional lives. When NL owners refused to meet with Ward to discuss player objections to the plan, the Brotherhood secretly recruited entrepreneurs to provide financial backing for the new Players' League in every NL city except Cincinnati (Buffalo was substituted instead as the eighth Players' League club).

Prior to formation of the Players' League, no AA players were affiliated with the Brotherhood, and, hoping to avoid this labor dispute, the AA had rejected the Salary Classification Plan. But 28 AA players neverthe-

Introduction

less jumped to the Players' League for the 1890 season, accounting for 23 percent of its roster spots. Eighty-one NL players—65 percent of the new league's roster spots—switched as well. The remaining 15 players, or 12 percent of the 124 players who participated in ten or more Players' League games, came from the minor leagues.

The Browns were ripe for plucking, largely because of Von der Ahe's temper. Until 1889, whenever Von der Ahe imposed unreasonable fines, Comiskey had been able to mediate on behalf of the players. He would wait for Von der Ahe's anger to subside and then convince the volatile owner to reward a previously fined player with a bonus for some extraordinary performance of recent vintage. However, in 1889 Von der Ahe installed his teenage son, Edward, as a new team official. Eddie Von der Ahe negated Comiskey's influence over his father; without Comiskey as a constraint, a flurry of fines and suspensions followed. Comiskey blamed the Browns' slip to second place on their internal turmoil and was quoted in *The Sporting News* as assigning responsibility for it to the younger Von der Ahe: "I was satisfied he was the mischief maker, as previous to his advent, I had always gotten along well with his father."[19] Seven alienated Browns, including Comiskey, jumped to the Players' League.

The 1890 season turned into a financial disaster for all three major leagues. For the first time since 1885 and only the second time since 1882, none of the leagues surpassed the one million mark in total attendance. The Players' League had cornered most of the game's best talent and drew the best total attendance among the three leagues (980,877). Yet the new league lost a reported $125,000, and its total deficit, counting construction costs of ballparks, reached $340,000. Since the Players' League maintained the NL's policies of 50-cent tickets and no beer sales or Sunday games, it lost support from a natural constituency of sympathetic working-class laborers.

The AA, depleted by Players' League raids on its players and NL raids on its franchises, suffered from a talent supply so diminished that Louisville rose from last place in 1889 to first place in 1890. But although half of the AA teams were now in undesirable small markets, most of their franchises did avoid direct competition with the other two leagues. Recent research reveals that, contrary to previous historical accounts, the AA did not finish a distant third in 1890 attendance figures but in fact outdrew the larger NL, attracting a total attendance of 803,200.

The NL finished last among the three leagues in attendance with a total of 776,042, and estimates of its losses ranged from $231,000 to $500,000. The NL benefited, however, from the business experience of Spalding, who bluffed the owners of the Players' League into believing that the NL remained resolved to continue the war through another season. The capitalists of the Players' League, who had anticipated profits from their baseball investments and instead acquired deficits, sold out the Brotherhood. Acting independently and in violation of their constitution, which called for governance by a 16-man senate of eight players and eight owners, the owners negotiated a settlement with their counterparts from the two older leagues. The Players' League therefore collapsed after only one year, but nearly all of its principal investors ended up owning shares in teams in either the NL or the AA.

In 1891, both the NL and AA exceeded the one million mark in total attendance, with NL attendance recovering more than 74 percent from the 1890 season and AA attendance increasing 46 percent. Comiskey returned to St. Louis, reunited with five of his old players, and again ran the Browns for Von der Ahe, who enjoyed the best attendance in the majors for the fourth time in ten years. Throughout most of the season, the Browns engaged in a neck-and-neck struggle atop the standings with the Boston Reds, the 1890 Players' League champions who were newcomers to the AA. In August 1891, amidst more fines and suspensions from the Von der Ahes, the Browns fell out of pennant contention.

Meanwhile, a squabble had erupted between the AA and the NL over the rights to returning Brotherhood players. When the NL signed a pair of former AA standouts who had jumped to the Players' League, the AA withdrew from the 1883 National Agreement that prevented each league from raiding the player rosters of the other. Pandemonium followed. In October and November 1891, the AA reached agreements with 13 players from the NL's ranks, while the NL signed 15 from AA squads. Having finished the 1891 season in second place again, Comiskey and six other discontented Browns bolted for National League offers.

Once the signing frenzy subsided, escalating salaries again concerned owners. The lack of a National Agreement had given marketplace freedom to the players, and to eliminate this privilege the NL moved to merge the two leagues into one. Von der Ahe was now offered the same terms of consolidation that he had sought since 1887. A three-man NL delegation of Byrne, Robison, and Brush (now owner of the Cincinnati Reds) met with Von der Ahe in St. Louis, and in December 1891 they hammered out a preliminary agreement that served as the cornerstone

Introduction

for consolidating the NL and the AA. Four AA clubs (St. Louis, Baltimore, Louisville, and Washington) would merge with four NL clubs (Chicago, Boston, New York, and Philadelphia) and four NL teams that had been raided previously from the AA (Pittsburgh, Cleveland, Cincinnati, and Brooklyn). All 12 clubs in the new "big league" would be granted local option regarding Sunday games, beer sales, and quarter tickets.

If the consolidation had taken place in 1887, Von der Ahe might have thrived in the NL. By the end of 1891, though, he had lost all remnants of his championship clubs. Even worse, Von der Ahe could no longer count on Comiskey, his sole source of managerial stability, to rebuild the Browns. In putting together his AA champions, Von der Ahe had accepted advice from Comiskey and other trusted scouts, sparing no expense and outbidding rivals for valuable players. But by the time he joined the NL, he could no longer afford free-spending tactics. He was overextended from purchasing property near Sportsman's Park, especially after real estate values plummeted in the late 1880s and left him heavily indebted to the Northwestern Savings Bank of St. Louis.

The collapse of real estate values, a leading economic indicator, perhaps should have forewarned Von der Ahe and the entire nation of an impending financial crisis, which arrived with the Panic of 1893 and developed into a full-scale depression that lasted through 1897. Thousands of overextended businessmen like Von der Ahe lost their businesses, and estimates of unemployment ranged from 25 to 33 percent. Had Von der Ahe heeded the warning signs and gotten out of the baseball business sooner, his achievements would have earned him recognition as one of the topmost owners in baseball history. As the owner of the Browns, the most successful and prosperous franchise in the AA, Von der Ahe had rescued baseball from its doldrums and elevated the game to new heights of popularity. From 1882 to 1891, his Browns led the major leagues in attendance four times, were the only AA team to defeat an NL team in the nineteenth-century version of the World Series, and became one of only four baseball teams prior to the 1950s to win four consecutive pennants. After the initial AA season in 1882, Von der Ahe had enjoyed nine successive winning seasons, with the Browns finishing either first or second in seven of them. Finally, he had been the central AA figure in the 1891 consolidation with the NL. A three-man NL delegation had sought him out and reversed their league's long-standing opposition to quarter tickets, beer sales, and Sunday games. If Von der Ahe had retired at this point, he probably would be enshrined in the National Baseball Hall of Fame alongside his contemporaries such as Spalding and Hulbert. In fact, despite Hulbert's induction into the Hall in 1995, with all 30 current major league teams playing Sunday games, serving beer in the ballpark, and directing their appeal to the masses, it is Von der Ahe's vision of the baseball business, not that of Hulbert and the pre–1892 National League, that lives today.

Part III: Another Major League Arises Out of the West, 1892–1903

The National League reneged on one aspect of the consolidation agreement. Initially the new "big league" was supposed to receive a name befitting the merger of the old rivals—the "American League." At the last moment, though, National League owners rejected the idea because it gave first billing to the word "American" rather than "National." Instead, in 1892 the "big league" took the field under the long-winded banner of the "National League and American Association." Sportswriters soon shortened the title to the simpler "National League." This had unfortunate consequences for historical truth. Since the name of the "National League" survived and the name of the "American Association" vanished, most modern historians—rather than grasping the December 1891 consolidation as the merger of business interests that it actually was—have assumed the National League unequivocally won the baseball war over the American Association.[20]

The consolidated "National League" remained the only major league through 1899. In its first season of 1892, the Cincinnati Reds, bolstered by the addition of Comiskey and six former Browns, topped the NL in attendance while the Browns, despite losing Comiskey, the other ex-Browns, and suffering their first losing season since 1882, were third. The Philadelphia Phillies, now the only major league team in the city without competition from the Athletics of the AA, finished second in attendance and went on to lead the NL in attendance for four of the next eight years (1893, 1895, and 1899–1900).

Meanwhile by 1895, nearing the end of his career as a player, Comiskey desired to emulate Spalding and move beyond a successful playing career into the realm of ownership. After acquiring the Sioux Falls, Iowa, Cornhuskers in the Western League, he moved it to St. Paul, Minnesota, where he operated the club as the St. Paul Saints for the next five seasons.

Introduction

In 1900, Comiskey gambled on transferring the franchise to his hometown of Chicago and, along with Western League president Ban Johnson, renamed the Western League as the American League and proclaimed the new organization to be a major league ready to challenge the business monopoly of the National League. In reality, the AL remained very much a regional league, with no clubs east of Buffalo, New York, until 1901, when it took on more of a national identity. First, it dispensed with its franchises in Kansas City, Minneapolis, Indianapolis, and Buffalo. Then it invaded the large Eastern cities of Philadelphia, Boston, Washington, and Baltimore (whose franchise transferred to New York prior to the 1903 season). The AL balanced out their new Eastern clubs with Chicago, Detroit, Cleveland, and Milwaukee in the West. Detroit, Cleveland, Washington, and Baltimore were former members of the NL, and all except Detroit had been recently dropped by the NL following the 1899 season when it downsized to eight clubs. The AL also bolstered its major league claims by raiding NL players, who were eager to jump to the AL for pay raises after the monopolistic NL had slashed player salaries to a maximum of $2,400 shortly after the consolidation with the AA. Of 182 AL players in 1901, 111 (or 61 percent) had previously played in the NL.

With the NL Chicago entry playing on the west side of town under the nickname of Orphans (due to the 1899 departure of Anson, their longtime player-manager), Comiskey took up residence on the south side of Chicago under the nickname of the White Sox. Jim Hart, who had succeeded Spalding as president of the Chicago Nationals, did not believe Comiskey could be successful on the South Side, which was largely composed of immigrant groups such as the Irish, Poles, and Lithuanians. However, after winning the inaugural AL pennant in 1900, the White Sox repeated against stiffer competition in 1901 and, in the process, outdrew the NL Chicago entry by 73 percent. A year later, the Philadelphia Athletics, using the traditional local nickname, won the 1902 AL pennant under the leadership of Connie Mack, a former catcher with Washington and Pittsburgh of the NL and Buffalo of the Players' League, and more than tripled the attendance of the NL Phillies (who had led the NL in attendance in two of the preceding three seasons).

In St. Louis, Von der Ahe had endured seven successive losing seasons in the NL from 1892 to 1898 and, rather than following a long-range rebuilding project, had pursued a misguided plan to build a new ballpark which failed to disguise his bad team. A disastrous 1898 fire at his new Sportsman's Park, located at Vandeventer Avenue and Natural Bridge

St. Louis and the Midwest and the Frontier of MLB

Road, further deteriorated Von der Ahe's finances and led to him losing control of the Browns in a foreclosure case brought by the Mississippi Valley Trust Company. The team was sold at public auction on March 14, 1899. Frank and Stanley Robison, brothers who owned a streetcar line and the Spiders baseball team in Cleveland, took over ownership of the St. Louis NL franchise. They introduced bright red uniforms that quickly led to the team being called the Cardinals. Also, since attendance in Cleveland had lagged behind the Browns despite seven successive winning seasons by the Spiders, the Robisons reckoned that a winning team would return St. Louis to the ranks of the best-drawing cities in baseball. Therefore they transferred the best of their Spiders to St. Louis, which enjoying its first winning season since the AA folded, trailed only Philadelphia in attendance, and drew a city-record of 373,909 spectators. Two years later in 1901, with Mack and the AL Athletics making inroads on the attendance of the NL Phillies in Philadelphia, the St. Louis Cardinals finished fourth in the NL with a record of 76–64 and topped the major leagues with a franchise record 379,988 spectators, averaging over 5,000 for each home game and accounting for one-fifth of the total NL attendance.

This rejuvenation of St. Louis baseball attracted the attention of the AL. On November 5, 1901, AL President Ban Johnson and Comiskey signed a five-year lease for the original Sportsman's Park on Grand Avenue and, two weeks later, the AL transferred their last-place Milwaukee Brewers to St. Louis. When the new AL entry arrived, they staked a claim to both the past and present of St. Louis baseball. Appealing to tradition, they took over the lease of the original Sportsman's Park and adopted the nickname of the Browns. Capturing as much as they could of current St. Louis baseball, the new Browns signed seven players off the Cardinals' roster, including a pair of future Hall of Famers, shortstop Bobby Wallace, coming off a season in which he had led NL shortstops in assists and double plays and had hit .324 with 91 runs batted in, and left fielder Jesse "The Crab" Burkett, who had just won his third NL batting championship with a .376 average and led the league with 142 runs scored. The 1902 Browns finished second in the AL with a record of 78–58, only five games behind the Philadelphia Athletics, and established themselves as early local favorites, outdrawing by 20 percent the neighborhood rival Cardinals in the battle for St. Louis, major league baseball's westernmost market until the 1950s.

Overall, in 1901 and 1902, attendance in the AL slightly surpassed

Introduction

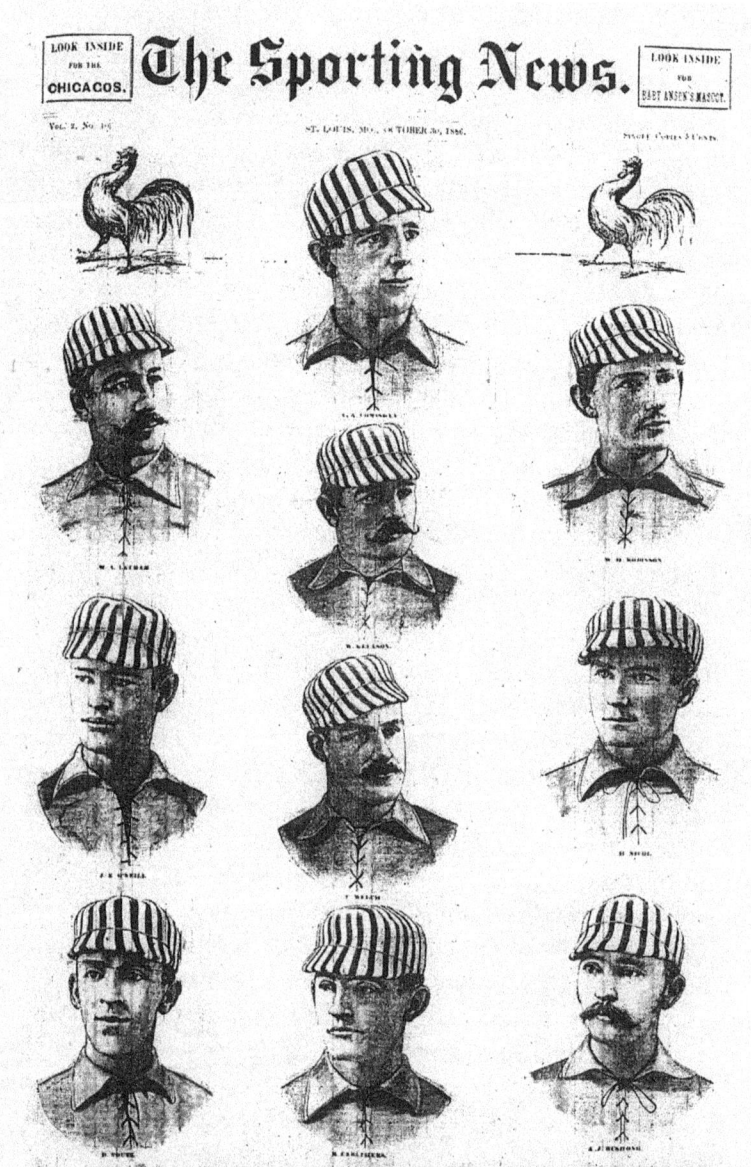

The Sporting News, born in 1886 in St. Louis, touted their hometown Browns for being victorious in the World Series in October (State Historical Society of Missouri).

the NL by eight percent. NL owners had seen enough and sought a peace agreement. They initially offered Ban Johnson a consolidation along the lines of the December 1891 consolidation between the NL and the AA, but riding high, Johnson wisely held out for an equal partnership with the NL. The AL and NL entered their own National Agreement in early 1903, enabling an annual World Series between their champions to start that October. The "Fall Classic" has been played every year since, with the exceptions of 1904 and 1994.[21] The hegemony of these two major leagues has been only briefly challenged by the short-lived Federal League of 1914–1915.

Although Eastern clubs were clearly necessary for larger markets, a national identity, and East-West rivalries, the Middle West had provided the impetus for the formation of the National League, the American Association, and the American League, the three most important major leagues in the history of baseball. Western values had ensured that the game would maintain beer sales, Sunday games, and ticket prices that were marketed to the masses. The spirit of the Middle West profoundly affected the development of major league baseball.

1

The Cardinals' Family Robison

> I have decided to make a change in managers and will not need your services any longer. I feel that you have not tried hard during the past year. The club has not made nearly as much money as it did in 1911. You do not seem to take much interest in the club.
> —Helene Robison Britton's October 22, 1912, letter of termination to Roger Bresnahan[1]

For 52 seasons, from 1902 through 1953, the NL Cardinals and the AL Browns fought for the hearts of the baseball fans of St. Louis. After raiding seven players from the Cardinals roster, the Browns, who had finished last in the AL as the Milwaukee Brewers, rose to second place in the AL in 1902 with a record of 78–58, the best finish for a St. Louis club since 1891. The decimated Cardinals dropped from fourth to sixth place in the NL with their record declining from 76–64 to 56–78, the first of nine straight losing seasons. In seven of eight seasons from 1902 to 1909, the Browns outdrew the Cardinals.

During this woeful period of baseball, the Cardinals acquired an aging, 36-year-old first baseman, Jake Beckley, in 1904. Beckley, a native of Hannibal, Missouri, was equally renowned for his prowess as a hitter, which earned him election to the Hall of Fame, and his notoriously erratic left throwing arm. True to his reputation, Beckley often employed his war cry of "Chickazoolah" effectively at the plate, batting .325, but in a rare good defensive play involving his throwing, overshot first base while fielding a bunt by the Pirates' Tommy Leach, retrieved the ball from the outfield, and dove for home at the same time as Leach, tagging him out and breaking two of Leach's ribs in the process.

The superiority of the Browns peaked in 1908. For the second succes-

Boom and Bust in St. Louis

Stanley Robison became president of the Cardinals upon the death of his brother Frank in 1908 (Library of Congress).

sive season, the Cardinals lost over 100 games, finished last in the National League standings, and had the worst attendance in the NL. Meanwhile the Browns benefited from the acquisition of Rube Waddell, an eccentric, future Hall of Fame left-hander who was the most flamboyant pitcher in the game. Despite leading American League pitchers in strikeouts for six years in a row, Waddell had worn out his welcome with the Philadelphia Athletics. He won 19 games in 1908 and kept the Browns in the thick of a four-team pennant race until September. The Browns' fourth-place finish and 83–69 record were the best results for a St. Louis club since their own 1902 debut. Waddell's magnetism enabled them to welcome 618,947 customers to Sportsman's Park, shattering the St. Louis attendance record and tripling the crowds of the Cardinals at League Park, renovated and renamed by the Robisons but still located on the same site at Vandeventer Avenue and Natural Bridge Road as the 1898 fire that had eventually driven Chris Von der Ahe out of the baseball business.

Sportsman's Park, converted from a corn field on Grand Avenue in 1866 and rebuilt in 1881 with proceeds from beer sales at Von der Ahe's saloon, would be renovated again by ticket sales from Rube Waddell's left

1. The Cardinals' Family Robison

arm. Robert Lee Hedges, a carriage maker and the Browns' absentee owner from Cincinnati, utilized profits from the 1908 season to modernize the ballpark. At the forefront of a movement away from hazardous wooden parks, he constructed a double-decked concrete and steel grandstand. His poverty-stricken rivals, the Cardinals, defied repeated warnings from the building commissioner about the dangers of their wooden ballpark, which in 1916 became the last all-wooden major league facility.

Frank Robison passed away on September 25, 1908, with the Browns' popularity over his Cardinals at an all-time high. He was succeeded as Cardinals president by his brother, Stanley. The Browns, largely because of the unpredictabil-

Upon the death of Stanley Robison during spring training of 1911, he was succeeded by Helene Robison Britton, Frank's daughter, who became the first female owner of a major league team (Library of Congress).

ity of Waddell, could not sustain their success of 1908. They tumbled to seventh place in 1909 and, after releasing Waddell in August of the next season, all the way to the American League basement in 1910. The Cardinals were not much better, but they improved enough to emerge from the bottom of the National League standings to seventh place in 1909 and 1910. In 1910, for only the second time in nine years of competition against the Browns, the Cardinals outdrew their neighborhood rivals.

On March 24, 1911, while spring training was underway for the Cardinals at West Baden, Indiana, Stanley Robison died. Helene Robison Britton, the daughter of Frank Robison, inherited the Cardinals upon her uncle's death. She rejected overtures to sell the ballclub and became the first female owner of a major league team. Dubbed "Lady Bee" by the press corps, Britton made few initial changes to the Cardinals, other

Boom and Bust in St. Louis

than renaming their ballpark from League Park to Robison Field to honor her father and uncle and encouraging women's attendance by relocating ticket sales from the predominately male bastion of saloons to a more female-friendly environment of drugstores. On the field, she followed the policy of her Uncle Stanley in giving a free hand to Cardinals manager Roger Bresnahan.

Bresnahan, acquired in December 1908 from the New York Giants for pitcher Bugs Raymond and outfielder Red Murray, had transformed the Cardinals. He acquired many new starters through trades. Bresnahan shared catching responsibilities and brought over his Giants teammate, Steve Evans, to play right field. From the Cincinnati Reds, he secured second baseman Miller Huggins, center fielder Rebel Oakes, and third baseman Mike Mowrey. He kept only first baseman Ed Konetchy and left-handed pitcher Slim Sallee from the club that he inherited. Konetchy, purchased in 1907 for $1,000 from La Crosse of the Wisconsin State League, had quickly established himself as one of the best-fielding first basemen in major league baseball, but his batting average hovered around .250. When Bresnahan arrived in 1909, he tutored Konetchy as a batter, instructing him to stop pulling everything and to hit to the opposite field. From 1909 through 1912, Konetchy hit .298, topping the team in runs batted in each year and batting average in each year except one. Sallee, known for his flashes of pitching brilliance, was nevertheless notorious for disappearing on extended drinking sprees. Bresnahan suspended him in 1909, and, frustrated, Sallee quit the team for the remainder of the season. Additional disappearances by Sallee and suspensions by Bresnahan followed in 1910, but in 1911, Sallee seemed to be fulfilling his potential. His record was 15–9 in late August, when he succumbed to his fondness for alcohol again. Bresnahan suspended him for the remainder of the season and finally taught Sallee that he could not survive solely on his pitching abilities. Beginning with spring training of 1912, Sallee became a much more dependable ballplayer both on and off the diamond. Only 35–36 after four major league seasons, he lasted ten more seasons in the majors and eventually finished with a win-loss record of 174–143.

In 1911, Bresnahan's combination of holdovers and newcomers jelled. The Cardinals stayed in a five-team pennant race until August. Their subsequent swoon, partly attributable to Sallee's suspension, dropped them to fifth place, and they barely finished with a winning record of 75–74. Nevertheless, by enjoying a winning season for the first time in a decade, the Cardinals pulled in a franchise-record 447,768 fans, double the

1. The Cardinals' Family Robison

attendance of the American League's last-place St. Louis Browns. Bresnahan's 1911 team turned a profit of $165,000. Lady Bee utilized these unexpected earnings to pare down the Cardinals' outstanding debts and rewarded Bresnahan with a new five-year contract for $10,000 a year and 10 percent of the profits.

This agreement lasted only one season, due to constant bickering between Bresnahan and Britton. First, Bresnahan persistently tried to buy the Cardinals, long after Britton explained that she had no intention of selling. Second, suspicious that Huggins might be angling for his job, Bresnahan attempted to trade the popular second baseman. Lady Bee intervened to block the trade of her favorite player. Then, with the Cardinals' record slipping toward their final mark of 63–90, Britton questioned her manager's strategy. Bresnahan, exploding into an outburst of expletives, expressed his belief that women were incapable of sharing baseball insights.

At the end of her second season as a baseball owner, Britton fired one future Hall of Famer as manager and replaced him with another, Miller Huggins. She also successfully negotiated a buyout of the last four years of Bresnahan's contract, settling with him for $20,000, after he had demanded $40,000 and she initially offered $2,500. Although Huggins would gain greater acclaim for guiding the New York Yankees to six pennants in eight years from 1921 to 1928, he might have done a better job of managing the Cardinals to a pair of third-place finishes in 1914 and 1917. The Yankees had wealthy owners who used their pocketbooks to purchase 15 players from the Boston Red Sox alone, while the Cardinals were too poor even to modernize their archaic ballpark.

In Huggins' first year, the Cardinals continued their downward spiral, falling from sixth in 1912 to last in 1913. Future prospects seemed equally bleak, especially after starting outfielders Evans and Oakes jumped to the rival Federal League. Huggins filled these holes in the "three-for-five deal" with Pittsburgh. This trade cost the Cardinals three significant players (Konetchy, Mowrey, and pitcher Bob Harmon) in return for two-thirds of their 1914 outfield, half of their infield, and a pitcher. Although the Cardinals might have missed the services of Harmon, who won 23 games for their last-place 1913 team, their 1914 pitching staff nevertheless led the league with a 2.38 earned run average, with "Spittin' Bill" Doak winning 19 games and boasting the lowest ERA in the NL at 1.72, and Sallee winning 18 games and finishing fifth in the league with a ERA of 2.10. Of the new position players, Dots Miller, the primary replacement for Konetchy at first base, led the 1914 Cardinals with a .290 batting average and finished

Boom and Bust in St. Louis

fourth in the league with 88 runs batted in; left fielder Cozy Dolan hit only .240, but created havoc on the bases with 42 stolen bases, third in the league; and right fielder Chief Wilson led NL outfielders in fielding percentage and assists, averaged .259 with 73 runs batted in, and tied for second in the league with 12 triples. On August 26, in the first game of a doubleheader played in front of a capacity crowd of 30,000 at Robison Field in St. Louis, Huggins scored the game's only run while Doak shut out the Giants on only four hits, moving the Cardinals into a first-place tie with New York. However, Giants ace Christy Mathewson countered with a two-hit shutout of his own in the nightcap, knocking the Cardinals back out of first place, and ultimately both the Cardinals and Giants were passed in the standings by the "Miracle Braves" of Boston, who rose from last place on the Fourth of July to win the NL pennant and sweep the highly favored defending champion Philadelphia Athletics in the 1914 World Series. Still, the Cardinals improved in 1914 to 81–72 and finished in third place, their best showing since Chris Von der Ahe had taken the franchise into the National League in 1892.

During the next two seasons, though, the team failed to sustain any momentum. Their record plummeted to sub–.500 again, and they fell back to the second division. Furthermore, the culmination of the Federal League war changed St. Louis baseball in favor of the Browns. The rival Feds had tried for two years to establish a third major league, but confronted with dwindling attendance and mounting debts, most of its investors accepted a $600,000 buy-out offer from the two older leagues. As part of this peace agreement, the owners of the Chicago and St. Louis Federal League teams acquired major league clubs. Phil Ball, owner of the St. Louis team, paid $425,000 to Robert Lee Hedges for the Browns and Sportsman's Park.

Lady Bee now faced a far more dangerous adversary. She had moved to St. Louis in 1913 and, as a hometown owner with a better ballclub than the Browns, had swung public opinion toward the Cardinals. Ball, a wealthy St. Louis businessman who earned millions from his ice-manufacturing plants, stalemated her hometown advantage and could draw from deeper reservoirs of capital.

In 1916, Ball combined his holdovers from the St. Louis Federal League team with the old Browns to finish 79–75, snapping the Browns' seven-year losing skid. Attendance had declined to a franchise-low of 150,358 in the last year of Hedges' ownership, but doubled under Ball. Meanwhile, the inconsistent Cardinals dropped to the bottom of the

1. The Cardinals' Family Robison

National League. Their attendance had surpassed the Browns for five of the previous six years, but fell 33 percent short of the 1916 Browns.

Besides these professional setbacks, Britton endured the disintegration of her marriage. A single mother of two, she longed for financial security and decided to sell the Cardinals and their ballpark for $375,000. She offered them to Huggins and her attorney, James Jones. While Huggins hurried to his hometown of Cincinnati in search of investors, Jones stayed in St. Louis and closed the deal. He had encouraged civic leaders to purchase stock, and his sales campaign gave birth to the "Knothole Gang," a promotional idea linking support for the Cardinals with battling juvenile delinquency. Businessmen, for each share purchased, received a season pass that they could dispense to a local youth. The Knothole Gang also benefited the Cardinals by developing future generations of loyal fans. The syndicate that Jones put together would soon produce a pair of executives, Branch Rickey and Sam Breadon, who would take the Cardinals to the top of the National League.

The 1888 American Association champion St. Louis Browns, last of Charles Comiskey's four consecutive champions, were also the last St. Louis team to win a pennant for 38 years (Library of Congress).

2

Branch Rickey, Sam Breadon and Creation of the Farm System

> I do not feel that the farming system we have established is the result of any inventive genius—it is the result of stark necessity. We did it to meet a question of supply and demand of young ball players.
> —Hall of Fame baseball executive Branch Rickey, quoted in the *Sporting News*, Dec. 1, 1933[1]

Part I: Branch Rickey: From the Browns to the Cardinals

The brief playing career of Branch Rickey, a former Browns catcher, ended with an injury to his throwing arm. Rickey became the baseball coach at the University of Michigan from 1909 to 1911 and, while in Ann Arbor, earned a law degree. Diagnosed with tuberculosis, he moved temporarily to the mountainous climate of Boise, Idaho, where he opened a law practice. He missed baseball, though, and in 1913 returned to St. Louis as presidential assistant to Robert Lee Hedges, owner of the St. Louis Browns. Late in the 1913 season, Rickey was named manager of the last-place Browns, and he led them to fifth in 1914 and sixth in 1915. When Phil Ball purchased the Browns from Hedges, Ball brought his manager along with him from the St. Louis Federal League club, thus supplanting Rickey. Ball retained Rickey in the front office as business manager, but Rickey felt unappreciated and disenchanted. In January 1917, James Jones, who

2. Branch Rickey, Sam Breadon and Creation of the Farm System

had just organized the syndicate that purchased the Cardinals from Helene Robison Britton, extended Rickey a generous offer to leave the Browns for their neighborhood rivals. Rickey promptly accepted an offer that doubled his salary and made him team president of the Cardinals.

Miller Huggins, much like Rickey with the 1916 Browns, now felt like the odd man out with the Cardinals. After trying and failing to buy the Cardinals, he had seen Jones bring in Rickey to run them. Huggins took the Cardinals to third place with a record of 82–70 in 1917 and then departed to become the manager of the New York Yankees. In the World War I–shortened season of 1918, Rickey went into military service, and the Cardinals sank to last place. In 1919, Rickey undertook the dual role of field manager and Cardinals president, but the team barely improved to seventh. The following season, though, laid the foundation for future greatness.

Future Hall of Fame first baseman Sunny Jim Bottomley was the first graduate of the farm system of the St. Louis Cardinals (**National Baseball Hall of Fame**).

Part II: Sam Breadon: From the Model-T to the Cardinals

> [Sam Breadon] was, of course, incomparably the most able and successful owner the Cardinals ever had. With money he had earned for himself he bought into a bankrupt organization, reorganized and refinanced it, and made it the dominant club in the league.... From 1926 through 1946, the National League had

Boom and Bust in St. Louis

eight world champions. Six of them represented St. Louis.

—Red Smith on Sam Breadon, *New York Herald Tribune*, April 22, 1949[2]

Sam Breadon, an affluent automobile dealer who introduced the Model-T to St. Louis, emerged as the leading figure of the syndicate that bought the Cardinals from Mrs. Britton. Breadon started with a mere $200 purchase of four shares in 1917, but shortly afterwards at the first shareholder's meeting, invested another $1,800 for 36 additional shares. The Cardinals were soon on the verge of defaulting on a scheduled payment to Helene Robison Britton, and Breadon protected his investment by loaning them $18,000. In 1920, Breadon made another $5,000 investment and became team president, with Rickey being demoted to vice-president. Breadon immediately streamlined the team's board of directors from 25 to seven, increasing his authority over the organization and ending the brief era of civic ownership. He continued to add stock and, after purchasing 1,048 more shares in November 1922, had acquired majority control of the Cardinals. By 1923, when the Cardinals completed the process of paying off Mrs. Britton, Breadon controlled 78 percent of the club's stock.

Breadon and Rickey were total opposites. Rickey, a Republican teetotaler from rural Ohio, advocated Prohibition and avoided the ballpark on Sundays. Breadon, an Irish Democrat from New York City, toasted special occasions with his whisky glass and manipulated weekday sprinkles to schedule Sunday doubleheaders. Nevertheless, beginning in 1920, Breadon and Rickey worked together effectively to establish the Cardinals as the best ballclub in the National League.

Their first big step came when Breadon convinced Phil Ball, owner of the American League St. Louis Browns and Sportsman's Park, to rent Sportsman's Park to the Cardinals for an annual payment of $35,000 and half of maintenance expenses. Then they sold the site of the Cardinals' old ballpark to the Board of Education, which tore down the ballpark to build Beaumont High School. Finally, rather than using the $275,000 proceeds as a nest egg, Breadon invested the money to develop Rickey's notion of a farm system.

Part III: Creation of the Farm System

Your typical Cardinal rookie is a poor boy of rudimentary education, bursting with base hits and ambition,

2. Branch Rickey, Sam Breadon and Creation of the Farm System

> a lean whip-muscled kid who can run and throw all day. He may not know the right side of the plate for his fork, but he knows it for his bat. He comes to town like Yankee Doodle, like Young Hickory, Andy Jackson himself. He wants money, but more than that he wants to play baseball and play it always. Around him grow up the historic tall tales of the pioneers. He can out-holler, out-sing, out-race, out-smart, out-fight, out-throw, anybody, anyplace, anytime.
> —Lloyd Lewis, Civil War historian and sports editor of the *Chicago Daily News*, in the introduction to J. Roy Stockton's *The Gashouse Gang and a Couple of Other Guys* (1945)[3]

Various major-league clubs had previously arranged to farm out a few of their promising prospects to gain seasoning in the minors, but Rickey and the Cardinals created the modern concept of a farm system. The Cardinals were unique in concentrating on scouting and developing young, unproven players. They assigned recruits to a low-classification minor-league team, such as Fort Smith (Ark.) of the Western Association. If a youngster showed promise there, the Cardinals advanced him to a higher-classification minor league team, like Houston of the Texas League. The Cardinals owned 50 percent of the Fort Smith club and, after starting with 18 percent, eventually acquired full ownership of the Houston club. As their farm system grew, the Cardinals continued to purchase minor league teams, but they also developed working agreements with others. Under a working agreement, the Cardinals provided financial support to the minor league team and received an option on their players.

This approach marked a radical break with the past, when independent minor league teams auctioned off their best players to the highest-bidding major league club. The Cardinals usually could not compete against wealthier major league clubs for top minor leaguers, and their infrequent winning seasons had relied on managers pulling off shrewd trades for major league veterans. Jesse Haines, a pitcher hailing from the same rural Ohio roots as Rickey, was purchased in 1919 for $10,000 from Kansas City of the American Association. He would win 210 games over the next 18 seasons in a Hall of Fame career with the Cardinals and also would be the last minor leaguer that the Cardinals purchased from an independent minor league club. After 1920, the Cardinals would harvest their own crop of minor leaguers from their own farm clubs.

A tragedy, though, provided a setback for the Cardinals in the early

Boom and Bust in St. Louis

1920s. Their left fielder, Austin McHenry, who only turned 26 in September 1921, had become a star that year, finishing third in the NL batting race with a .350 average and fourth in home runs (17) and runs batted in (102). He only played one more season, still batting over .300 for 1922 (.303) and his five-year career (.302) before a brain tumor drove him out of the line-up and took his life in November at the age of 27. After rising to third place in 1921 and 1922, the Cardinals fell to fifth in 1923 and sixth a year later, despite an increased influx of talent from the farm clubs.

Sunny Jim Bottomley, a future Hall of Fame first baseman, was the farm system's first graduate. A native of the farming and mining community of Nokomis, Illinois, Bottomley was the son of a coal miner. He had already suffered the loss of a brother, who survived military service in World War I, but not a cave-in at the local mine. Seeking to avoid the same fate, Jim Bottomley hired himself out as a blacksmith's apprentice, played on an area semipro ballclub, and attracted the attention of the Cardinals with a letter that expressed his love of baseball and desire to play for them. Rickey answered the letter and, by August 1922, Bottomley was batting .348 for Syracuse of the International League. The Cardinals promoted him to the majors, and he proceeded to hit .325 and drive in 35 runs in 37 games. For the following eight years, he was unchallenged as the Cardinals' first baseman, averaging 145 games per year with 20 homers, 118 runs batted in, and a .325 batting average. Bottomley was quickly joined by another Illinois native and former Cardinals farmhand, outfielder Ray Blades, who batted .301 and lasted ten years with the Cardinals, despite being slowed by leg and knee injuries. Over the next three years, many other players followed the same trail as Bottomley and Blades, working their way through the farm system to the Cardinals.

Rickey was far better at developing farm products than at managing them.. On Memorial Day 1925, with the Cardinals mired in last place, Breadon fired Rickey as field manager. Breadon believed, correctly as it turned out, that his club would be better off with Rickey focusing on front-office responsibilities and presiding over the fertile farm system. Although Rickey and Breadon occasionally overlapped each other's primary fields of expertise, Breadon was generally in charge of hiring and firing managers. Rickey was usually responsible for overseeing player development through the farm system, making trades, and negotiating salaries.

The managerial responsibilities were handed to the Cardinals' second baseman, Rogers Hornsby, then on his way to a sixth consecutive National League batting championship and his second Triple Crown for leading

2. Branch Rickey, Sam Breadon and Creation of the Farm System

the league in home runs, runs batted in, and batting average. Upon being named manager, Hornsby had just turned 29, an age old enough to possess the wisdom of a veteran and still young enough to recall the troubles of youngsters seeking to establish themselves in the majors.

Hornsby's background helped him to relate to the young Cardinals farmhands. A member of the Cardinals since September 1915, Hornsby had been discovered prior to the creation of the farm system. The Cardinals had acquired his contract for $500 from Denison (Tex.) of the Western Association. Aside from the faith of scout Bob Connery, the scrawny 19-year-old kid seemed woefully lacking in credentials. Connery, despite the fact that Hornsby had hit no higher than .277 in the Western Association and racked up 28 errors in the field, promised to reimburse the Cardinals their purchase price if Hornsby failed. In a late-season trial with the Cardinals, Hornsby had hit only .246 and committed eight errors in 18 games at shortstop. Miller Huggins, the manager, thought the youngster needed more minor league seasoning and told Hornsby that the Cardinals might want to farm him out. Hornsby, back in the days before farm systems were formed, had misunderstood. He got the idea that Huggins wanted him to work on a farm and bulk up. Hornsby went back to Texas, labored all winter on his uncle's ranch, and reported to spring training with 30 extra pounds on a newly muscular physique. From 1916 through 1919, he emerged as a star, averaging .311 and playing each of the four infield positions. In 1920, firmly established at second base, Hornsby hit .370 and started his six-year run of National League batting championships. Over the next five years, Hornsby topped the .400 mark three times and averaged .402 for the entire span.

Nicknamed "The Rajah," Hornsby understood the psychology of young players better than Rickey and therefore enjoyed immediate success. Rickey, verbose and theoretical, had bored ballplayers by diagramming strategy on a blackboard. Hornsby, profane and earthy, threw the blackboard out of the clubhouse. Whereas Cardinals prospects such as center fielder Taylor Douthit, left fielder Chick Hafey, and third baseman Les Bell had shuttled back and forth between the minors and the parent club during Branch Rickey's tenure as manager, they stuck with the Cardinals under Hornsby. Also, shortly after gaining command, Hornsby demanded that the Cardinals recall 22-year-old shortstop Tommy Thevenow, who had played briefly for them in 1924, from their Syracuse farm club. Bell believed that, for young players weary of Rickey's professorial soliloquies, Hornsby had simplified the task at hand: "All he ever asked

Boom and Bust in St. Louis

of anybody was that they give him all they had out on the field."⁴ After changing leaders, the 1925 Cardinals climbed from the National League cellar to the first division. They finished fourth with a record of 77–76 (13–25 under Rickey and 64–51 with Hornsby).

This improvement renewed hope for the upcoming season, but the Cardinals were not the only St. Louis club looking with optimism toward 1926. Their landlords, the St. Louis Browns, after losing the 1922 American League pennant by a single game to the New York Yankees, had rebounded from two ensuing losing seasons with an 82–71 record and third-place finish in 1925. Phil Ball was so encouraged over the Browns' prospects for 1926 that he enlarged the seating capacity for Sportsman's Park from 24,000 to 34,000. He had good reason to believe the Browns would be the primary beneficiaries of this expansion. After all, in his ten years of running the Browns, they had outdrawn the Cardinals in eight of those seasons. However, in 1926, the Cardinals brought St. Louis a pennant after a 38-year drought and suddenly were celebrated as the city's most beloved ballclub.

Branch Rickey expanded his farm system and sustained its success with the financial support of Sam Breadon (National Baseball Hall of Fame).

Baseball Commissioner Kenesaw Mountain Landis, always an opponent of the farm system, had refrained from taking action against it because Pittsburgh Pirates owner Barney Dreyfuss and Detroit Tigers owner Frank

2. Branch Rickey, Sam Breadon and Creation of the Farm System

Navin had both advised him that the farm system would collapse from its own weight. Instead, the farm system not only allowed the Cardinals to win in 1926, but it proved to be a sustainable and renewable system of player development that enabled the Cardinals to win nine pennants and six World Series between 1926 and 1946. They would outdraw the Browns in 27 of 28 years from 1926 to 1953 (every year except 1944, when the Cardinals defeated the Browns in the first World Series played exclusively west of the Mississippi). Finally in 1954, the Browns moved to Baltimore and became the Orioles.

Commissioner Kenesaw Mountain Landis opposed development of the farm system (Library of Congress).

3

The Rajah's Redbirds of 1926

> I've always played hard. If that's rough and tough, I can't help it. I don't believe there's any such thing as a good loser. I wouldn't sit down and play a game of cards with you right now without wanting to win. If I hadn't felt that way I wouldn't have got very far in baseball.
> —Rogers Hornsby, quoted in *Sport Magazine* in August 1955[1]

Part I: Winning the Pennant

Les Bell, one of the Cardinals' farm hands who settled into the parent club's starting lineup under Hornsby, was the son of a Harrisburg, Pennsylvania, railroad worker who did not want him to follow in his father's footsteps: "Railroading was a tough job in those days, real tough. So it was the old story of a father wanting to see his son do better than he did. But I told him he didn't have to worry—I had my sights set on playing ball." The Cardinals discovered him in 1920, while he was hitting .329 for Lansing, Michigan, of the Central League. Although a Detroit Tigers scout had placed Bell there, the Cardinals signed him, and he worked his way through the rungs of the Cardinals' farm system at Syracuse, Houston, and Milwaukee. After shuttling between the minors and the Cardinals in 1923 and 1924, Bell became the Cardinals' starting third baseman in 1925, hitting .285 with 11 homers and 88 runs batted in. He recalled that Hornsby in 1926, on the first day of spring training at San Antonio, had challenged the Cardinals: "If there's anybody in this room who doesn't think we're going to win the pennant, go upstairs now and get your money and go home, because we don't want you around here."[2]

3. The Rajah's Redbirds of 1926

The message had an important underlying meaning to Bell, Tommy Thevenow, Taylor Douthit, and Chick Hafey. Hornsby regarded these young players, who had spent years shuttling between the Cardinals and their farm clubs, as established major leaguers capable of carrying the Cardinals to the top of the National League standings. All of these Cardinals would respond positively to Hornsby's confidence in them. Bell would lead the Cardinals in 1926 with a batting average of .325, and he finished in the top five of the National League with 17 home runs and 100 runs batted in. Thevenow, an Indiana native recalled to the Cardinals on Hornsby's request in 1925, topped National League shortstops in putouts and assists and hit a productive .256 with 63 runs batted in.

Douthit and Hafey fulfilled the faith of a University of California–Berkeley history professor, Charles E. Chapman, who was a friend of Branch Rickey and had signed both of them to Cardinals contracts. Douthit, born in Little Rock, Arkansas, moved as a child with his family to California and earned a bachelor's degree in agricultural studies at UC–Berkeley. Hafey, originally a pitcher, was a native of Berkeley. In 1923, both Douthit and Hafey played for Fort Smith in the Western Association, and during spring training, Rickey heard the crack of the ball off Hafey's bat and immediately ordered the conversion of the future Hall of Famer into an outfielder. Douthit batted .305 for Fort Smith, and Hafey hit .284 with 16 home runs. In 1924, each young outfielder improved on his minor league batting average, with Douthit hitting .322 for St. Joseph (MO) of the West-

Rogers Hornsby likely accomplished what no other manager will ever match in 1926, leading his team to their first pennant in 38 years and an upset triumph in the World Series, but still losing his job (National Baseball Hall of Fame).

Boom and Bust in St. Louis

ern League and Hafey .360 for Houston of the Texas League. Both earned trials with the Cardinals, but were sent back to the minors for more seasoning. After they were recalled by the Cardinals in 1925, however, Hornsby kept them in the majors. Douthit hit .308 in 1926, his first full season as the Cardinals' starting center fielder, and won the nickname of "The Ball Hawk" by leading National League outfielders in putouts. Hafey, recalled by the Cardinals after Ray Blades injured his leg in mid–July 1925, got the opportunity to play regularly in the majors and hit .323 for the rest of the season. In 1926, though, Blades had recovered and reclaimed his starting position in left field. Hafey, relegated to part-time duty, was hitting only .241 on August 30 when Hornsby inserted him back into the starting lineup after Blades seriously damaged his knee trying to climb a chicken-wire fence to catch a fly ball. Blades never completely recuperated, so by hitting .302 down the stretch drive of a pennant race and raising his season average to .271, Hafey seized his opportunity to become an everyday starter.

The rest of the starting lineup of the 1926 Cardinals arrived via trade. On May 23, 1925, a week before Hornsby became manager, Branch Rickey acquired catcher Bob O'Farrell from the Chicago Cubs. An Illinois native, O'Farrell had grown up as a fan of the Chicago White Sox, but became the starting catcher for their cross-town rival. A foul ball had fractured his skull in 1924, and, while unable to play, O'Farrell became expendable when his job was taken over by a future Hall of Fame catcher, Gabby Hartnett. For the Cardinals, O'Farrell hit .293 in 1926, led National League catchers in putouts, and was named the League's Most Valuable Player. Thevenow, Douthit, and O'Farrell solidified the middle defense of the Cardinals.

On June 14, with the Cardinals contending for the pennant, they obtained right fielder and future Hall of Famer Billy Southworth, a 33-year-old veteran of four teams, in a trade with the New York Giants. The Cardinals' offense, composed predominately of right-handed hitters, gained another powerful left-handed batter to pair with Bottomley. Southworth was a native Nebraskan, and a family friend—Buffalo Bill Cody, the famous Pony Express rider, scout, and showman—nicknamed him "Billy the Kid" after the notorious New Mexico gunfighter. "Billy the Kid" hit .317 in 99 games with the Cardinals and ended in the top five of the league with 16 homers and 99 runs batted in. He moved into the second spot of their batting order behind Douthit and in front of Hornsby, Bottomley, and Bell. All five batters hit over .300 except Bottomley, who finished at .299, and, following Douthit, each of the next four drove home over 90 runs, topped by Bottomley's league-leading total of 120 runs batted in. The potent offense

3. The Rajah's Redbirds of 1926

of the 1926 Cardinals led the National League in runs scored (917), hits (1,541), and home runs (90).

Eight days after the acquisition of Southworth, the Cardinals claimed future Hall of Fame pitcher Grover Cleveland Alexander, another Nebraskan, for the $4,000 waiver price. Alexander had been raised on a farm and, as a child, developed his pitching skill from hunting wild turkeys with rocks. Joe McCarthy, the rookie manager of the Chicago Cubs, had released the 39-year-old Alexander, already a winner of 318 games. In his Cardinals' debut, Alexander thrilled a capacity crowd of 37,000 at Sportsman's Park with a 10-inning, 3–2 victory over McCarthy's Cubs. He notched nine wins against seven losses in three months for the Cardinals and posted a staff-best 2.91 earned run average.

The Cardinals moved into first place on their last home stand of the regular season, which lasted from August 14 through September 1. After opening the home stand with 11 wins in 15 games, they hosted a crucial five-game series against the defending World Series champion Pittsburgh Pirates. When the Pirates arrived at Sportsman's Park, they were tied for first place with the Cincinnati Reds, and the Cardinals were only a game back in third place. On August 29, Alexander and Pirates pitcher Vic Aldridge dueled to a 2–2, ten-inning tie. This tie had to be replayed, and since the Cardinals were not scheduled for any home games after September 1, the five-game series was condensed to three days. Doubleheaders were played on both August 30 and 31, followed by a single game on September 1. The two teams split the first doubleheader, leaving the standings exactly the same. However, the Cardinals made a significant breakthrough in the second doubleheader. They won the opener, 6–1, behind the pitching of a product from the coal-mining region of Pennsylvania, Bill Sherdel, who was supported by home runs from Bell and Hafey. In the nightcap, the Cardinals turned to rarely-used Allen Sothoron, a 33-year-old veteran pitcher in his 11th major league season. When the major leagues banned the spitball in 1920, Sothoron was one of 17 practitioners of the pitch who were permitted to continue using it. An Ohio native, he had won 20 games for the St. Louis Browns in 1919, but was now more of a coach than an active pitcher. In one last burst of glory, though, he allowed just three hits and defeated the Pirates, 2–1. Hafey drove in the Cardinals' first run and scored the second in the seventh inning. Meanwhile in Chicago, the Cubs beat the Reds for the second time in three days, permitting the Cardinals to spring from third place to sole possession of first (a half-game ahead of the Reds and a game up on the Pirates). On September 1, the Cardinals

Boom and Bust in St. Louis

faced the Pirates' ace, Ray Kremer, who had shut them out on only two hits in the first game of the doubleheader of August 30. Hornsby chose to go with a better-rested pitcher, Art Reinhart, a left-handed Iowa native who appeared more often as a reliever than a starter. The Cardinals shelled Kremer for 11 hits in just over six innings, and Reinhart breezed to a 5–2 victory. Following four wins in a row, the Cardinals departed on their closing, month-long road trip in first place, a game ahead of the Reds and two games in front of the Pirates.

The road trip started with a doubleheader in Chicago. In the opener, Alexander held his former Cubs teammates to three hits, winning 2–0. He also had two hits in three at-bats and scored the game's first run, the only one he needed. The Cardinals clobbered the Cubs, 9–1, in the nightcap, pounding 13 hits against Sheriff Blake and a succession of relievers. Both Southworth and O'Farrell had three hits, but Hornsby inflicted the most damage with a couple of hits, including a home run, scoring twice and driving home three runs. Flint Rhem, a hard-throwing and hard-drinking farm product from South Carolina, was the pitching beneficiary of the Cardinals' offensive onslaught and scattered six hits in a complete-game performance.

The Cardinals took off for Cincinnati and a weekend showdown against the Reds, now two games back. The Reds won on Friday and Saturday, throwing the National League race into a tie. Alexander pitched the Cardinals back into first place, 7–3, in the Sunday finale. He was supported by a 12-hit attack, led by Thevenow's three hits and two runs batted in.

The next stop was another three-game showdown in Pittsburgh, where the Pirates were lurking in third place, 3½ games behind the Cardinals. After splitting a Labor Day doubleheader, the Cardinals won the rubber game, 8–0, with Sherdel scattering nine hits in a shutout performance and Hornsby driving in three runs. They also picked up a game on the Reds and left Pittsburgh with an advantage of two games over Cincinnati and 4½ games over the Pirates.

However, the Cardinals faltered against the Braves, the league's hottest team in September. After losing three of four contests in Boston, they again fell into a first-place tie with the Reds. Upon reaching Philadelphia for a six-game series, though, the cozy dimensions of Baker Bowl—merely 272 feet down the right-field line and only 300 feet in the power alley of right-center—provided a cure for the Cardinals' offense. The Cardinals took the first five games of the series, outscoring the Phillies, 59–11. Their offensive explosion was primarily fueled by lead-off hitter Douthit, with

3. The Rajah's Redbirds of 1926

an average of .478, a dozen runs, and three steals, and cleanup hitter Bottomley, with an average of .579, a dozen runs batted in, and two homers. Although the Cardinals lost the last outing in Philadelphia, 3–2, they still left town in first place, 1½ games ahead of the Reds, who won twice in Brooklyn but fell off the pace by losing the last two of a three-game series against the Giants at the Polo Grounds.

The Reds journeyed next to Boston, where they dropped three straight to the red-hot Braves. By battering Brooklyn 15–7 at Ebbets Field, the Cardinals extended their lead to 2½ games. The trio of Southworth, Bottomley, and Bell combined for ten hits (including four triples, two doubles, and a home run), eight runs scored, and eight runs batted in, supplying the brunt of the Cardinals' 17-hit barrage. On September 24, the final Friday of the regular season, the Reds lost again in the first game of a doubleheader at Philadelphia. Their sixth consecutive loss gave the Cardinals an opportunity to clinch the pennant later that day against John McGraw's Giants.

Sherdel held the Giants to one run in eight strong innings of relief, and Southworth slammed a game-winning home run into the upper deck of the right-field stands of the Polo Grounds. The 6–4 victory provided sweet revenge for both Southworth and the Cardinals. McGraw, the highly influential Giants manager who won ten pennants between 1904 and 1924, had traded away Southworth and expressed confidence that the sweltering summertime heat in St. Louis would prevent their clubs from ever winning a pennant.

Part II: Winning the World Series

> The Yankees were at the epicenter of the baseball world while the Cardinals toiled away at the western fringe of the major leagues. The Yankee franchise was among the most profitable and publicized in baseball. The Cardinals received limited press coverage and the team's ownership had a long history of struggling to generate adequate revenues.
> —Paul E. Doutrich, describing the contrasts in the 1926 World Series participants in *The Cardinals and the Yankees, 1926*[3]

The Cardinals completed the regular season with a record of 89–65, two games ahead of the second-place Reds. The New York Yankees won

Boom and Bust in St. Louis

the American League championship, and, since the World Series opened in New York, the Cardinals waited there for a week. Throughout this interval, the Cardinals wearied of listening to the talk of the town, which believed that the Yankees would easily prevail. The stage was set for one of the greatest World Series upsets. The Yankees, appearing in their fourth Series in six years, were heavy favorites over the Cardinals, whose .578 winning percentage was worse than any champion in the first half-century of the National League. The Cardinals' chances hinged on using off-speed pitching—the change-ups of Sherdel, curves of Alexander, and knuckleballs of Jesse Haines—to slow down the offense of the Yankees' "Murderer's Row," who had led the majors in runs scored and home runs.

Sherdel, 16–12 in the regular season, lost a pitching duel in the opener to Herb Pennock, 2–1, but in Game Two, Alexander retired the last 21 Yankees to even matters with a 6–2 victory. The Cardinals' offense, limited to only three hits in the opening game, recovered with a dozen hits, including an inside-the-park home run by Thevenow and a more conventional three-run smash into the right-field bleachers by Southworth.

The Cardinals returned home to St. Louis and, in a downtown parade, received exuberant greeting from a million fans. They took the Series advantage when Haines, 13–4 in the regular season, pitched a shutout and slugged a two-run homer in a 4–0 win. In Game Four, Yankees hitters feasted on the fastballs of Flint Rhem, who had won 20 games in the regular season. After being held to a total of 15 hits in the opening three contests, the Yankees lashed out 14 hits against Rhem and a procession of relievers in Game Four alone. Babe Ruth paced the attack with three home runs, and the Yankees won a 10–5 rout. Hornsby then returned the Yankees to a steady diet of off-speed pitching. In the last contest at Sportsman's Park, Sherdel took a 2–1 lead into the ninth inning, but ultimately lost another hard-luck decision to Pennock, 3–2, in ten innings.

Back at Yankee Stadium, the Cardinals staved off elimination, 10–2, behind the pitching of Alexander and four runs batted in, including a home run, by Bell. In the seventh and deciding game, Haines carried the Cardinals into the seventh inning, clinging to a 3–2 lead provided on Thevenow's two-run single. With two on, two out, and two strikes on Lou Gehrig, his control wavered. He threw four straight balls to load the bases. The veteran knuckleball artist, bleeding profusely, had developed blisters on the knuckles of his throwing hand, rendering his trademark pitch ineffective. Although Haines volunteered to go after the Yankees

3. The Rajah's Redbirds of 1926

with fastballs, Hornsby sagely avoided that tactic and instead called for Alexander from the bullpen.

According to legend, Alexander had been dozing, either sleeping off a hangover from an all-night binge or perhaps still inebriated. The myth borrows a cloak of plausibility from Alexander's personal problems. A sergeant in the 89th Infantry Division, Alexander had served in the trenches of the western front during World War I, emerging shell-shocked, deaf in one ear, and prone to epileptic seizures. At a time when alcoholism seemed more socially acceptable than epilepsy, then stigmatized as akin to demonic possession, Alexander masked his symptoms of epilepsy with his fondness for booze.

After the call from Hornsby, Alexander ambled to the mound and confronted Tony Lazzeri, a 22-year-old rookie who had driven home 114 runs in the regular season. The old pitching master carved up the youngster with the precision of a surgeon, striking him out with a high-inside fastball that Lazzeri tagged but pulled foul and a pair of low and away curves.

In the eighth inning, Alexander retired the Yankees in order on a grounder and two pop-ups, and he faced the top of their vaunted batting order in the ninth. Earle Combs and Mark Koenig both grounded out to Bell, and Alexander went to a full count with Ruth before walking him. Ruth promptly attempted to steal second, but O'Farrell gunned him down, giving the World Series championship to the Cardinals.

According to the *St. Louis Post-Dispatch*, local fans immediately responded as if a "city-wide detonation" had occurred: "It was as if dynamite had been planted in a hundred scattered spots and all touched off at the same instant. The downtown exploded in noise. Two minutes after the din was deafening. Automobile horns and sirens, back-firing of motors, tin horns, bells that had been muffled in silence, all turned loose." This pandemonium persisted throughout a "nine-hour rampage."[4]

For the next 70 days, fans rested on their laurels until December 20, when the Cardinals traded Hornsby to the Giants. The emotions of local fans again erupted, only this time in anger, threatening to boycott the Cardinals in protest. The St. Louis Chamber of Commerce adopted a resolution that criticized the trade, and protesters draped black crepe paper on Sam Breadon's home and his automobile agency. Jim Gould, a sportswriter for the *St. Louis Star*, vowed never to cover another Cardinals game.

Breadon dealt Hornsby, who had averaged .359 in a dozen seasons with the Cardinals, because of a confrontation during the September stretch drive. Breadon had scheduled an exhibition game on a rare day off. Hornsby thought the Cardinals needed a day of rest and, in front of the team, branded Breadon as a penny-pincher more concerned with pocketing spare change from a meaningless exhibition than with winning the pennant. His diatribe concluded with the suggestion, as longtime *Post-Dispatch* sportswriter J. Roy Stockton paraphrased, of "a palpably impossible disposition of all exhibition games."[5] Breadon smoldered over this insubordination, and Hornsby's fate was already virtually sealed before winning the pennant and World Series. Afterward, Breadon briefly reconsidered, agreeing to Hornsby's request for a $50,000 contract. However, unsure about how long he could put up with Hornsby, he refused Hornsby's demand for a three-year contract and instead offered only a one-year deal. Negotiations broke down, and Breadon traded Hornsby.

Hornsby, having spent his entire career with the Cardinals, entered a nomadic phase that took him to five different teams in the final 11 years of his playing career. Sometimes he served as a player-manager and, on other occasions, solely as a player. Hornsby, even as a baseball gypsy, could always hit and averaged .357 for the remainder of his Hall of Fame career. However, after leaving the Cardinals, his managerial reputation suffered. O'Farrell, who succeeded him as Cardinals manager, later recalled: "Hornsby was a great manager as far as I'm concerned. That year in St. Louis he was tops. He never bothered any of us. Just let you play your own game…. Of course they say later on he couldn't get along with his players. Got a little bossy, they say. Seems like he changed. But as far as I'm concerned he was great."[6]

4

Managerial Merry-Go-Round

> We almost won the pennant again in 1927. Lost out to the Pirates by only one and a half games. But we *didn't* win it, so the following season I wasn't the manager any more, and I found myself traded to the Giants in 1928.[1]
> —Bob O'Farrell, quoted in Lawrence Ritter's *The Glory of Their Times* (1966)

Fortunately for Sam Breadon, his December 1926 trade with the New York Giants swapped future Hall of Famer second basemen. In exchange for Rogers Hornsby, he acquired Frank Frisch, the Giants' veteran second baseman and captain, who had undergone his own falling-out with John McGraw. Frisch was a product of New York City, like Breadon, and in 1919 joined the Giants straight out of Fordham University. As a Giant, he hit .318, played on four consecutive pennant-winners from 1921 to 1924, and led the league one season apiece in runs, hits, and stolen bases. In 1927, his first year with the Cardinals, Frisch batted .337, led the majors in stolen bases with 48, and played second base better than anybody. He topped all major league second basemen in fielding percentage, double plays, and assists (setting an all-time single-season record for assists by a second baseman that still stands), Breadon always regarded Frisch's season to be the best individual performance of any Cardinal. Thanks to Frisch, Breadon withstood the local furor over the Hornsby deal and honed his ability to view popular players as dispensable cogs. He viewed the Hornsby for Frisch trade as a personal epiphany: "I knew then that it was the ball club that counted. I never again feared trading a player."[2]

Breadon was just as willing to fire managers as to trade players. Bob O'Farrell, after replacing Hornsby as manager, piloted the 1927 Cardinals to 92 victories, three more than their championship season a year earlier.

Boom and Bust in St. Louis

THE NEW SPIRIT OF ST. LOUIS.

More than four years after Charles Lindbergh's solo flight across the Atlantic aboard the *Spirit of St. Louis,* the World Series performance of Pepper Martin turned him into a Lindbergh-style hero in this cartoon of October 9, 1931, drawn by Daniel Fitzpatrick, in the *St. Louis Post-Dispatch* (State Historical Society of Missouri).

However, the Cardinals fell 1½ games short of the Pittsburgh Pirates and wound up second. Frisch blamed Branch Rickey for costing the Cardinals another pennant. After shortstop Tommy Thevenow broke his ankle, rather than calling up 15-year veteran and future Hall of Famer Rabbit Maranville from their higher-classification Rochester farm club, Rickey promoted a 21-year-old Texan, Heinie Schuble, from their lower-classification Danville (IL) farm club. For months, Schuble struggled in the field, committing 29 errors in 65 games, before Rickey finally relented and brought up Maranville. Breadon, dissatisfied with a near miss, dismissed O'Farrell and appointed Cardinals coach Bill McKechnie as manager.

4. Managerial Merry-Go-Round

McKechnie, who had managed the 1925 Pirates to the World Series championship, benefited from Rickey enjoying a better year in the front office than in the preceding season. First, prior to the start of the 1928 season, Rickey traded third basemen with the Boston Braves, acquiring a seven-year veteran, Andy High, and $25,000 for Les Bell, who had slumped at the plate after his banner 1926 season. An Illinois native, High would hit .287 for the Cardinals over the next four seasons, originally as the starting third baseman and later as a valuable utility infielder. Second, with Thevenow slow to recover from his broken ankle, Rickey resisted the temptation to turn to a younger alternative than the 37-year-old Maranville, a Massachusetts product who had led the Braves to the 1914 World Series title. Third, on May 1, Rickey traded O'Farrell, still troubled from a broken thumb suffered in 1927, to the Giants for right fielder George Washington Harper, a native of southern Arkansas. Harper, hitting .305 in 99 games with the Cardinals, driving in 58 runs, and blasting 17 homers, filled a gap created when Billy Southworth chose to launch a managerial career with the Cardinals' Rochester farm club. Fourth, on May 11, Rickey engineered a deal with the Philadelphia Phillies and secured a replacement for O'Farrell as catcher. He obtained Jimmie Wilson, a local Philadelphian with five years of major league catching experience, for an undisclosed amount of cash and two inexperienced rookies, catcher Spud Davis and outfielder Homer Peel. Wilson served as the Cardinals' regular backstop for the next six years, averaging .281 and leading National League catchers in putouts three times and assists twice. At the end of his run, the Cardinals traded him back to the Phillies for Spud Davis, by then an experienced catcher.

These newcomers joined the Cardinals' nucleus of Frisch, Taylor Douthit, Chick Hafey, and Sunny Jim Bottomley. Frisch averaged an even .300 and topped all National League second basemen in fielding average, while Douthit batted .295 and again led National League outfielders in putouts. Hafey hit .336, homered 27 times, and drove in 111 runs. Bottomley, batting .325 and leading the league with 31 home runs and 136 runs batted in, won the National League's Most Valuable Player Award. Bill Sherdel, Jesse Haines, and Grover Cleveland Alexander headed the veteran pitching staff with 21, 20, and 16 wins respectively. This talented team attracted a St. Louis attendance record of 761,574 that would stand for 18 years and turned a profit of $444,737.

McKechnie, like O'Farrell, guided the Cardinals to another three-game improvement in wins. Unlike in 1927, though, the improvement in 1928

Boom and Bust in St. Louis

enabled the Cardinals to take the National League pennant. On June 15, the Cardinals moved into first place to stay, and their 95 wins held off the Giants by two games. For the second time in three years, the Cardinals enjoyed the last laugh on McGraw following a mid-season trade. In 1926, after acquiring Southworth from the Giants, the Cardinals had clinched the pennant on a Southworth homer against McGraw's Giants. Two years later, they obtained Harper from the Giants and, on September 20, won a crucial showdown between the two contenders, 8–5, when Harper, who had overheard McGraw refer to him as a "dumb bastard" before the trade, hit three home runs and literally thumbed his nose at McGraw after each one.[3]

On September 29, the final Saturday of the regular season, the Cardinals clinched the pennant in their next-to-last game, defeating the Braves, 3–1, in Boston. They scored all three of their runs in the top of the first inning, keyed by Bottomley's run-scoring triple. Sherdel, winning his 21st game, made that lead stand up with three innings of relief help from Flint Rhem. The Cardinals faced the New York Yankees again in the World Series, but all comparisons with the 1926 World Series began and ended there. The Yankees, who had romped over the Pirates in four straight games in the 1927 World Series, also swept the Cardinals in 1928. Breadon, in response, demoted McKechnie to his minor-league team in Rochester and promoted Southworth, a Series hero who had hit .345 for the victorious Cardinals in 1926.

Southworth, later one of the Cardinals' best managers, was not yet ready for big-league managerial responsibilities. He had to manage veterans who had been his teammates and, in trying too hard to exert his authority, alienated his former friends. By July, with the Cardinals floundering at 43–45, Breadon recalled McKechnie to St. Louis and sent Southworth back to Rochester.

McKechnie returned to a different Sportsman's Park from the one he had left the preceding fall. Phil Ball, the owner of the St. Louis Browns and Sportsman's Park, had tired of watching the Yankees' left-handed duo of Babe Ruth and Lou Gehrig drive homers into his right-field pavilion (only 320 feet from home plate and later reduced in 1931 to 310 feet). Therefore, on July 5, 1929, Ball installed a wire screen in front of the right-field pavilion that reached a height of 33 feet. Now, to hit a home run, a batter had to hit the ball over the screen and onto the right-field pavilion roof. Otherwise, balls hit off the screen remained in play, often leading to doubles and triples. The right-field screen of Sportsman's Park,

4. Managerial Merry-Go-Round

therefore, affected playing conditions similarly to the left-field wall at Boston's Fenway Park.

After McKechnie's return, the 1929 Cardinals pulled themselves above .500, finishing fourth at 78–74. Breadon intended to keep McKechnie as manager for 1930, but McKechnie accepted the job security of a five-year offer from the Braves and hopped off the Cardinals' managerial merry-go-round. McKechnie, a low-key Pennsylvanian, later guided the Cincinnati Reds to consecutive pennants in 1939–1940 and became the first manager to take three different clubs to the World Series, a feat that earned him selection to the Hall of Fame.

During the Roaring 20s, the Cardinals had turned a profit of $1,481,081. Major league baseball had reflected the general affluence of the decade. Every club, except the Boston Red Sox, had made money during the decade, and ten clubs had earned more than a million dollars. The Cardinals had ranked third in the National League and fifth in the majors for earnings in the 1920s.

The year of 1930 marked the first baseball season of the Great Depression, and the major leagues initially weathered the economic storm well, with 14 of 16 clubs enjoying profits. Spurred by pennant-winning seasons in both 1930 and 1931, the Cardinals profited $576,181 in the first two years of the Great Depression. They topped the majors in 1931 with earnings of $345,263, but most clubs did not fare nearly as well. By 1931, economic realities took a toll on major league baseball, and the majority of clubs lost money. Although the National League as a whole still turned a profit in 1931, the American League suffered a deficit, with six of its eight clubs losing money.

For his manager in 1930, Breadon turned to Cardinals coach Gabby Street, an Alabama native who had served as a sergeant in World War I. A different manager directed spring training camp for a sixth successive season. Street, however, became the first Cardinals manager since Rickey to survive two full seasons and, in the process, won two straight National League pennants. He inherited the same Cardinals lineup that had won the 1928 pennant for Bill McKechnie, except for the left side of the infield and the right fielder.

The Cardinals converted their third baseman for the last two years, Andy High, into a utility infielder and occasional pinch-hitter. The third base job was put into the hands of Sparky Adams, a Pennsylvania product and eight-year veteran purchased from the Pirates. Adams held the starting job for two years, averaged .303, and scored 98 runs in 1930 and

Boom and Bust in St. Louis

97 more in 1931. Shortstop had been a troublesome spot for the Cardinals ever since Thevenow broke his ankle in 1927. The Cardinals never believed that Thevenow fully recovered, so they primarily used the veteran Maranville to man the position in 1928. In December, they traded Thevenow to the Philadelphia Phillies and sold the 37-year-old Maranville to the Boston Braves, his original team. This left the shortstop position to be filled at spring training of 1929 between two Pennsylvania prospects from the farm system. Eddie Delker got the first crack at the position, but he failed to hit enough. Charley Gelbert, a product of Lafayette College, soon took over and proved to be the shortstop that the Cardinals had sought. He kept the position for the next four seasons, batting .281, until a tragic hunting accident virtually ended his career.

Despite his dazzling 1928 season, the Cardinals also sold their 36-year-old right fielder George Washington Harper to the Boston Braves in the same transaction as Maranville. As his replacement, the Cardinals turned right field over to Ernie "Showboat" Orsatti, a farm product from Hollywood, California. Orsatti hit .332, but was eventually relegated in 1930 to a backup role behind another farm product, George Watkins, a Texan who could hit with more power than Orsatti and was coming off a .337 season for the Rochester farm club. Watkins patrolled right field for the Cardinals for four years, hitting .313 and averaging 11 home runs and 66 runs batted in.

The Cardinals' pitching staff also underwent several changes in 1930. Alexander was gone. In August 1929, after undergoing rehabilitation for alcoholism, the pitching hero of the 1926 World Series had returned to the Cardinals and shut out the Pirates. Shortly afterwards, as a reliever, he entered a tied game against his original team, the Phillies. The Cardinals won the game in extra innings, and Alexander earned his 373rd major league win, all in the National League. His victory broke the record for National League wins, previously held by Christy Mathewson. It would be the last win of Alexander's career. Alexander fell off the wagon, celebrating his record-setting victory with a drinking binge that left him unavailable to pitch. Sam Breadon, out of sentimental affection for Alexander, paid him for the rest of the season and sent him home to Nebraska. Seventeen years later, in 1946, New York sportswriter Joe Reichler uncovered a box score from May 21, 1902, in which Mathewson pitched and, under modern scoring rules, would have been credited with a win. Reichler got the official records changed, giving Mathewson 373 wins and a share of the record with Alexander.

4. Managerial Merry-Go-Round

Bill Sherdel, who had hitherto spent his entire 13-year career with the Cardinals and won 153 games for them, was traded in June 1930 to the Boston Braves. In exchange, the Cardinals received a future Hall of Fame pitcher, Burleigh Grimes, the last legal spitball pitcher. Although he did not rely exclusively on the spitball, Grimes constantly employed it as a psychological weapon, bringing his glove always up to his mouth and planting the idea in the hitter's head that every pitch might be a spitball.

Grimes, who grew up in Wisconsin and worked as a boy in a logging camp, won 13 games after joining the Cardinals. Haines also contributed 13 victories, and "Wild Bill" Hallahan, nicknamed for his control problems rather than his lifestyle, topped the Cardinals' staff with 15 wins. Hallahan, a native of Binghamton, New York, had been a young reliever on the Cardinals' 1926 World Series champions, but was shipped back to the minors to learn how to command his outstanding fastball. He never gained complete control of it, leading National League pitchers in walks three times. However, Hallahan mastered enough control to lead the league in strikeouts twice and win an average of 14 games a year for the Cardinals from 1930 to 1935.

The 1930 pennant race was a four-team affair, with the Cardinals rising from fourth to first in the last month of the season. As late as August 8, the Cardinals trailed the front-running Brooklyn Robins by a dozen games. They won 18 of their last 24 games in August and, although still entering September in fourth place, had definitely interjected themselves into the race. Brooklyn had dropped to third and was only a half-game ahead of the Cardinals, the second-place Giants were 1½ games ahead of the Cardinals, and the front-running Chicago Cubs were 4½ games up on the Cardinals. The Cubs were the defending league champions and, after moving into first place in August, appeared ready to justify their status as pre-season favorites.

Beginning on September 8, though, the Cubs stumbled at Ebbets Field, where Brooklyn swept three straight games. The red-hot Robins, nicknamed for their manager Wilbert Robinson, went on to sweep a four-game series from Cincinnati and run their winning streak to 11 games. They had moved into first place, a game ahead of the Cardinals, whose 10–2 September record made them the second-hottest team in the league.

These two contenders faced each other in a three-game showdown at Ebbets Field, beginning September 16. In the opener, Hallahan won a pitching duel against his counterpart, future Hall of Famer Dazzy Vance,

Boom and Bust in St. Louis

in front of a capacity crowd of 30,000. The game was scoreless through nine innings. In the top of the tenth, the Cardinals pushed across the only run. High, playing because Gelbert had been injured in an eighth-inning collision at second base, doubled to right-center and scored on Douthit's single to right. Brooklyn threatened in the bottom of the tenth, loading the bases with one out, but Hallahan induced Al Lopez to ground into a game-ending double play. The teams were now in a virtual first-place tie, although the Cardinals were one percentage point ahead. On the next day, they were tied three-all in the top of the ninth, with two Cardinals on base and two out, when Street sent High to the plate to pinch-hit for the pitcher. High delivered again, doubling off the right-field wall to score the deciding runs in the Cardinals' 5–3 victory. Grimes completed a three-game sweep for the Cardinals on September 18, defeating Brooklyn, 4–3. Although the Cardinals were limited to five hits, three were decisive extra-base hits. After Frisch tripled in one run, Bottomley blasted a two-run homer. Douthit later tripled and scored the Cardinals' fourth run.

The Brooklyn Robins never recovered, losing the next four games and falling to fourth place. The rejuvenated Cubs, winning seven of their final eight contests and the last six in succession, still gave chase to the Cardinals. However, the Cardinals successfully fended off their challenge, taking four of five games in Philadelphia and, after returning home to St. Louis, two straight from the Pirates. Their offense again capitalized on the cozy dimensions of Baker Bowl, as in the September stretch drive of 1926, to pummel the Phillies into submission, outscoring Philadelphia, 53–33, in the five-game series. The Cardinals continued their offensive onslaught at Sportsman's Park, defeating the Pirates, 9–0 and 10–5. Their weeklong scoring binge, spearheaded by Bottomley with a .556 average and 14 runs batted in and Watkins with 12 runs batted in and a .607 average, culminated with the Cardinals clinching the National League pennant on the final Friday of the regular season. Haines won the 10–5 pennant-clincher, and Watkins paced the assault on Pirates pitchers with three hits, three runs batted in, and a home run. With the pennant already in hand, Street allowed a 19-year-old farmhand to make his major league pitching debut on the last day of the regular season. Dizzy Dean, signed earlier in the year when a Cardinals scout discovered him pitching semipro ball for San Antonio Public Utilities, threw a three-hitter and beat the Pirates, 3–1, giving the Cardinals 39 wins in their last 49 games and a September record of 21–4. The Cardinals, with a season record of 92–62, finished two games

4. Managerial Merry-Go-Round

ahead of the second-place Cubs, and the Giants and Robins trailed by five and six games respectively.

In the 1930 World Series, the Cardinals clashed with the defending champions, the Philadelphia Athletics, who easily won the opening two games behind their powerful pitching duo of Lefty Grove and George Earnshaw. Upon returning to St. Louis, though, the Cardinals rallied, taking the third game on a 4–0 shutout by Hallahan and then evening the series when Haines defeated Grove, 3–1. The fifth game was a pitching duel with Grimes matching Earnshaw for seven innings and Grove in relief for eight innings of scoreless ball. In the top of the ninth, with one out and a runner on first, Grimes faced the Athletics' top slugger, Jimmie Foxx. Earlier in the Series, Grimes had fooled Foxx, pretending to load up a spitball and striking Foxx out with a curve instead. When Grimes tried the same ploy again, Foxx was not deceived, crushing the curveball deep into the left field bleachers and giving the Athletics a 2–0 victory. Following a travel day to Philadelphia, the Athletics' manager, Connie Mack, gambled by bringing Earnshaw back to pitch with only one day of rest. Hallahan, with three days of rest, should have been far stronger. Ironically, it was Hallahan who had to leave the game early, departing with blisters on his throwing hand after just two innings of work. The Cardinals trailed, 2–0, at the time, and Earnshaw made the lead hold up in a 6–1 Series-clinching win.

Unlike in 1928, when Breadon fired McKechnie for being swept in the World Series, Breadon believed that the Cardinals had put up a spirited fight in the 1930 Series loss. Street was retained as manager and, in 1931, guided the Cardinals to one of their greatest seasons. For the first time, the Cardinals won 100 games, finishing with a record of 101–53. They took over first place on May 30, never relinquished it, and coasted to the National League pennant, 13 games ahead of the second-place Giants. Then, avenging their World Series loss of the preceding year, they defeated Philadelphia in seven games and derailed the quest of the Athletics to become the first team to win three straight World Series titles.

The composition of the 1931 Cardinals differed only slightly from their roster of the year before. Ripper Collins, once a coal miner in Pennsylvania, was coming off a year of hitting .376 and socking 40 home runs for the Cardinals' Rochester farm club. He shared time in 1931 with Bottomley at first base, hit .301, and drove home 59 runs in 89 games. Paul Derringer, a 23-year-old pitcher, was also promoted to the Cardinals after leading the International League with 23 wins for Rochester. Derringer

Boom and Bust in St. Louis

had been raised on a Kentucky tobacco farm, and his family had been active in the 1904–1908 Black Patch War that tobacco planters in Kentucky and Tennessee waged against the price-fixing purchasing tactics of the monopolistic American Tobacco Company, owned and operated by James Duke. In 1931, Derringer topped all National League pitchers in winning percentage with an 18–8 record. Finally, at the mid–June trading deadline, Rickey dealt Douthit to the Cincinnati Reds. From 1926 through 1931 Douthit had averaged .303 for the Cardinals and, as their center fielder, established career and single-season fielding records that still stand. He had just belted eight consecutive hits, boosting his average to .331. Rickey nevertheless believed the 30-year-old Douthit had lost a step and cleared center field for 27-year-old Pepper Martin, who had hit .363 in 1930 for Rochester and was earning nearly $10,000 a year less than Douthit. Martin, an Oklahoman whose father had participated in the Land Rush of April 22, 1889, averaged an even .300 in the regular season and turned the 1931 World Series into a personal showcase. He batted .500, stole five bases, and set a Series record with 12 hits that stood for 33 years.

While Martin did not win the World Series single-handed for the Cardinals, there were moments when it seemed that way. The World Series opened in St. Louis for the first time since 1887, but Grove put a damper on the excitement, pitching the Athletics to a 6–2 victory. Hallahan, who had led the National League with 19 wins, countered with a three-hit shutout in the second game, and Martin scored both of the Cardinals' runs against Earnshaw. In the second inning, with one out, Martin stretched a single into a double with a headfirst dive into second base, stole third, and scored on a sacrifice fly. He led off the seventh with a single, stole second, and went to third on a groundout. On Gelbert's suicide squeeze bunt, Martin slid home safely beneath the tag of catcher Mickey Cochrane. After two games, Martin had four hits in seven at-bats, and of the Cardinals' four runs, he had scored two and drove in one.

The series moved to Philadelphia, where local fans respectfully gave Martin a standing ovation and booed President Herbert Hoover, who was blamed both for the Great Depression and for still defending Prohibition. Boos for the President turned into a chant of "We want beer!"[4] Meanwhile, Martin had two more hits and two runs scored to support Grimes, who threw a two-hitter and beat Grove and the Athletics, 5–2. Earnshaw evened the series the next day with a 3–0 triumph, in which he allowed only two hits, both by Martin. The Cardinals again took the Series lead in the fifth game, 5–1, behind the pitching of Hallahan and the offense

4. Managerial Merry-Go-Round

of Martin, whose four runs batted in included a two-run homer into the upper deck of the left-field pavilion. After five games, Martin had 12 hits in 18 at-bats, and of the Cardinals' 14 runs, he had scored five and driven in another five.

When the Series returned to St. Louis, Grove allowed Martin only a walk and defeated the Cardinals, 8–1, forcing a seventh and deciding game. Earnshaw held Martin hitless again. However, Martin's walk and stolen base were crucial in the Cardinals' two-run first inning. High, subbing for an injured Adams at third base, led off with a single to left and, when Watkins also singled to left, advanced to second. After Frisch moved up the runners with a sacrifice bunt, Earnshaw faced Martin and unleashed a wild pitch, allowing High to score. Martin subsequently coaxed a walk from Earnshaw and stole second. His steal left first base vacated and, therefore, when Cochrane dropped a third strike to Orsatti, he had to throw to first to retire Orsatti. As soon as Cochrane threw to first, Watkins broke from third and scored on an errant return throw from Foxx.

High singled to center in the third inning and scored when Watkins walloped a homer over Sportsman's Park right-field pavilion. High and Watkins scored all four of the Cardinals' runs in the seventh game and accounted for all five of their hits. Grimes, a 17-game winner in the regular season, protected their 4–0 lead all the way to the ninth inning, when the Athletics scored twice and had the potential tying runs on base with two outs. Street summoned Hallahan from the bullpen. The Cardinals' ace faced the Athletics' leadoff man, Max Bishop, who drove a sinking liner into center field. Martin raced in and, appropriately, made the catch for the final out. The 1931 World Series had transformed him from a relatively obscure player into a national celebrity, the Associated Press "Athlete of the Year." Martin, with the World Series winner's share of $4,467.59, virtually doubled his 1931 salary of $4,500, and his sudden fame landed him an off-season vaudeville contract that guaranteed $1,500 a week for a nine-week tour. Halfway through the tour, though, Martin quit and offered an explanation true to his principles and rural roots: "I ain't an actor; I'm a ballplayer. I'm cheating the public and the guy who's paying me the $1,500. Besides, the hunting season's on in Oklahoma, and that's more important business."[5]

Over a six-year span, thanks to the fertile farm system and a few wise trades, the Cardinals had won four pennants and two World Series. They had split World Series appearances against two of the most famous teams in baseball history, the 1926–1928 New York Yankees and the 1929–1931

Boom and Bust in St. Louis

Philadelphia Athletics, denying each of them the chance to become the first team to win three consecutive World Series. After the Cardinals claimed the 1931 World Series, the *St. Louis Post-Dispatch* editorialized that the "series of the century" had provided the city with an economic and psychological release from the stresses of the Great Depression: "The hotels have been crowded to capacity, banishing for the time being the specter of depression. The shops have, of course, shared in the harvest.... The emotional value of the series cannot be put down in figures, but surely it must be worth a good deal in times like the present to divert the national mind from the besetting cares and anxieties."[6] However, since the Cardinals relied on their farm clubs to be renewable sources of player development, they would soon need to part with more of their old heroes to make way for new prospects.

5

Rise and Decline of the Gas House Gang

> They certainly have that something which makes them a more interesting outfit to watch than perhaps any great club of the past. They are a hell-roaring, hard-riding bunch of baseball cowboys.... Their dashing play and drastic expedients stood out in sharp contrast against the workaday play of the Tigers.
> —Wilbur Wood, sports editor of the *New York Sun*, on the victorious performance of the St. Louis Cardinals in the 1934 World Series[1]

The farm system matured into a self-sustaining bonanza. It produced an abundant surplus of players, permitting the Cardinals to choose the cream of the crop and sell their leftovers to other major league clubs. The Cardinals plowed back proceeds from sales of unproven youngsters and aging veterans into further expansion of the farm system. Thus, they constantly duplicated their recipe for success, stocking their roster with farm products and supplementing it with occasional trades for veteran players.

Three members of the Cardinals' World Series champions of 1931 were traded before the first pitch of the 1932 season. In December, two months after starring in the seventh game of the World Series, 34-year-old Andy High and 38-year-old Burleigh Grimes were both traded. Chick Hafey had won the National League batting championship in 1931 with a .349 average, despite missing spring training while holding out for more money. He was only 28 years old and, in the last five seasons, had hit .338 and averaged 23 home runs with 100 runs batted in per year. However, when he held out again in the spring of 1932, the Cardinals shipped him to the Cincinnati Reds.

Friction soon developed on the team. In their pennant-winning

Boom and Bust in St. Louis

years of 1930–1931, the press had referred frequently to manager Gabby Street's reliance on the guidance of veteran players. Street apparently resented this and, in the spring of 1932, advised returning veterans that he was the Cardinals' only boss. Veteran leaders, such as Sunny Jim Bottomley, Frank Frisch, and Jimmie Wilson were already embittered over the trades of three fellow veterans, and they now felt completely unappreciated. Street claimed that Frisch, the National League's Most Valuable Player in 1931, had not exerted as much effort in 1932 as in the two previous pennant-winning seasons. Frisch complained of being forced to play with multiple injuries, a problem that the presence of High could have alleviated.

Furthermore, although Ernie "Showboat" Orsatti hit .336 as Hafey's replacement in left field, he lacked the power of Hafey. The Cardinals finally addressed this problem in September, when they called up 20-year-old

Dizzy Dean (left) shakes hands with his younger brother Paul (right). In the Cardinals' championship season of 1934, the Deans pitched 49 of the Cardinals' 95 wins in the regular season and all four victories to defeat the Detroit Tigers in the World Series (Charles Trefts, Photographer, State Historical Society of Missouri).

5. Rise and Decline of the Gas House Gang

Joe "Ducky" Medwick from their Houston farm club. Medwick, a native of Carteret, New Jersey, who had turned down a football scholarship to Notre Dame to sign with the Cardinals, was batting .354 with 26 homers and 111 runs batted in for Houston and, in 26 games with the Cardinals, hit .349. He manned left field for the Cardinals until June 1940 and, like Hafey, blazed his way to the Hall of Fame. In his seven full seasons with the Cardinals (1933–1939), Medwick averaged .337 with 20 home runs and 123 runs batted in per year.

With his motto of "base hits and buckerinos" and occasional indifference to defense, though, Medwick did not endear himself to the veteran Cardinals. Frisch pointedly protested: "I have never seen a base-hit hound yet who was of much use to his ball club." The brashness of the team's leading pitcher, 21-year-old Dizzy Dean, also frustrated team elders. After winning 26 games in 1930, 25 with two farm clubs and the final game of the regular season for the Cardinals, Dean would have won a spot in the Cardinals' 1931 starting rotation based on his pitching ability, but the Cardinals shipped him back to their Houston farm club to teach him a lesson in humility. Dean won 26 games for Houston and remained as boastful as ever. Just two months after making the Cardinals in 1932, he was already questioning his standard rookie salary of $3,000 and the entire salary structure of the defending world champions. "There's guys on this club makin' four times the dough I'm makin', but I'm nine times a better pitcher. That ain't fair."[2]

The 1932 Cardinals—beset by the loss of traded players, a rift between the manager and their veteran players, and another rift between the veterans and younger players—were a demoralized crew that dipped to sixth place, with a losing record of 72–82. Many changes loomed on the horizon.

Bottomley was the last position player to participate in all four of the Cardinals' World Series appearances between 1926 and 1931. In 1931, he hit .348 to fend off a challenge for the first base job from Ripper Collins. A year later, still sharing first base with Collins, Bottomley had his batting average dip to .296 in 91 games with 11 home runs and 48 runs batted in, compared to Collins' .279 average in 149 games with 21 homers and 91 runs batted in. At the age of 31, Bottomley had hit .325 in 11 years with the Cardinals, the same average that he had posted in his major league debut in 1922. However, on December 17, 1932, the Cardinals traded Bottomley to the Cincinnati Reds, choosing the 27-year-old Collins for his youth, lower salary, and versatility to play the outfield. After winning the first base job from one future Hall of Famer, Collins was the Cardinals' unchallenged first baseman from 1933 to 1935, before another future Hall of Fame farm product, Johnny "The Big Cat" Mize, began to push him aside. In his three years as the Cardinals' full-time first baseman, Collins hit .320 and averaged 23 home runs and 106 runs batted in per year.

Also, in the off-season of 1932, shortstop Charley Gelbert virtually ended his career when he shot himself accidentally in the leg while hunting. He missed the next two seasons and, even after returning to the majors in 1935, was never close to being the same player again. Desperate for a shortstop, Branch Rickey was forced to trade one of the Cardinals' best young pitchers, Paul Derringer, and their aging third baseman, 38-year-old Sparky Adams, to the Cincinnati Reds on May 7, 1933, to obtain Leo "The Lip" Durocher, who had been suspended from high school in Springfield, Massachusetts (and never returned) for retaliating against a male science teacher for slapping him by whacking the teacher across the back with one of "those big window-lifter poles they used to have in school rooms."[3] For four years, Durocher ably filled their needs at shortstop, twice leading National League shortstops in fielding average and hitting .268 with a yearly average of 62 runs batted in. In 1937, though, Durocher slumped to a batting average of only .203, prompting the Cardinals to trade him to the Brooklyn Dodgers. Meanwhile, Derringer would win 20 or more games for the Reds four times in six years from 1935 to 1940. Because of Gelbert's hunting accident, the arrival of Durocher was crucial for the Cardinals, but the loss of Derringer was certainly felt as well.

In July 1933, with the Cardinals barely above the .500 mark at 46–45, Breadon replaced Street as manager with Frisch. Under Frisch, the Cardinals improved to a record of 36–26 for the remainder of the 1933 season, but still finished fifth. Following the season, the Cardinals traded two 33-year-old veterans, right fielder George Watkins and catcher Jimmie Wilson. Watkins was dispatched to the New York Giants, while Wilson was sent to the Philadelphia Phillies for 29-year-old Spud Davis, who replaced Wilson behind the plate. Davis, from Birmingham, Alabama, hit .300 in 1934. However, while injured, he lost his job to 22-year-old Bill DeLancey, a native of Greensboro, North Carolina. Davis, in an era when veterans frequently shunned youngsters trying to take their jobs, provided catching tips to DeLancey and also helped his fellow Southerner to learn the traits of National League hitters. Frisch noticed the unselfishness of Davis and, when managing the Pittsburgh Pirates in the 1940s and Chicago Cubs in the 1950s, hired Davis as a coach.

5. Rise and Decline of the Gas House Gang

DeLancey was one of four members of the Columbus (OH) farm club, champions of the American Association in 1933 and victors in the Junior World Series over the Buffalo Bisons, champions of the International League, who played major roles in transforming the Cardinals into 1934 World Series champions. For Columbus in 1933, DeLancey slugged 21 homers, drove in 97 runs, and averaged .285, and, a year later, in 93 games with the Cardinals, he hit .316 with 13 home runs and 40 runs batted in. Rickey considered DeLancey one of the three best catchers he had ever seen, but unfortunately, DeLancey only played two full seasons with the Cardinals before contracting tuberculosis, which halted his baseball career and caused his premature death at the age of 35.

Burgess Whitehead, a product of the University of North Carolina and the regular shortstop for Columbus in 1933, later compared the champion Columbus Redbirds to the 1934 St. Louis Cardinals as "hustling, winning types of ball clubs."[4] In 1934, filling the Cardinals' dire need for a utility infielder like Andy High, he hit .277 in 100 games and saw considerable action at second base, shortstop, and third base. Only 24 years old, Whitehead appeared to be the heir apparent to the aging Frisch at second base. However, after earning All-Star recognition in 1935, Rickey traded him to New York, where Whitehead started at second base and batted .282 on consecutive pennant-winners for the Giants in 1936 and 1937. He appeared in the All-Star Game again in 1937 and led National League second basemen in putouts, double plays, and fielding percentage.

Paul Dean, the younger brother of Dizzy Dean, was promoted to the Cardinals after winning 22 games for Columbus in 1933. As a 21-year-old rookie in 1934, he trailed only his older brother on the Cardinals' pitching staff. Finally, Jack Rothrock, once a longshoreman on the docks of San Pedro, California, took over as the Cardinals' starting right fielder. Unlike the other three Columbus graduates, the 29-year-old Rothrock was not a young product of the Cardinals' farm system. He had averaged .280 in five seasons with the Boston Red Sox from 1925 to 1929 and, in 1928, became the first major leaguer to play all nine positions in a single game. A broken leg disrupted his career in 1930 and, although Rothrock returned in 1931 to play in 133 games and hit .278, he got off to a slow start in 1932. The Red Sox sold him to the Chicago White Sox on April 30, but his struggles continued. Altogether, Rothrock batted only .196 in 1932 and fell out of the majors. Attempting to fight his way back, he accepted a minor-league contract with Columbus in 1933. Rothrock enjoyed an outstanding season there, hitting .347, and in 1934, was the only Cardinal to play every inning of every game. He hit .284 for the Cardinals, scored 106 runs, and was hailed as the club's unsung hero by everyone from Frisch to Albert Monroe Dean, father of Dizzy and Paul Dean.

The support from the Columbus farm club could not have arrived at a more crucial time for the Cardinals. Sam Breadon had lost a reported $200,000 on the Cardinals from 1932 to 1933 and, haunted by a fear of going from riches to rags, was reconsidering his commitment to baseball. Although second-generation farm products had started for previous Cardinals champions, no Cardinals club composed primarily of second-generation farm products had won a championship until 1934. The year of 1934 would reaffirm the vitality of the farm system and strengthen the connection between Breadon and the Cardinals.

The Cardinals returned to the top of the baseball world with the fabled "Gas House Gang." The term "gas house gang" conveyed connotations of the working-class neighborhoods of major cities. Gene Karst, hired by the Cardinals as the first major league public relations director, widely distributed background information about the Cardinals' second-generation of farm products. Perceptive writers were well aware of the working-class origins of many Cardinals. Karst influenced enough stories written about individual players that their collective working-class affiliations eventually coalesced into the team identity of the "Gas House Gang," which blended rural and urban players from coast to coast and truly resembled a cross-section of the American working-class. First baseman Collins, the coal miner from Pennsylvania, only pursued a baseball career when his union went on strike. Pepper Martin, who transferred to third base for the Cardinals from 1933 to 1935, had been a jack-of-all-trades in his native Oklahoma, where he worked as a farmer, ranch hand, well digger, posthole digger, and garage mechanic. His Italian-American replacement in center field, Orsatti, who averaged .306 in his nine-year career with the Cardinals from 1927 to 1935, had worked in Hollywood setting up props and occasionally as a stunt man. Left fielder Medwick, the son of Hungarian immigrants, had grown up in Carteret, New Jersey, where his father labored at a saw mill that produced ties for the Reading Railroad. The top pitchers were a pair of Arkansas-born brothers, Dizzy and Paul Dean, who had toiled throughout their youth as migratory cotton pickers across the Southwest.

Dizzy Dean, after winning 20 games in 1933, startled reporters the following spring with his prediction that he and his younger brother would win 45 games for the 1934 Cardinals. He was wrong. Paul Dean earned 19

5. Rise and Decline of the Gas House Gang

victories in his rookie season, while Dizzy garnered 30 despite being suspended for a week in August for skipping an exhibition game in Detroit. As late as September 4, though, the Cardinals trailed the defending world champion New York Giants by seven games. Rumors were rampant that Frisch would be fired as manager and that Breadon would sell the Cardinals, who might move elsewhere.

However, with 20 wins in their last 25 games, the Cardinals silenced these rumors and overtook the Giants on the last weekend of the season. They caught the Giants largely as a result of winning 13 of 22 head-to-head confrontations, with Dizzy and Paul Dean combining to go 12–2 against the Giants. Jimmy Powers, a sportswriter with the *New York Daily News*, attributed the phenomenal success of the Deans at subduing the Giants to a rural-urban conflict: "Does anyone appreciate the resentment small-town citizens hold for citizens of big cities? This explains more than anything the success of the Dean brothers…. Tell them they are going to pitch a nine-inning contest they more or less mechanically turn in an excellent job. If you tell them to pitch against the New York Giants their eyes glow fanatically, they snatch the horsehide and stride to the mound, nostrils breathing fire." On the final weekend, while Paul and Dizzy defeated the Cincinnati Reds in St. Louis, the Brooklyn Dodgers took on the Giants at the Polo Grounds. Back in January, exhibiting a rare moment of levity with the press, Giants manager Bill Terry had joked: "Is Brooklyn still in the league?"[5] After the Dodgers knocked the Giants out of pennant contention with two wins, Terry was haunted by his words and never again displayed a sense of humor with the press. The Cardinals, with a record of 95–58, edged the Giants for the pennant by two games.

Then they came from behind again to upset the favored Detroit Tigers in seven games in a fiercely fought World Series. "Members of both teams," reported W. J. McGoogan of the *St. Louis Post-Dispatch*, "were sliding into bases with spikes waist high with no quarter asked and none given."[6] The Deans pitched St. Louis to all four wins in the World Series, and Dizzy Dean was acclaimed as National League Most Valuable Player and Associated Press Athlete of the Year. In just a few weeks of late September and early October, the "Gas House Gang" claimed their fame and earned their name.

Although radio broadcasts of World Series games dated back to 1921, the 1934 World Series was the first one to have a commercial sponsor, with the Ford Motor Company shelling out $100,000 for the rights to air the series. The two participating teams split 58 percent of the windfall,

Boom and Bust in St. Louis

while their players received the remaining 42 percent of the proceeds. The 1934 World Series games also constitute the oldest existing radio broadcasts of the World Series, and, prior to the opening game in Detroit, with the Tigers appearing in their first World Series in 25 years, announcer Graham McNamee observed on CBS Radio, "Detroit is more hungry for this series than any other city in my recollection." Pat Crawford, a veteran reserve infielder from North Carolina and the National League's leading pinch-hitter in 1934, recalled that the Cardinals were greeted with "jeering insults" at the Detroit train station and were kept up most of the night by a loudspeaker outside the Book-Cadillac Hotel blaring "Hold That Tiger" over and over again. However, the next day, the Tigers appeared to be the team that was rattled. They committed five errors in the opening three innings, and behind four hits by Medwick and a 13-hit attack, Dizzy Dean coasted to an 8–3 victory. *New York World-Telegram* sports columnist Joe Williams described the Cardinals as looking "like a bunch of boys from the gas house district who had crossed the railroad tracks for a game of ball with the nice kids."[7]

In Game Two, Wild Bill Hallahan led 2–1 going into the ninth inning, but the Tigers rallied to tie the game and then win it in the 12th inning against Cardinals reliever Bill Walker. Paul Dean regained the series lead for the Cardinals with a 4–1 win in the first game played in St. Louis. The Tigers then evened the series for a second time, 10–4, with Walker again taking the loss in relief of Tex Carleton. Dizzy Dean, who had entered the game as a pinch-runner, was knocked unconscious when he was hit in the head by a throw by Tigers shortstop Billy Rogell. In the last game at St. Louis, an obviously woozy Dizzy returned to the mound and was beaten, 3–1.

The Cardinals faced elimination when they returned to Detroit, received another hostile reception at the train station, and heard many more choruses of "Hold That Tiger" from the loudspeaker outside the Book-Cadillac Hotel.[8] Paul Dean won his second game of the series, 4–3, and drove in the winning run off Tigers ace "Schoolboy" Rowe with a single that scored Durocher. Dizzy Dean then shut out the Tigers in the seventh game, 11–0, and, in the Cardinals' key seven-run third inning, tied a World Series record with two hits in one inning. In the sixth inning, Medwick tripled to drive in Martin and increase the Cardinals' lead to 8–0. He slid hard into third base and became entangled with Tigers third baseman Marv Owen. After Medwick and Owen got into a brief skirmish, Medwick scored on Ripper Collins' fourth hit of the day, pushing the Cardinals'

5. Rise and Decline of the Gas House Gang

advantage to 9–0. When Medwick tried to take his left field position for the bottom half of the sixth inning, Detroit fans pelted him with fruit and bottles, halting the game for 20 minutes. Finally Commissioner Kenesaw Mountain Landis removed Medwick—the Cardinals' leading hitter in the World Series with a .379 average—from the game for his own protection. Each of the Cardinals' starters in the seventh game had at least one hit and scored at least one run. Dan Daniel, a colleague of Williams at the *World-Telegram*, summarized the Cardinals' World Series championship as a triumph of the "gas house gang" over "nice boys from the right side of the tracks."[9]

The Cardinals drew one-fourth of their total of 325,056 spectators during the final frantic week of the pennant race. The Gas House Gang's stretch drive symbolized the survival of America's common man against all odds. The proceeds from the World Series enabled Breadon to turn a profit of $109,229, when just a month earlier *The Sporting News* had reported that he had another $100,000 shortfall staring him in the face. Breadon believed major league baseball had turned the corner toward recovery and decided not to sell the Cardinals. Indeed, the Cardinals lost money in only one other season of the 1930s, and their overall profits of $788,777 in the decade surpassed all National League teams except for the Giants.

Folklore quickly embraced the never-say-die spirit of the 1934 Cardinals and, in the process, elevated the Gas House Gang into one of the most famous teams of baseball history, despite its lack of sustained success. The Gas House Gang lacked pitching depth and depended too much on the Deans. In 1934, Dizzy and Paul Dean accounted for over half of the Cardinals' victories, 49 of 95. Nevertheless, in November 1934, the Cardinals traded Tex Carleton, whose 16 wins had trailed only the Deans on the 1934 pitching staff, to the Chicago Cubs. Carleton, who had grown up on a cattle ranch in Comanche County, Texas, and attended Texas Christian University, was a cantankerous teammate. He had fought Medwick and deeply resented the popularity of Dizzy and Paul Dean. Carleton joined a Cubs staff that included two other farm products of the Cardinals, Lon Warneke and Bill Lee. Warneke, who had already won 62 games for the Cubs from 1932 to 1934, and Lee, who had pitched in 1933 for the Cardinals' championship farm club at Columbus, would both win 20 games for the 1935 Cubs. Carleton chipped in 11 more victories, giving Chicago a trio of pitchers who were gifts from the Cardinals and won 51 games for the Cubs.

Boom and Bust in St. Louis

Meanwhile, Dizzy and Paul Dean combined for 47 of the Cardinals' 96 victories in 1935, and, in August, when the Cardinals again passed the Giants and took over first place, it appeared that they would pitch the Cardinals into another World Series. However, the Cubs went on a 21-game winning streak in September and overtook the front-running Cardinals by four games.

Paul Dean tore cartilage in his right shoulder in June 1936 and never fully recovered. That year the Cardinals tied the Cubs for second place with an 87–67 record, even though Dizzy Dean won 24 games and led the league in games pitched, innings, complete games, and saves. Dizzy averaged 24 wins a year from 1932 to 1936 and, in 1937, had 12 wins at mid-season. He started the 1937 All-Star Game and needed only one out to finish his three-inning stint, when Earl Averill of the Cleveland Indians smashed a liner off the big toe of Dean's left foot. The ball caromed to an infielder, and Averill was retired at first base, but Dizzy Dean's left big toe became his Achilles' heel. He limped back into action two weeks later and placed an unnatural strain on his throwing arm. He suffered a shoulder injury that abruptly halted his brilliant Hall of Fame career. The Cardinals tumbled to fourth place and wasted an MVP year from Medwick, who won the Triple Crown with 31 homers, 154 runs batted in, and a .374 batting average, the last NL player to do so.

On April 16, 1938, the Cardinals peddled Dizzy Dean to the Chicago Cubs for $185,000 and three players, including Missouri-born pitcher Curt Davis, who would win 22 games for the 1939 Cardinals. Amazingly, even without his fastball, Dizzy Dean parlayed guile and control into a 7–1 record in spot starts and actually helped the Cubs win the pennant. Although 3–1 for the Cardinals, Paul Dean only managed to pitch in five games. Virtually without either Dean for a full season, the Cardinals fell back to sixth place with a 71–80 record, which cost Frisch his job. Frisch had played the final 11 seasons of his 19-year Hall of Fame career with the Cardinals, compiling a batting average of .312, twice leading the league in stolen bases, and playing for four pennant-winners and a pair of World Series champions.

With the departure of Frisch as manager, only Medwick in left field and Pepper Martin as a reserve outfielder and occasional third baseman remained from the original Gas House Gang of 1934. Medwick, after his Triple Crown season of 1937, became increasingly embittered with the Cardinals' salary structure. Although the Cardinals had fared better than most clubs during the Great Depression, their average annual profit

5. Rise and Decline of the Gas House Gang

had declined from around $148,000 in the 1920s to around $78,000 in the 1930s. This decline in profits had caused the Cardinals to cut corners whenever possible and become more tightfisted than ever in contract negotiations. They cut Medwick's salary after both the 1938 and 1939 seasons, citing his declining production. In 1938 and 1939, Medwick had batted .327 and averaged driving in 120 runs and hitting 18 home runs. In 1938, he had even led the National League in runs batted in for the third successive season. Medwick never believed he had been properly compensated, and he was outraged over his salary being cut for All-Star performances, simply because they failed to match his career-best season of 1937. The moody slugger became even more prone to lackadaisical play in the outfield, which antagonized his teammates and particularly the pitching staff. On June 12, 1940, the Cardinals traded Medwick to the Brooklyn Dodgers.

Pepper Martin, the last member of the original Gas House Gang, hit .316 in 86 games with the 1940 Cardinals. He then accepted an offer to manage in the Cardinals' farm system. During World War II, Martin briefly returned to the Cardinals, hitting .279 in 40 games in 1944 and being part of a third World Series championship club. He still holds the World Series record for the highest batting average, .418, of any player with over 50 at-bats in Series play. Martin was a career .298 hitter, led the National League in stolen bases three years, and scored over 120 runs in a season three times.

When Martin rejoined the Cardinals in 1944, despite war-time manpower shortages, the Cardinals still boasted a far deeper pitching staff than the Gas House Gang had enjoyed. The farm system had yielded abundant harvests throughout the late 1930s and early 1940s, and, unlike with the second generation of farm products, Rickey had restrained himself from selling or trading too many pitchers from the third generation of farm products.

6

St Louis Swifties

> I don't think that I was ever as proud to be with a ball-club as I was to be one of the 1942 St. Louis Cardinals. I've played with other great clubs, but I would have to say that one topped them all.
> —Enos Slaughter, who played on four World Series champions, two with the Cardinals (1942 and 1946) and two with the New York Yankees (1956 and 1958)[1]

The transition from a second to a third generation of farm products had already started in the managerial tenure of Frank Frisch. Terry Moore, Alabama-born but St. Louis-raised, had replaced Ernie "Showboat" Orsatti as the Cardinals' starting center fielder in 1935. He roamed center field for the Cardinals for the next eight years, then spent three seasons in the military during World War II, and reclaimed his center field position for another three years after the war. In 11 years with the Cardinals, Moore was a four-time All-Star, hit .280, and, as an excellent fielder, topped National League outfielders in putouts twice and fielding average once. Johnny "The Big Cat" Mize, a Georgian, displaced Ripper Collins at first base in 1936, and the Cardinals traded Collins to the Chicago Cubs after the season. Mize, in six seasons with the Cardinals, batted .336 and averaged 26 homers and 109 runs batted in per season. Enos "Country" Slaughter, raised on a North Carolina farm, signed with the Cardinals in 1934 at a tryout camp in Greensboro, North Carolina. In 1937, he led the American Association with a .382 batting average for the Cardinals' Columbus (OH) farm club and, a year later, took over the Cardinals' right field position from Pepper Martin, who had returned to the outfield in 1936 following three years as the third baseman. Slaughter did not relinquish the right field position in his Hall of Fame career for the next 16 years, except for three seasons in military service during World War II.

6. St Louis Swifties

In 13 seasons with the Cardinals, while leading National League outfielders twice in assists and once apiece in putouts and fielding average, he hit .305, drove in an average of 88 runs per year, and batted .381 in ten All-Star Game appearances.

The trio of Frisch, Durocher, and Pepper Martin, at second base, shortstop, and third base respectively, would be replaced in the infield by a trio of farm products: Don Gutteridge, Stu Martin, and Jimmy Brown. All three of the new infielders were capable of playing multiple positions. The Cardinals used Gutteridge, a native of Pittsburg, Kansas, primarily as a third baseman and occasionally at shortstop. They moved around the two North Carolinians, Martin and Brown, much more. Stu Martin saw action at all four infield positions, but usually played either second or third base. Brown varied, season to season, from being the club's primary second baseman, shortstop, or third baseman, or dividing time between all three positions. All three infielders were effective hitters. Gutteridge averaged .268 in five seasons from 1936 to 1940, and, over the same span, Martin hit .269. Brown, a North Carolina State product and the starting second baseman for the National League in the 1942 All-Star Game, batted .282 in seven seasons with the Cardinals from 1937 to 1943. Martin, a National League All-Star in his rookie season of 1936, did not appear in the All-Star Game that year. Winning pitcher Dizzy Dean had started the game with three shutout innings, and, staked to an early lead, National League manager Charley Grimm stuck with his starters to secure the National League's first victory in four All-Star Games. After Bill DeLancey's

Stan Musial, only 21, in his first full major league season of 1942 (National Baseball Hall of Fame).

catching career was tragically shortened by tuberculosis, another farm product, Mickey Owen, emerged as his successor behind the plate. Owen, a native Missourian born in Nixa, was a fiery competitor like DeLancey, but not nearly as good a hitter. Nevertheless, he held the catching job for four years from 1937 to 1940, battling his way to a .257 batting average.

Sam Breadon had replaced Frisch, a personal favorite of his, as manager with Ray Blades, a personal favorite of Branch Rickey. Blades imposed a prohibition on the Cardinals more drastic than the Twentieth Amendment, which forbade only production and sale of alcoholic beverages but not consumption, by banning beer-drinking on his team. He also had an unique manner of handling his pitchers. In those days, it was not rare to use a starter in relief, but Blades took the practice to a different level. For example, in 1939, three Cardinals pitchers finished among the top four of the National League in games pitched. This strategy actually worked well in 1939, when the Cardinals finished second with a record of 92–61, only 4½ games behind the Cincinnati Reds. The flip side occurred the following year. Sore-armed pitchers contributed to the Cardinals stumbling to a 14–24 start, and Blades was fired by Breadon on June 7.

Breadon replaced Blades with another personal favorite of his own, Billy Southworth. Southworth had changed considerably since failing as the Cardinals' manager in 1929. His years as a minor league manager, dealing with young players like he had been in his big-league debut of 1913, had mellowed Southworth into a kinder and more considerate leader. Enos Slaughter, one of the young stars on the Cardinals, regarded Southworth as a father figure. Shortly after taking charge in 1940, Southworth won the goodwill of his players with an important gesture, permitting the Cardinals to stop in New York City and watch a championship boxing match on their way to a series in Boston.

This paternal, fatherly approach differed from the feisty, hot-tempered style of Blades, and the Cardinals responded positively to the change. Under Southworth, the Cardinals completed the 1940 season with a 69–40 record, moving from sixth place to third in the final standings. The relaxed leadership of Southworth allowed young farm products to flourish. Max Lanier, a left-handed pitcher from North Carolina, had been signed by Frank Rickey, the brother of Branch Rickey and a Cardinals scout who specialized in recruiting North Carolina because he enjoyed hunting and fishing there. Lanier was rarely used in 1938 and 1939, but he blossomed under Southworth's tutelage and posted a 64–41 record for five years from 1940 to 1944. Marty Marion, a South Carolinian and descendant of the

6. St Louis Swifties

Revolutionary War hero Francis "The Swamp Fox" Marion, emerged from the farm system in 1940 and hit .278 in his rookie season, firmly establishing himself as the Cardinals' shortstop. In 11 seasons, from 1940 to 1950, Marion was named to eight All-Star teams, batted .264, and topped National League shortstops in fielding four times.

Shortly after Southworth became manager, the Cardinals traded Ducky Medwick to the Brooklyn Dodgers, and on June 18, 1940, six days after the trade, the Cardinals faced the Dodgers in Brooklyn. On their way to Ebbets Field, Medwick and the Dodgers' manager, Leo Durocher, exchanged taunts with Bob Bowman, the Cardinals' starting pitcher and a West Virginia native, in the elevator of the New Yorker Hotel. In the bottom of the first inning, following three consecutive Brooklyn hits, Bowman unleashed a fast ball that hit Medwick in the head, knocking him unconscious. A bench-clearing brawl ensued between the two teams, and the Dodgers' chief executive, Larry MacPhail, launched an unsuccessful attempt to ban Bowman from baseball permanently. The incident fueled the Cardinals-Dodgers rivalry of the 1940s, which was further inflamed when the two teams battled down to the last weekend of the season for the National League pennant in both 1941 and 1942.

In December 1940, the Dodgers also acquired Cardinals catcher Mickey Owen. Another aspect of the Cardinals-Dodgers rivalry concerned the way that the clubs had been constructed. The Cardinals, fielding a young team mostly harvested from their farm system, were always ready to sell established veterans and reinvest the proceeds back into the farm system. In contrast, the Dodgers were a wealthier club, composed primarily of established veterans who had been purchased from poorer teams. Many of the Dodgers, in fact, had been obtained from the Cardinals. In 1940 alone, for instance, MacPhail paid Breadon $185,000 for Medwick, Owen, and pitcher Curt Davis, who won 22 games for the Cardinals in 1939 but was winless in 1940 when included in the June deal for Medwick. The Dodgers' center fielder, Pete Reiser, had been a farmhand of the Cardinals, until Commissioner Kenesaw Mountain Landis freed him and 90 other players in the so-called "Cedar Rapids Decision" of March 1938. Finally, Durocher had gone from being the shortstop and captain of the Gas House Gang to being the manager of the Dodgers.

Walker Cooper, another farm product and the son of a rural mail-carrier, replaced Owen as the Cardinals' catcher. In the process, he became the battery mate of a fellow native of Atherton, Missouri, his older brother Mort Cooper, one of the Cardinals' pitchers. In the opening week

Boom and Bust in St. Louis

of the 1941 season, though, Walker Cooper separated his shoulder diving to tag a runner at the plate, and this injury marred his rookie season. He ended up sharing catching duties with veteran Gus Mancuso, acquired in the Owen trade. Cooper hit only .245 in his injury-plagued debut. Furthermore, his brother Mort, although setting a career high with 13 wins, underwent surgery to remove bone chips from his elbow and was sidelined for six weeks. However, once their health was restored, the Cooper brothers came back strong. Walker Cooper batted .305 from 1942 to 1944 and averaged 10 home runs and 73 runs batted in per year, while Mort won 65 games from 1942 to 1944 and suddenly emerged as a consistent 20-game winner (22 in 1942, 21 in 1943, and 22 again in 1944).

The growing depth of the Cardinals' pitching staff became increasingly apparent in 1941. It featured six pitchers who won between 10 and 17 games, and in late August, the Cardinals called up a 20-year-old lefthander from New Orleans, Howie Pollet, who had won 20 games against only 3 losses with a minuscule 1.16 earned run average for their Houston farm club. After joining the Cardinals, Pollet posted a dazzling 1.93 earned run average, while winning five games with just two losses.

In the infield, the Cardinals had promoted second baseman Frank "Creepy" Crespi from their farm system. Crespi, a St. Louis native from the Italian-American community of The Hill, hit .279 in 1941 and led National League second basemen in putouts and double plays. Jimmy Brown settled at third base and batted .306. Late in September, with Brown hindered by a broken finger, the Cardinals called up a 23-year-old third baseman, George "Whitey" Kurowski, from their Rochester farm club. Kurowski, a native of Reading, Pennsylvania, whose father was a coal miner, had endured the tragic death of an older brother in a cave-in. He desperately desired to avoid following his father's footsteps into the mines, and baseball provided an outlet. After being called up by the Cardinals, Kurowski hit .333 in four games.

Ernie Koy, a 30-year-old veteran obtained from the Dodgers as part of the Medwick deal, initially replaced Medwick in left field. He hit .310 for the remainder of the 1940 season, but was sold in May 1941 to make room for a 24-year-old farm product from Nebraska, Johnny Hopp, who hit .303 in 1941. However, in August, right fielder Slaughter broke his collarbone in a collision with center fielder Terry Moore and, shortly afterward, Moore was hit in the head by a pitch. For a while, the Cardinals relied on a pair of veteran reserve outfielders, 29-year-old Coaker Triplett, who hit .286, and 38-year-old Estel Crabtree, who hit .341.

6. St Louis Swifties

By mid–September, though, the Cardinals called up Stan Musial, a 20-year-old youngster, from the Rochester farm club. Musial was born in the industrial town of Donora, Pennsylvania, to a father who had immigrated from Poland and a mother of Czech descent. His father, Lukasz Musial, worked in the shipping department of the wire mill, but in 1932, when American Steel and Wire virtually shut down, Lukasz was only able to work one day a week at best. Pennsylvania had more workers on relief than any other state, and the Musials, like so many other Depression-era Pennsylvanians, were forced to accept flour and other necessities from the Red Cross and other charities. Stan Musial later maintained that his family never went hungry, although he pointedly complained about the monotony of their diet: "There was always something to eat, cabbage soup, cabbage salad, steamed cabbage, and every other kind of cabbage. No more cabbage for me. I can't even look at it."[2]

In 1938, he signed with the Cardinals as a pitcher and started his professional baseball career with Williamsburg, West Virginia, in the Class D Mountain State League for $65 a month. After a shoulder injury ended his pitching career, Musial turned to playing the outfield and, in 1941, advanced in a single season from Class C ball in Springfield, Missouri, to Rochester in the International League and then to the majors. In 12 games with the Cardinals, Musial hit a torrid .426. He played 21 more seasons with the Cardinals in his remarkable Hall of Fame career. Musial would win seven batting championships, three Most Valuable Player Awards (in 1943, 1946, and 1948), and hit for a lifetime average of .331. His 24 All-Star appearances have been equaled only by Willie Mays and Hank Aaron, and Musial, who won the 1955 All-Star Game for the National League with a walk-off homer in the bottom of the 12th inning, still holds the career record for All-Star Game home runs with six.

The Cardinals finished 1941 with an outstanding record of 97–56, but it was only good enough for second place, 2½ games behind the Dodgers. They blamed losing the pennant on their injuries, but the injuries actually provided Pollet, Kurowski, and Musial opportunities to showcase their abilities. These three players all earned roster spots in 1942, and each played a significant role in the most successful era of Cardinals baseball history.

On December 11, 1941, the same week that the United States entered World War II, the Cardinals shipped Mize, their six-time All-Star first baseman, to the New York Giants. In exchange, they received $50,000 and three players, although only catcher Ken O'Dea actually played for

Boom and Bust in St. Louis

the Cardinals. O'Dea, a native of Lima, New York, and originally a product of the Cardinals' farm system, backed up Walker Cooper for the next three years and hit .255. When Cooper went into military service early in the 1945 season, O'Dea became the Cardinals' primary catcher for the rest of the year, hitting .254 and leading National League catchers in fielding.

The Cardinals initially replaced Mize with Ray Sanders, a Missourian born in Bonne Terre, who had driven in 120 runs and hit .308 at Columbus (OH) in 1941. By mid–June, though, Southworth turned to Hopp, the starting left fielder in 1941 who had lost his job to Musial. When the military draft began draining major league rosters in 1943, Hopp bounced back to the outfield, and Sanders once again became the starting first baseman. Hopp hit .292 for the Cardinals from 1941 to 1945, while Sanders batted .279 from 1942 to 1945. Neither Sanders nor Hopp packed the power of Mize. In 1942, Sanders and Hopp combined to hit eight home runs and drive in 76 runs, compared to Mize's six-year average of 26 home runs and 109 runs batted in.

Both Sanders and Hopp were far faster than the massive Mize, though, and their speed contributed to the Cardinals' new nickname of "St. Louis Swifties." Willard Mullin, a *New York World-Telegram* cartoonist, devised the name "St. Louis Swifty" for his drawing of a riverboat gambler who represented the Cardinals in his sketches. The nickname accurately described the Cardinals' style of play in the 1940s. Unlike Whitey Herzog's "Runnin' Redbirds" of the 1980s, the Cardinals of the 1940s did not make extensive use of stealing bases. However, in the 1940s, the Cardinals ran the bases very aggressively, taking an extra base whenever possible. Casey Stengel, then managing the Boston Braves, described the Cardinals in 1942 as a "track team that ran like uncaged rabbits."[3]

From 1935 to 1941, the Cardinals were runners-up four times, but had not won a pennant. The drought would be broken in 1942 with a third generation of champion players. All of the 1942 Cardinals, except for pitcher Harry "Gunboat" Gumbert and reserve outfielder Coaker Triplett, were homegrown products of the farm system. They were one of the youngest champion clubs ever, averaging just 26 years old, with six players in their first full major league season. Musial, the most notable of the newcomers, teamed with center fielder Moore and right fielder Slaughter to form a stellar outfield trio who roamed far and wide to chase down fly balls. Slaughter and Musial, with averages of .318 and .315 respectively, finished second and third in the National League batting race.

6. St Louis Swifties

In June, when Southworth replaced Sanders with Hopp as the starting first baseman, he also moved Brown from third base to second and installed Kurowski at third base. Crespi, who had sparkled at second base in 1941, was relegated to utility infield duty at second base and shortstop. Crespi went into military service in 1943 and, after breaking his leg in a service game, suffered a career-ending injury when he immediately broke the leg again in a hospital wheelchair race. Kurowski would remain the Cardinals' third baseman until injuries forced him out of the starting lineup in 1948. In his six seasons as a starter, he was named an All-Star five times, averaged 17 home runs, 82 runs batted in, and a .293 batting average per year, and twice led the league's third basemen in fielding. In 1942, Kurowski batted .254 with nine home runs and 42 runs batted in. He combined with Slaughter, who hit 13 homers, and Musial, with 10 home runs, to account for over half of the meager 60 home runs struck by the 1942 Cardinals. Although the Cardinals merely ranked sixth in the National League in home runs, they led the league in batting average (.268) and runs scored (775).

Their pitching staff boasted the lowest earned run average in the National League (2.55). Mort Cooper, the National League MVP, headed the staff and led the league with 22 wins, 10 shutouts, and an earned run average of 1.78. Johnny Beazley, a rookie from Nashville, Tennessee, trailed only Cooper with 21 wins and a 2.13 earned run average. A deep pitching corps backed up the two aces. A pair of pitchers, Max Lanier and relief specialist Howie Krist, won 13 games apiece. Gumbert won nine while dividing time as a starter and reliever, and two more pitchers, Pollet and Ernie White, overcame sore arms early in the season and won seven games apiece.

The Cardinals got off to a sluggish 15–15 start and spent nearly the entire season trying to catch the defending National League champion Dodgers. As late as August 5, St. Louis trailed Brooklyn by ten games. However from August 11 to September 10, the Cardinals took 27 out of 32 games, including three of four versus the Dodgers at Sportsman's Park from August 24 to 27, and when they met the Dodgers again at Ebbets Field for the last two contests between the contenders, the Dodgers were only two games in front of the hard-charging Cardinals. Southworth had his two Dodger-killers, Mort Cooper and Max Lanier, ready to pitch, and they gave him a key advantage in battling managerial wits with fellow future Hall of Famer Leo Durocher. Prior to the series, Cooper was 4-1 against the Dodgers for the season, while Lanier was 4-2. In the opener,

Boom and Bust in St. Louis

on September 11, Cooper led the Cardinals past the Dodgers 3-0, pitching a three-hit shutout, singling twice, and scoring twice. A day later, behind Kurowski's two-run homer, Lanier defeated the Dodgers, 2-1. The Cardinals had finally caught the Dodgers.

Both teams had Sunday doubleheaders scheduled for September 13. The Cardinals split in Philadelphia, salvaging the nightcap, 3–2, on a game-winning home run by Moore, their captain. Meanwhile in Brooklyn, the Reds swept the Dodgers, moving the Cardinals into first place. After that, the Dodgers recovered to win nine of their next 11 games, but the Cardinals refused to yield, winning nine of 10 contests to push their advantage to a game and a half.

On the final day of the regular season, September 27, the Dodgers played a game in Philadelphia, while the Cardinals hosted a doubleheader against the Chicago Cubs. The only hope for the Dodgers was to force a tie by winning their game while the Cubs swept the Cardinals. The Dodgers did their job, winning their eighth consecutive game and completing the season with 104 wins against just 50 losses. It would not be enough. Southworth started Ernie White in the first game against the Cubs. White, a South Carolinian, had been scouted by former Gas House Gang player Pat Crawford, who himself had been born and raised in South Carolina before moving to North Carolina. In 1941, White had won 17 games, but plagued with arm trouble in 1942, entered the game with only a 6–5 record. However, he stymied the Cubs on only five hits while the Cardinals, paced by Moore's three hits and three runs batted in, bashed 11 hits and rolled to a 9–2, pennant-clinching victory. Musial recorded the final putout, tracking down and snagging a long fly ball to left off the bat of Cubs catcher Clyde McCullough and, decades later, still vividly recalled "the joy" of the moment.[4] Southworth rested his regulars in the nightcap, but Beazley and the subs still beat the Cubs, 4–1, for the Cardinals' seventh successive win. The "St. Louis Swifties" had won 41 of their last 48 games, finishing with a record of 106–48 and nipping the Dodgers by two games. The 106 wins of the 1942 Cardinals, still the franchise record, were the most for a National League club since the Pittsburgh Pirates won 110 in 1909, and the Dodgers tied a major-league record set by the 1909 Cubs for the most games won by a runner-up.

In the *St. Louis Globe-Democrat*, Martin J. Haley, who had witnessed the spectacular 1934 stretch drive of the Gas House Gang, nevertheless embraced the sizzling finish of the 1942 Cardinals as "the most amazing performance in all major league baseball history." Dizzy Dean, the

6. St Louis Swifties

ace hurler of the Gas House Gang, had retired early in the 1941 season and soon returned to St. Louis as a baseball announcer for KWK, one of two radio stations to air broadcasts of Cardinals games. He quickly became the most popular announcer in town, garnering 82 percent of the audience for Cardinals radio broadcasts. After the Cardinals clinched the 1942 pennant, Dean proclaimed above the din of the clubhouse that the current Cardinals were superior to the Gas House Gang and then assured everyone listening: "Folks, I'm broadcasting to you about the greatest team in baseball, and they will run them Yankees right out of the ballpark."[5]

Despite dethroning the Dodgers in one of the most heated of pennant races, the Cardinals entered the World Series as heavy underdogs to the New York Yankees, defending world champions who had won five of the last six World Series. In the opening game at Sportsman's Park, the veteran Yankees appeared invincible and took a 7–0 lead into the bottom of the ninth. Yet the youthful Cardinals staged a furious rally. They scored four runs, drove future Hall of Famer Red Ruffing from the mound, and actually got Musial to the plate with the bases loaded and two out. There would be no joy in St. Louis on that day, though, as reliever Spud Chandler retired Musial on a grounder to first. Momentum had, however, shifted for the duration of the Series. Musial delivered in the clutch the next day, singling home Slaughter in the bottom of the eighth inning and snapping a three-all tie. Beazley, who had shut the Yankees out on five hits through seven innings, gave up three runs on three hits in the top of the eighth. He surrendered successive singles to start the ninth, but Slaughter threw out pinch-runner Tuck Stainback at third. Given this reprieve, Beazley retired the next two Yankees, nailing down the 4–3 victory.

The Cardinals then swept three games at Yankee Stadium. White, assisted by a spectacular catch from each of his outfielders for three successive outs in the sixth and seventh innings, pitched a 2–0 shutout. It was the first time that the Yankees had been shut out in a World Series game since the Cardinals' Jesse Haines performed the feat in the third game of the 1926 World Series. Brown, the Cardinals' leadoff hitter, drove in Kurowski for one run and scored on Slaughter's single for the other. Game Four, tied 6–6 after six innings, boiled down to a battle of the bullpens. Lanier blanked the Yankees for the final three innings, and Walker Cooper singled Slaughter home with the go-ahead run. The Cardinals added a couple of insurance runs, the last one on a run-scoring single by Lanier, to salt away a 9–6 triumph. Beazley then wrapped up the Series, 4–2, with

Boom and Bust in St. Louis

Kurowski clouting a two-run homer in the top of the ninth to provide the margin of difference.

The mighty Yankees, winners in eight straight World Series since losing to the Cardinals in 1926, had fallen to yet another youthful band of Cardinals. They would win their next seven Series appearances before losing again. If the Cardinals had not upset them in 1926 and 1942, the Yankees would have won 18 consecutive World Series appearances between 1923 and 1953. For the Yankees' star center fielder Joe DiMaggio, the 1942 World Series would be his only loss in 10 Series appearances. Frank Graham, a New York sportswriter with the *Sun*, commented that the confidence of the Yankees had finally met its match in the brashness of the young Cardinals: "The Yankees have finally found a team that they can't frighten to death just by walking out on the field and taking a few swings in batting practice. The Cardinals haven't been around and they don't read the papers; the chances are they don't even know these are the Yankees they are playing."[6]

James Dawson, reporting from the victorious visiting clubhouse of Yankee Stadium, observed in the *New York Times* that "few clubhouses have matched the Cardinals quarters in reckless abandon." The young, rambunctious Cardinals celebrated by raucously singing tunes like "Good Old Mountain Music" and hoisting onto their shoulders everyone from Southworth to Beazley to Kurowski (still holding his bat with which he had struck the Series-clinching homer) to Branch Rickey and even Commissioner Kenesaw Mountain Landis and National League President Ford Frick, who when finally lowered by the World Series champions, huffily protested: "I never saw anything like this. Let me out of here."[7]

After the 1942 season, the military draft depleted major league rosters, so World War II actually prevented the Cardinals from performing at their peak again. Before Opening Day 1943, the war deprived the Cardinals of Beazley, Slaughter, and Moore. Beazley, while in the military, hurt his arm in a service game and was never the same again. During the course of the 1943 season, military service also summoned Pollet and Brown. Pollet, 12–7 with the Cardinals in 1941 and 1942 combined, had posted an 8–4 record for 1943 and was leading the league with a 1.75 earned run average. He missed all of the next two seasons and then, in five post-war seasons from 1946 to 1950, won 77 games against 51 losses.

Even so, the Cardinals were not as hard-hit as most clubs. They retained eight key players from their 1942 champions for the 1943 and 1944

6. St Louis Swifties

seasons (the Cooper brothers, catcher Walker and pitcher Mort; first baseman Sanders; shortstop Marion; third baseman Kurowski; outfielder Musial; first baseman-outfielder Hopp; and pitcher Lanier). Mort Cooper, Sanders, Marion, Kurowski, and Hopp were all classified 4-F, physically unfit for service. Dependent families enabled both Musial and Lanier to receive draft deferments, and Walker Cooper had a low-level draft priority due to a leg injury that would limit his capacity for military service. By the last year of World War II, though, Musial, Lanier, and Walker Cooper would all join the military.

Branch Rickey, whose contract with the Cardinals expired after the 1942 season, did not receive a contract extension from Sam Breadon, who blamed Rickey for the violation of baseball rules that resulted in Commissioner Kenesaw Mountain Landis' "Cedar Rapids Decision" of 1938. Furthermore, now retired from the automobile business, Breadon had free time on his hands and believed that he had gained enough baseball expertise to dispense with the expense of Rickey, whose take of $50,000 plus a percentage of the profits had totaled $88,000 in 1941. One month after the 1942 season, Rickey became president and general manager of the Dodgers, replacing Larry MacPhail, who entered military service. For the next couple of seasons, though, Rickey could do little to help the Dodgers, while Breadon did little to hurt the Cardinals.

Musial moved from left field to right in 1943, won his first of seven batting championships with a .357 average, and won the first of his three MVP Awards. Mort Cooper won 21 games, leading the league for a second successive season. Both Musial, with an average of .347, and Cooper, with 22 wins, dropped to second in the league in 1944, and shortstop Marty Marion won the MVP for spearheading a defense that established a league record for fielding percentage. Given their available talent, nobody was stunned when the Cardinals won 105 games each year and cruised to the National League title.

In the 1943 World Series, the Cardinals were favored to repeat their victory over the Yankees of the preceding year. Despite having fewer holdovers than the Cardinals, the Yankees reversed the outcome and took the Series in five games. The Cardinals' only win came in the second game, when Mort Cooper overcame the experiences of four previous ineffective starts against the American League in the 1942 World Series and the All-Star Games of 1942 and 1943. Making the moment more poignant, Cooper and his brother, catcher Walker Cooper, had learned earlier in the day of their father's death from a heart attack.

Boom and Bust in St. Louis

On the last day of the 1944 regular season, the St. Louis Browns captured their only American League pennant, allowing Sportsman's Park to host the first World Series played entirely west of the Mississippi River. In contrast to the Cardinals relying upon key components of previous championship clubs, the Browns had cobbled together their champions from available spare parts. Thus the underdog Browns enjoyed the sentimental support of many St. Louis fans over the heavily favored Cardinals.

This first all-St. Louis match-up in the World Series posed a dilemma for the opposing managers, Southworth and Luke Sewell of the Browns. Due to war-time housing shortages in St. Louis, the managers were sharing an apartment at Lindell Towers. With both teams playing home games at Sportsman's Park, the Cardinals and Browns—and their managers—could never be at home at the same time. When the Cardinals were in town, Sewell's wife and two teenage daughters vacated their Lindell Tower home for Dayton, Ohio, where the Sewells lived in the off-season; when the Browns were in town, Southworth's wife and nine-year-old daughter returned to Columbus, Ohio, where the Southworths lived in the off-season. The arrangement worked flawlessly until both teams made it to the World Series (the Cardinals and Browns did not face each other during the regular season, as such interleague play would not begin until 1997). Sewell won a coin flip for the apartment, but another resident of Lindell Towers who was out of town loaned his apartment to the Southworths for the World Series.

For the first half of the "Streetcar Series," (so named because with two teams from the same city, travel needs could be met by city streetcars rather than by trains), the Browns held the upper hand. Sewell made a surprising pitching choice of Denny Galehouse, just 9–10 in the regular season, to start the opening game against Cardinals ace Mort Cooper. Cooper held the Browns hitless until the fourth inning, when right fielder Gene Moore singled with two outs. George McQuinn, the Browns' first baseman who would lead all hitters in the series with a .438 average, followed with a two-run homer onto the roof of the right-field pavilion. They were the only hits allowed by Cooper, but no more were needed as Galehouse shut out the Cardinals until finally allowing one run in the ninth inning. The Cardinals escaped with a 3–2 win in 11 innings the next day on a walk-off, pinch-hit single by O'Dea, the backup catcher obtained in the Mize trade, only because three errors by the Browns allowed two unearned runs to send the game into extra innings. Nelson Potter, a 19-game winner and the Browns' top pitcher, committed two of the errors himself

6. St Louis Swifties

on a bunt by Max Lanier. The Browns bounced back to take the Series advantage again in Game Three with a 6–2 triumph behind their 17-game winner, Jack Kramer.

The turning point for the Series came early in the fourth game. In the top of the first inning, with one out and Cardinals center fielder Johnny Hopp on first base after hitting an infield single, Musial pounded a pitch from Sig Jakucki over the right-field pavilion for a two-run homer. Harry "The Cat" Brecheen, a left-handed pitcher from Oklahoma who had moved up from the Cardinals' farm system due to war-time absences and posted a 16–5 record in the regular season, made those runs stand up in a 5–1 win that evened the Series. The fifth game featured another pitching duel

Stan Musial joined the Cardinals in September 1941 at age 20 and, except for a year in the Navy in World War II, played every year with them until he retired at the age of 42 after the 1963 season. He holds Cardinals career records for runs batted in (1,951), runs (1,949), hits (3,630), home runs (475), doubles (725), triples (177), and batting championships (7) (National Baseball Hall of Fame).

Boom and Bust in St. Louis

between Galehouse and Cooper, but Cooper got the best of Galehouse this time, with the Cardinals winning, 2–0, on home runs by first baseman Ray Sanders and left fielder Danny Litwhiler. Lanier, another lefty who had won 17 games in the regular season, clinched the World Series title with a 3–1 win in the sixth game. The margin of difference came in the Cardinals' three-run fourth, when an error by Browns shortstop Vern Stephens prolonged the inning, allowing Cardinals second baseman Emil Verban and Lanier to drive in two unearned runs.

In the end, the Cardinals did not prevail solely because of holdovers from their 1942 club. The Browns had holdovers as well, including McQuinn, their best player in the Series, and, for the Cardinals, Brecheen, Litwhiler, and Verban were all war-time replacements. The biggest difference in the 1944 World Series was defense. The Cardinals committed only one inconsequential error, compared to ten committed by the Browns, including crucial mistakes that cost them the second game and provided the margin of difference in the sixth.

In contrast to the elation of upsetting the mighty Yankees in the 1942 World Series, the Cardinals reacted to winning the "Streetcar Series" more with a sense of relief. Marion explained the Cardinals' perception of the 1944 World Series: "We thought we were just going to walk through them. Who in hell's the Browns, you know. By the time we got in that first game, we found out they were a pretty good ball club.... We had a hell of a time beating those boys. They were tough."[8]

7

Slicing the Baloney Too Thin

> When all else about the 1946 Series, a cliffhanging upset for the Cards, has been reduced to bloodless statistics, Enos Slaughter's break for home will be remembered, retold, elevated into the kind of myth baseball and America love the most—a story of individual effort, "hustle," playing hard, putting out the extra effort.
> —Tom Wicker, "Enos Slaughter, on His Toes" (1979)[1]

In the last war-time season of 1945, the Cardinals lost Max Lanier, Danny Litwhiler, Stan Musial, and Walker Cooper to the military. Mort Cooper, disillusioned over an ongoing salary squabble with Sam Breadon, was traded on May 23 to the Boston Braves for $65,000 and pitcher Red Barrett, who won 21 games for the Cardinals. The contract dispute with Mort Cooper had started following the 1943 season. After leading the league in wins for the second straight season, Cooper had asked for a contract of $17,500, while Breadon had offered only $12,000. Breadon, citing government controls on salaries and prices, claimed that he could not pay a salary over the pre-war maximum of $13,500 that he had paid Terry Moore. This had indeed been the case in 1942, but the government had relaxed the salary controls by 1944, and Breadon had misled Mort Cooper. Even worse, Breadon had impugned his ace pitcher's patriotism: "Certainly, at a time like this, it is unwise for players who have been excused from military service for some reason or another to publicize their dissatisfaction with the contracts which have been sent to them. I do not think it makes very good reading for persons who have their boys on the fighting fronts."[2] Mort Cooper lowered his contract demand and signed for 1944 on terms acceptable to Breadon. However, after winning the 1944

Boom and Bust in St. Louis

World Series, both Cooper brothers and Marty Marion, the reigning National League MVP, held out before the 1945 season. Breadon again resorted to hiding behind the 1942 government salary controls. Marion, though, wrested a $15,000 contract from Breadon. At that point, Breadon agreed to give the Coopers contracts for $15,000 as well. Although Mort Cooper bought Marion a new hat for getting him a raise, he still resented that Breadon had lied to him for over a year. When he skipped a starting assignment in Boston and went back to St. Louis instead, Breadon traded him to the Braves. Walker Cooper was in military service at the time, but this series of events would also number his days as a Cardinal.

Enos Slaughter, with his Mad Dash in the bottom of the eighth inning of the seventh game, scored the winning run of the 1946 World Series for the Cardinals (National Baseball Hall of Fame).

Despite winning 95 games in 1945, the Cardinals finished second, three games behind a Cubs club that the Cardinals defeated in 16 of 22 head-to-head confrontations. After the season, Billy Southworth departed for a more financially lucrative offer to run the Braves. In five full seasons as the Cardinals' manager, he averaged 102 wins a year, and, bracketed by a pair of second-place finishes in 1941 and 1945, guided the Cardinals to three consecutive pennants from 1942 to 1944, the last National League team to do so. For his replacement, Breadon turned to Eddie Dyer, a veteran manager in the Cardinals' farm system. Dyer had managed many Cardinals on their way to the majors. Enos Slaughter, who had considered Southworth a father figure, regarded Dyer as an older brother. Dyer would make a smooth transition to the big leagues in 1946, far smoother than the Cardinals themselves adapted to the first post-war season.

The Cardinals entered 1946 with a surplus of players at second base,

7. Slicing the Baloney Too Thin

catcher, first base, and the outfield, thanks to returning war-time veterans, returning war-time replacements, and farm prospects eager to reach the majors. Breadon responded as usual to this type of pleasant dilemma, choosing the players to keep on the Cardinals and selling the leftovers to other clubs.

For example, on January 5, 1946, Breadon sold Jimmy Brown, the starting second baseman on the 1942 World Series champions, to the Pittsburgh Pirates for $30,000. Brown had been a valuable player for the Cardinals, starting at various times at second base, shortstop, and third base, while hitting .282 in seven seasons. Nevertheless, he was 35 years old and, because of military service, had not played in the majors since the early portion of the 1943 season. Under those circumstances, Breadon did well to receive $30,000 for Brown, who retired after playing only one season with Pittsburgh. The Cardinals had plenty of other options at second base.

On the same day, though, Breadon sold Walker Cooper, the starting catcher on three consecutive pennant-winners from 1942 to 1944, to the New York Giants for $175,000. Breadon suspected that Walker Cooper might hold a grudge against him over the bitter contract negotiations that had concluded with Breadon trading Mort Cooper, Walker's older brother, in May 1945. During the off-season of 1945–1946, Walker Cooper alluded to a disagreement in the minors with Eddie Dyer and told Breadon that he preferred not to play for Dyer. Dyer thought his problem with Walker Cooper was trivial and could be solved, but Breadon used it as an excuse to sell his All-Star catcher to the Giants.

The sale of Walker Cooper was, unquestionably, a major mistake. Breadon, impressed by the performance of Ken O'Dea as the starting catcher in 1945 when Cooper was in military service, thought Cooper's longtime backup could handle catching responsibilities for 1946. Under this plan, a couple of youngsters, 23-year-old Del Rice, who had backed up O'Dea in 1945, and a 20-year-old rookie, Joe Garagiola, could gain seasoning backing up O'Dea. Unfortunately, O'Dea was three years older than Walker Cooper and, entering his 12th major-league season at the age of 33, nearing the end of his career. He had been a .259 hitter before 1946, but bothered by a bad back, batted only .123 in 22 games with the Cardinals. Breadon sold him to the Boston Braves on July 8, and O'Dea retired after the season.

This left the Cardinals' catching job in the hands of the two youngsters, Rice and Garagiola. On May 2, Breadon traded Emil Verban, the

Boom and Bust in St. Louis

Cardinals' starting second baseman in 1944 and 1945, to the Philadelphia Phillies for a four-year veteran catcher, 29-year-old Clyde Kluttz. The trio of Rice, Garagiola, and Kluttz shared catching duties in 1946. None of the trio could compare with Walker Cooper. Kluttz, from North Carolina, hit .268 in 52 games and was sold to the Pittsburgh Pirates on December 26, 1946. Both Garagiola and Rice were better defensively than offensively. Garagiola, a St. Louis product from the Italian-American neighborhood of The Hill, batted .244 before being traded to the Pirates on June 15, 1951, while Rice, a native of Ohio, hit .241 before being traded to the Milwaukee Braves on June 3, 1955. Meanwhile, Walker Cooper continued as a starting catcher for seven seasons from 1946 to 1952, hitting .281 and averaging 17 home runs and 69 runs batted in. An All-Star in each of his last three full seasons with the Cardinals, he was selected for five more consecutive All-Star teams from 1946 to 1950.

If not for the devious double-dealing of Branch Rickey, the Cardinals could have replaced Walker Cooper with a Hall of Fame catcher, Yogi Berra. In 1942, Berra and his neighborhood friend Garagiola journeyed from The Hill to Sportsman's Park for a tryout camp. Rickey, in his last year with the Cardinals before leaving for the Dodgers, signed Garagiola for the Cardinals but passed on Berra. A year later, Rickey tried to sign Berra for the Dodgers. His plan backfired because Berra had already signed with the Yankees. In a decade from 1947 to 1956, Berra played on Yankees teams that defeated the Dodgers in five of six World Series. However, if Berra had signed with his hometown Cardinals as he wanted, the Cardinals might have been in those World Series rather than the Dodgers.

On February 5, 1946, exactly one month after the sales of Jimmy Brown and Walker Cooper, Breadon shipped outfielder-first baseman Johnny Hopp to the Boston Braves for $40,000. In April, he also sold first baseman Ray Sanders to the Braves for another $25,000. In these two deals, Breadon sold the two players who had combined to start at first base for the Cardinals for the four preceding seasons and left the position solely in the hands of an unproven 25-year-old rookie from St. Louis, Dick Sisler, whose father George had been a Hall of Fame first baseman for the St. Louis Browns. The Cardinals should have kept either Hopp or Sanders as an insurance policy at first base, in case Sisler stumbled, just as they had kept Sunny Jim Bottomley for the first two years of Ripper Collins' career or Collins for the first year of Johnny Mize's career. Hopp, a reserve outfielder as well, would have been the better choice. As it turned out, Sisler did struggle, forcing the Cardinals to move Stan Musial from left field

7. Slicing the Baloney Too Thin

to take over the starting position at first base. Musial hit .365 to win his second batting championship and second Most Valuable Player Award. Forced to learn how to play first base on the job, he led National League first baseman in errors in 1946, but eventually became an excellent defensive first baseman. However, although Musial later led National League first basemen in assists and double plays, he led the league in fielding average three times as an outfielder and none as a first baseman.

Furthermore, even though Musial solved the problem at first base, his departure from left field created another dilemma. Breadon had kept two reserve outfielders, a 25-year-old rookie right-handed batter from Chicago, Erv Dusak, and a 29-year-old veteran left-handed batter, Harry "The Hat" Walker, a Mississippi native who had hit .299 for the Cardinals in 1942 and 1943 as a reserve outfielder and then a wartime fill-in in center field in 1943. Apparently, Breadon chose to keep Walker over Hopp, another 29-year-old left-handed batter who hit .291 for the Cardinals from 1940 to 1945 and, in different years, had been their primary starter at first base and all three outfield positions. Logic should have dictated that, given their similarity in age and batting average, that Breadon keep Hopp over Walker because of Hopp's greater versatility, particularly his ability to provide insurance for Sisler at first base. If Breadon had kept Hopp, then Hopp could have replaced Sisler, allowing Musial to stay in left field. In that case, the Cardinals would have been starting the same outfield and first baseman that they had used while chasing down the Dodgers for the pennant in 1942 and defeating the Yankees in the World Series.

As it was, with Hopp gone, Walker took over in left field for Musial and batted only .237 while Hopp was an All-Star hitting a robust .333 for Boston. A year later, Walker was still hitting only .200 when Breadon sold him to Philadelphia, where he hit .371 and won the National League batting championship. Over five seasons from 1946 to 1950, with Hopp playing for three National League teams and Walker for four, Hopp was clearly a more consistent player, hitting .308 (with seasons ranging from a low of .278 to a high of .340) compared to Walker's .297 (with seasons ranging from a low of .207 after rejoining the Cardinals in 1950 to his high of .363 in 1947).

Also, while it was more excusable to keep a 25-year-old prospect, Dusak, over a 29-year-old wartime fill-in, Danny Litwhiler, Breadon again made the wrong choice. Dusak, in six seasons as a right-handed batter and reserve outfielder for the Cardinals, averaged 15 runs batted in, and four homers, and batted .244. Litwhiler, in six years as a right-handed batter

Boom and Bust in St. Louis

and reserve outfielder for the Braves and Cincinnati Reds, averaged 30 runs batted in, and eight homers, and batted .276.

At second base, Breadon had two returning wartime replacements, Lou Klein and Emil Verban. Klein, a native of New Orleans, hit .287 as the Cardinals' 1943 starter, but when he entered military service, Verban took over second base from 1944 to 1945 and batted .268 while leading National League second sackers in double plays in 1944 and fielding average in 1945. Breadon kept Klein and traded Verban, another wrong decision. In this case, though, Breadon's decision could easily be forgiven since the Cardinals ended up with a second baseman far better than Klein or Verban, Red Schoendienst, who had been a wartime replacement in left field in 1945. Schoendienst was a product of Germantown, Illinois, 40 miles on the opposite side of the Mississippi from St. Louis, whose father was a coal miner. Like millions of other young men in the nation, he had worked in President Franklin D. Roosevelt's Civilian Conservation Corps, but a freak accident had sent a nail flying into his left eye. His eye ailment, combined with a sore shoulder weakened from sliding head-first into bases, brought Schoendienst an early discharge from military service and the opportunity to play for the Cardinals in 1945. He hit .278 and led the National League in stolen bases with 26.

When Klein started slowly in 1946, Dyer gave increased playing time to Schoendienst at second base, which contributed to Klein accepting an offer from the Mexican League on May 23. Klein was hitting only .194 at the time and, upon returning to the Cardinals in 1949, batted just .219. He played one more season in the American League and averaged a mere .226. The scrappy Verban put together four solid seasons for the Phillies and Chicago Cubs from 1946 to 1949, hitting .279 and leading National League second basemen in assists twice and putouts once. But the Cardinals fortunately had Schoendienst as their second baseman for the next decade. From 1946 until he was foolishly traded in mid–June 1956, during the reign of terror of Frank "Trader" Lane as Cardinals general manager, Schoendienst was a nine-time All-Star whose game-winning home run in the 14th inning claimed victory in the 1950 All-Star Game for the National League.

The Mexican League had a more negative impact on the Cardinals' pitching staff. On May 23, besides raiding Klein, the Mexican League also signed two Cardinals pitchers, Freddie Martin and Max Lanier. Martin, a 30-year-old rookie from Oklahoma, had spent nearly all of World War II in the military. He had a 2–1 record with the Cardinals before signing with

7. Slicing the Baloney Too Thin

the Mexican League and, following his return to the Cardinals in 1949, compiled a record of 10–2 over the next two seasons. His career record of 12–3 indicated that, if he had not lost so much time to World War II and the Mexican League, Martin might have enjoyed a much more memorable major league career. Lanier was the biggest catch of the three Cardinals. At the time he headed south of the border, Lanier had a career record of 74–47 and was leading National League pitchers with a 6–0 record and a 1.93 earned run average. Furthermore, the left-handed hurler was a proven big-game pitcher. His record against the Dodgers had been 5–2 in 1942 and was already 4–0 in 1946. In World Series play, Lanier had a 2–1 record with a 1.71 earned run average and a .444 batting average. A persistently ailing left elbow, though, convinced Lanier to cash in on his pitching abilities while he still could.

The Cardinals were not the only team affected by the Mexican League. In addition to the three Cardinals defectors, 20 other major leaguers, including Dodgers catcher Mickey Owen, jumped to the Mexican League. Jorge Pasquel, who bankrolled the Mexican League, also attempted to sign the Cardinals' outfield of Musial, Moore, and Slaughter. All three turned him down, with Musial reportedly rejecting an offer of $200,000 ($75,000 down and a five-year contract for $25,000 a year). Breadon rewarded each of his three outfielders with a bonus of $2,500 for their loyalty. Ultimately, the Mexican League boosted the salaries of major league players. For example, Musial had signed a contract for $13,500 in 1946, but his next contract in 1947 paid him $31,000. Slaughter's 1946 contract was for $11,000, but he was earning $25,000 by 1950. For those who leaped to the Mexican League, they did not receive all of the money promised by Pasquel and were initially banned from returning to the majors for five years. Only a lawsuit won their reinstatement in 1949.

Lanier had been promised $125,000 by Pasquel ($25,000 down and a five-year contract for $20,000 a year). He stayed in Mexico for a year and a half and later explained: "Aleman was running for President, and I think there was some family relationship between him and Jorge Pasquel. Now the people in Mexico loved baseball. It was worked out so Aleman got the credit for us coming down there. They figured he'd get some votes out of it. And he did get elected. After the election Pasquel started cutting everybody. He cut me from $20,000 a year to $10,000. That's when we started going back."[3] Lanier was back in the United States by 1948, but was initially restricted to pitching on barnstorming tours or in a Canadian league. After the Mexican Leaguers won their lawsuit, he returned to the

Boom and Bust in St. Louis

Cardinals on July 2, 1949. Lanier compiled a 27–22 record for the Cardinals through 1951, perhaps still hindered by pains in his left elbow. His overall record with the Cardinals of 101–69 could have been much better if he had not missed all of two seasons (1947–1948) and large chunks of three other seasons (1945–1946 and 1949) due to World War II military service and the Mexican League misadventure.

The Cardinals could have used Lanier's prowess as a Dodger-killer. The Cardinals and Dodgers were again battling with the same ferocity as their tussles of 1941 and 1942, abetted by the presence of Branch Rickey as the newest ex–Cardinal turned Dodger. Leo "The Lip" Durocher, the Dodgers' manager and another former Cardinal, stirred the pot even further when he proclaimed that the Cubs, not the Cardinals, were the team the Dodgers would have to beat for the 1946 pennant. In response, Dyer vowed: "We'll show The Lip the team he has to beat."[4]

The Cardinals trailed the Dodgers by 7½ games on July 2, but won 12 of their next 15 outings. On July 14, when the Dodgers arrived at Sportsman's Park for a four-game series, the lead had been whittled down to 4½ games. The Cardinals swept the opening doubleheader, winning the first game, 5–3, behind four runs batted in by Slaughter (who led the NL in 1946 with 130) and then taking the nightcap, 2–1, in the 12th inning on the dramatic flourish of a Musial walk-off homer. Musial had four hits the next day, including another homer, and the Cardinals pounded the Dodgers, 10–4. Finally, in the fourth game, the Cardinals trailed, 4–3, in the bottom of the ninth. Erv Dusak, pinch-hitting with two runners on base, hit a home run to win the game, sweep the series, and forever earn the nickname of "Four Sack" Dusak.

For the rest of the season, the Cardinals and Dodgers waged a seesaw fight for first place. On August 25, tied for first, the rivals started another four-game series at Sportsman's Park. After splitting the series, they were still tied when the Dodgers left town. By September 12, when the contenders faced each other in a three-game series at Ebbets Field, the Cardinals had crept ahead by a game and a half. However, the Dodgers took two of the three games, reducing the Cardinals' lead to only a half-game.

Neither adversary could shake the other, and, entering September 30, the final day of the regular season, Breadon's Cardinals and Rickey's Dodgers were tied. Although the Cubs defeated the Cardinals, 8–3, the Cardinals stayed alive when the Braves, managed by the Cardinals' former skipper, Billy Southworth, beat the Dodgers, 4–0, on a shutout by former

7. Slicing the Baloney Too Thin

Cardinals ace Mort Cooper. The Cardinals and Dodgers finished deadlocked at 96–58, the first tie in major-league history.

The Cardinals, after forging the tie with 14 wins in 22 regular season contests against the Dodgers, now faced the Dodgers again in a best-of-three playoff that would determine the National League pennant. In the opener at Sportsman's Park, Howie Pollet pitched the Cardinals to a 4–2 victory, winning his 21st game with the support of battery-mate Joe Garagiola who had three hits and two runs batted in. Needing only one win at Ebbets Field to wrap up another crown, the Cardinals built an 8–1 advantage after eight innings. Every player in the Cardinals' starting lineup, including pitcher Murry Dickson, contributed at least one hit and either scored or drove home a run. The Dodgers tallied three times in the bottom of the ninth and loaded the bases with only one out. Harry "The Cat" Brecheen, beckoned from the bullpen, struck out successive Brooklyn batters to nail down the pennant.

The Cardinals entered the 1946 World Series in the underdog role that they relished. They faced the Boston Red Sox, triumphant in 104 contests and American League champions by 12 games. For six games of the World Series, the clubs traded victories. The Red Sox gained the upper hand three times; the Cardinals evened matters three times. The series started in St. Louis and Pollet led 2–1 with two outs in the ninth inning, but gave up a game-tying single and then lost in the tenth on a solo home run by Rudy York. Brecheen lifted the Cardinals' spirits the next day, pitching a four-hit shutout and driving in one run and scoring another in a 3–0 win.

After the series shifted to Boston, the Red Sox countered with a shutout by their 25-game winner, Boo Ferris, while York slammed a three-run homer in the first inning and the Red Sox cruised to a 4–0 victory. In Game Four, the Cardinals pounded the Red Sox, 12–3, with a 20-hit attack that included four hits apiece by Slaughter, Kurowski, and Garagiola. George Munger, only 2–2 in the regular season, was the pitching beneficiary of the Cardinals' offensive onslaught against losing pitcher Tex Hughson, a 20-game winner who had gotten the best of the pitching duel against Pollet in the opening game. The Red Sox responded by knocking Pollet out in the first inning of the fifth game, and, although the Cardinals rallied to tie it, reliever Al Brazle was beaten by the Red Sox, 6–3.

Back in St. Louis, the Cardinals forced a seventh and deciding game, 4–1, behind the pitching of Brecheen and a three-run third inning keyed by consecutive two-out hits by Musial, Kurowski, and Slaughter. The series came down to Game Seven at Sportsman's Park, where 36,143 spectators witnessed one of the most exciting contests in baseball history.

The teams were tied, 3–3, with two outs in the bottom of the eighth. Both of them had turned the game over to their bullpens, with Brecheen taking over for the Cardinals and Bob Klinger pitching for the Red Sox. Slaughter, aboard on a leadoff single, took off on a pitch to Harry "The Hat" Walker, who dropped a hit into left-center. Slaughter sped around the bases without stopping. As the relay throw reached Red Sox shortstop Johnny Pesky, Slaughter headed for home, gambling on the element of surprise. Pesky, with his back to the infield, could not see Slaughter turning third, and the roar of the crowd drowned out the directions of second baseman Bobby Doerr. When Pesky spotted Slaughter halfway home, he hastily heaved the ball to the plate, off-line and too late. Walker was officially credited with a double, although he actually took second on the throw home. In their accounts of the play, the Associated Press credited the daring of Slaughter and his club ("any runner except a Cardinal would have pulled up at third"), while the *New York Times* praised the blazing speed with which Slaughter covered the 270 feet between first base and home plate ("Country ran as perhaps he had never run before").[5]

In the top of the ninth, the Red Sox put runners on first and third with only one out, but Brecheen wiggled out of the jam and won his third game of the 1946 World Series. "Slaughter's Mad Dash" stood up as the deciding run of the Cardinals' 4–3 seventh-game victory, and it became known as the most famous base-running exploit in World Series history.

Prior to the playoff series against Brooklyn, a team party was held in St. Louis at Ruggeri's restaurant on The Hill. J. Roy Stockton, the longtime sports editor of the *St. Louis Post-Dispatch*, roasted Breadon with these words: "Sam, you've always liked to slice the baloney thin, but this year, you may have sliced it a little too thin."[6] Indeed, by only razor-thin margins, the 1946 Cardinals gave Sam Breadon his ninth pennant and sixth world championship, his fourth pennant and third world championship in the last five years. "Slaughter's Mad Dash" rang down the curtain on the glory years of the Breadon era. Breadon owned the team for only one more year, and the Cardinals did not win another pennant for 18 seasons.

In January 1947, Breadon formed the Cardinals' radio network and extended broadcasts beyond Sr. Louis for the first time, initially reaching out only to six stations and two states (by means of contrast, the St. Louis Cardinals radio network is currently the largest in major league baseball, with 111 affiliates in eight states, including the author's hometown station

7. Slicing the Baloney Too Thin

of KAGH in Crossett, Arkansas). However, since Breadon was an urbanite born and raised in New York City, he disliked the rural folksy charm of the most popular baseball announcer in town, former Cardinals ace pitcher Dizzy Dean, and instead gave exclusive broadcasting rights to Harry Caray and former Cardinals manager Gabby Street. Caray, who had ingratiated himself with Breadon by defending him when Stockton accused the Cardinals owner of cutting the baloney too thin, remained the Cardinals' primary play-by-play announcer through 1969.

Breadon had overseen the Cardinals through good times and hard times. His club had flourished during the Roaring Twenties and survived the hardships of the Great Depression and World War II. A post-war renaissance ensued as Americans, after 16 years scarred with either economic depression or wartime anxiety, flocked to major league ballparks and made the turnstiles click like never before. Baseball was made more accessible by the increased availability of night games, first started in 1935 in Cincinnati and introduced to St. Louis in 1940. In 1946 the Cardinals had surpassed one million in attendance for the first time and earned nearly $700,000, the largest windfall of Breadon's tenure. Altogether, in Breadon's 28 years as President, the Cardinals earned over $4 million.

8

Bing Devine Ends a Pennant Drought

> Back in 1964 we got a lot of national publicity because we began to wear rubber horror masks. It began in 1963, but it didn't get national attention until we won the pennant in 1964. We had all seen a horror movie on the Late Late Show in Milwaukee and the next day we went out and bought those masks. Ray Sadecki had a Wolf Man mask. Tim McCarver was the Hunchback of Notre Dame. I was Frankenstein. Another player was somebody else. We'd wear them on airplanes and scare the stewardesses and we'd wear them on the bus going to the ball park and we'd stick our heads out and get a double-take from passers-by. It sounds childish but it was fun, and it was the kind of thing that kept us together and gave us camaraderie.
> —Bob Gibson, from *Ghetto to Glory* (1968)[1]

In 1946, completing his fourth full season for the Cardinals, Stan Musial played in his fourth World Series and won his third world championship ring, his second batting championship, and his second Most Valuable Player Award. He played 17 more seasons with the Cardinals, winning his third Most Valuable Player Award and five more batting championships, without ever returning to the World Series. The Cardinals finished second to the Brooklyn Dodgers in 1947, to Billy Southworth's Boston Braves in 1948, and to the Dodgers again in 1949. Musial believed two factors prevented the Cardinals from sustaining a string of pennants through the 1940s. First, he blamed the sales of Johnny Mize and Walker Cooper: "With John Mize and Walker Cooper in our lineup all those years we would've been *unbeatable*." Enos Slaughter, a teammate of Musial and a fellow Hall of Famer, downplayed the sale of Mize but certainly concurred

8. Bing Devine Ends a Pennant Drought

on the significance of Sam Breadon's sale of Walker Cooper: "As far as I'm concerned, letting Walker go was the biggest mistake Breadon ever made. He may have parted with bigger names like Dean, Medwick, and Mize, but he was still able to develop a team that won four pennants in five years. I honestly believed that, with that tough raw-boned catcher behind the plate for us instead of the Giants, we could have remained a dynasty for another five or six years."[2]

The other reason advanced by Musial was that the Cardinals lagged far behind the Dodgers in pioneering racial integration. Breadon, suffering from the onset of cancer, reluctantly sold his beloved team in November 1947 to Robert Hannegan and Fred Saigh for $3.5 million. Hannegan, a fellow Irishman, was U.S. Postmaster General under longtime friend Harry Truman, but resigned from the President's cabinet to preside over the Cardinals. Unfortunately, ill health forced him to sell his shares in January 1949 to Saigh for $1 million. Given his friendship with Truman, an advocate of civil rights, Hannegan might have moved quicker to integrate the Cardinals than Saigh. An attorney of Syrian descent, Saigh openly defended his segregation policy, claiming the Cardinals were "a team for the South."[3] Multitudes of Southerners did attend the Cardinals' games in St. Louis, and the Cardinals' roster included numerous Southern players. Yet after the Cardinals integrated, their Southern fan base still traveled to home games in St. Louis, and, during the civil rights movement of the 1960s, the Cardinals developed team chemistry that became a model of racial harmony.

Another factor for the Cardinals' decline, not cited

Bob Gibson pitched the Cardinals to victories in the seventh game in both 1964 and 1967, winning the World Series MVP Award in each year (National Baseball Hall of Fame).

Boom and Bust in St. Louis

by Musial, was that their farm system failed to produce a fourth-generation crop of players in the late 40s and early 50s as talented as their predecessors. With Branch Rickey no longer presiding over the once-fertile farm system, the Cardinals lacked substitutes as strong as shortstop Marty Marion, third baseman Whitey Kurowski, or center fielder Terry Moore when injuries shortened their careers. Red Smith, a St. Louis sportswriter in the early 1930s who eventually went to New York and became a Pulitzer Prize-winning sports columnist, noted in September 1950 that the Cardinals would finish in the second division for the first time since 1938 and concluded: "Rickey conceived the chain-store idea in St. Louis. He made the Cardinal farms the most richly productive in baseball, able to furnish St. Louis with enough top-grade talent to dominate the league with a profitable supply left over for sale to other clubs. When he departed the farms went to seed." Without Rickey, Smith observed: "The simple fact is that the Cardinal farms have not produced an outfielder of note since Stan Musial came up, not an infielder of distinction since Red Schoendienst. Both were, of course, Rickey's boys, as were Enos Slaughter and Marty Marion and all of the others who kept the Cardinals on top until this year."[4]

In part, the Cardinals were victims of their own success. When Breadon and Rickey started the farm system, it was strictly unique to the Cardinals. However, after the farm system transformed the Cardinals into the most successful team in the National League, other clubs emulated the Cardinals' example and developed their own farm systems. Cardinals scouts suddenly faced fierce competition in locating young players to stock the farm clubs. After leaving St. Louis for Brooklyn, even Rickey realized that the Dodgers were an aging team with a poorly developed farm system that could not be overhauled quickly enough to provide replacements for veterans in the twilight of their careers. Rickey always defended integration on purely humanitarian grounds, but he also pragmatically admitted that he turned to signing African American players because they were "the greatest untapped reservoir of raw material in the history of the game."[5]

Saigh, who refused to tap into this reservoir of talent, had attained his wealth from wheeling and dealing in real estate. His financial practices eventually ran afoul of the Internal Revenue Service, and Saigh served 15 months in prison for income tax evasion. On February 20, 1953, before his incarceration, Saigh sold the Cardinals to the Anheuser-Busch Brewing Association for $3.75 million. August "Gussie" Busch took over the reins of the Cardinals and did not relinquish them until his death late in the 1989 season.

8. Bing Devine Ends a Pennant Drought

The landscape of St. Louis baseball changed again after Anheuser-Busch acquired the Cardinals. The rival Browns, following the 1933 death of Phil Ball passed through several owners and, in the quarter-century from 1926 to 1950, outdrew the Cardinals only in their single championship season of 1944. Nevertheless, in 1951, they ended up in the hands of Bill Veeck, who believed that he could run the Cardinals out of town. Although the Cardinals still surpassed the Browns' attendance, Veeck was pleased with his progress until the Anheuser-Busch purchase of the Cardinals. Afterward, unwilling to battle the vast financial reserves of Anheuser-Busch, Veeck looked to move the Browns. He was initially thwarted by the other owners, though, and had no choice except to spend the 1953 season in St. Louis, where his popularity had plummeted. Angry fans hung him in effigy at Sportsman's Park, and hundreds cancelled their season tickets. Desperate for revenue, Veeck sold Sportsman's Park to Anheuser-Busch for $1.1 million on the eve of the 1953 season. The Browns finished last in their lame-duck year, Veeck sold them to Baltimore investors, and they became the Orioles before the 1954 season.

Gussie Busch pumped in $1.5 million of corporate funds to redesign Sportsman's Park. He wanted to dub the field Budweiser Stadium in honor of his brewery's best-selling product. The proposed name change raised howls of protest, however, and Busch partly relented. He renamed Sportsman's Park as Busch Stadium and then introduced a new beverage, Busch Bavarian Beer. Most St. Louis residents simply continued calling their old ballpark Sportsman's Park. Dizzy Dean had proven resilient after Breadon banished him from broadcasting Cardinals games, and, with the growth of television, he became the first prominent national television broadcaster on the pioneering "Game of the Week" that aired first on ABC (1953–1954) and then CBS (1955–1965). When Dean visited St. Louis for the "Game of the Week," Busch pleaded with him to refer to the ballpark as Busch Stadium rather than Sportsman's Park. Dean came on the air and welcomed folks "to the grand old ballpark in St. Louis on Grand and Dodier," which all of Dizzy's fans knew was Sportsman's Park, where their hero had once pitched for the Gas House Gang.[6]

Although Gussie Busch's financial infusion enhanced the attractiveness of Sportsman's Park, it was harder for him to improve the Cardinals. When he took control, the Cardinals were still a winning club, but had fallen from pennant contention. In his initial year of 1953, the Cardinals finished third for the third successive season, trailing a pair of integrated teams (the Dodgers and the New York Giants). Seating at Sportsman's

Boom and Bust in St. Louis

Park had been integrated since 1944, and Anheuser-Busch marketed to all races. Gussie Busch saw no reason to maintain a segregated ball club and integrated the Cardinals with first baseman Tom Alston in 1954.

Busch not only integrated the Cardinals, but he also sought to revitalize the farm system through the "force-feeding" plan of 1954–1955, throwing youngsters into the fire to see if they withstood the heat.[7] On April 11, 1954, the Cardinals dealt their ten-time All-Star right fielder Slaughter to the New York Yankees for three minor-league prospects, including center fielder Bill Virdon, signaling the end of one era and the start of the youth movement. The force-feeding plan resulted in a losing record, the first since 1938, and the team was even worse the next year (68–86), coming in seventh. Despite these growing pains, many talented rookies emerged. In 1954 and 1955, six future All-Stars made their major league debut: third baseman Ken Boyer; a pair of first basemen-outfielders, Wally Moon and Joe Cunningham; and pitchers Larry Jackson, Luis Arroyo, and Brooks Lawrence. Moon was the National League Rookie of the Year in 1954, and Virdon won the award in 1955.

Busch was impatient for success, though, and in the words of *St. Louis Post-Dispatch* sportswriter Bob Broeg, often followed a "zig-zag course."[8] In 1956, he hired Frank Lane as general manager, who brought in Fred Hutchinson as the Cardinals' third field manager in Busch's four years of ownership. Under Hutchinson's leadership, the youthful Cardinals seemed on the verge of maturing. They boasted the best spring training record in baseball, and once the regular season commenced, seized the lead in the National League. Lane then tore this promising team apart with deals that defied baseball logic. In mid–May, for example, he traded away both of his shortstops and received two players, neither a natural shortstop, who combined to hit just .172 for the 1956 Cardinals. The next day, he sent Virdon to the Pittsburgh Pirates for Bobby Del Greco. Virdon, one of the best defensive center fielders in the game, hit .334 the rest of the season, while Del Greco batted .215.

These transactions decimated the Cardinals' middle defense and forced Hutchinson to play rookie second baseman Don Blasingame out of position at shortstop. Suddenly desperate to acquire veteran shortstop Alvin Dark from the Giants, Lane resorted to trading nine-time All-Star second baseman Schoendienst. As a Cardinal, Schoendienst had established credentials that would lead him to the Hall of Fame, batting .290 and topping National League second basemen in fielding average four times, putouts and assists three times, and double plays twice.

8. Bing Devine Ends a Pennant Drought

The Schoendienst trade left Musial as the Cardinals' last link to the 1946 Series champions. Shortly afterward, word leaked out that Lane intended to swap Musial to the Philadelphia Phillies for pitcher Robin Roberts. Musial threatened to retire rather than report to Philadelphia. Busch belatedly stepped in, blocked the trade, and revoked Lane's right to trade without his authorization.

The reign of terror of "Trader" Lane came to a close. Before it ended, Lane's bizarre trades had prevented the Cardinals' rebuilding project from running its course. The Cardinals fell from first to fifth and finished 76–78, their third consecutive losing season. In 1957, the Cardinals gave a glimpse of what might have been if the potential of force-feeding had been realized, finishing second (87–67) eight games behind the Milwaukee Braves, who had added Schoendienst as their second baseman. Lane, forewarned by Busch that his job depended on winning the 1957 pennant, moved on to the Cleveland Indians.

Musial remained a Cardinal, winning his seventh batting title in 1957 with an average of .351. Early in the 1958 season at Wrigley Field, he recorded his 3,000th hit, a pinch-hit double that rallied the Cardinals past the Chicago Cubs. Later, in 1967, when Musial was general manager of the Cardinals and Schoendienst was field manager, Musial once discovered Lane on the team bus talking to Cardinals players, stormed over, and bluntly told Lane, "Get the hell out of here."[9]

Busch replaced Lane as general manager with Bing Devine, a veteran executive in the Cardinals' farm system. Devine sought to overhaul the Cardinals as thoroughly as Lane, but with a coherent vision. Devine's rebuilding plan called for a faster club and made the entire pitching staff expendable to achieve that goal. Devine believed that, since scouts searched harder for pitchers and farm systems produced more pitchers, pitchers were plentiful. He would place a greater premium on acquiring position players, preferably position players with speed. Lane had moved Boyer, the National League's All-Star third baseman in 1956, to center field in 1957. Devine returned Boyer, a native of the Ozarks in southwestern Missouri, to third base and, in seven years from 1958 to 1964, Boyer won five Gold Gloves, batted .303, and averaged 26 home runs and 101 runs batted in per year (he also hit .348 in eleven All-Star Games). Almost assuredly the best third baseman in Cardinals history, Boyer possesses legitimate Hall of Fame credentials but has never been elected. This lack of appreciation for Boyer stemmed partly from a grudge held by Harry Caray, the Cardinals' primary play-by-play broadcaster for all 11 seasons Boyer spent

Boom and Bust in St. Louis

in St. Louis, because Boyer had once declined to be interviewed during the middle of a game that Caray was broadcasting from field level.

With Boyer entrenched at third base, Devine made three significant transactions between December 1957 and May 1960, parting with five pitchers for center fielder Curt Flood, first baseman Bill White, and second baseman Julian Javier. Devine had located half of the regular starting lineup for the 1964 champion Cardinals. The farm system, just as Devine had anticipated, provided a pair of quality starting pitchers, Ray Sadecki and future Hall of Famer Bob Gibson. In 1960, Devine added veteran pitcher Curt Simmons, who had been released by the Phillies. Sadecki, Gibson, and Simmons were the leading pitchers on the staff of the 1964 Cardinals, winning 20, 19, and 18 games respectively.

The Cardinals again struggled at the start of another rebuilding project. In 1958, after a fifth-place finish, Busch dismissed Fred Hutchinson and appointed Solly Hemus as manager. By 1961, with the Cardinals in sixth place, Busch lost patience with Hemus and replaced him with Johnny Keane, the Cardinals' fifth manager in Busch's nine years of ownership. Keane had been a Cardinals coach since 1959 and previously had managed for 20 years in their farm system. His first step as manager was to bridge the gulf that had developed between his predecessor and Flood and Gibson, African Americans who considered Hemus a racist. Hemus had frequently benched Flood and never gave Gibson a regular spot in the starting rotation. Keane soothed their discontent by giving them a shot, the only thing that Flood and Gibson needed to become All-Stars. Flood won seven successive Gold Gloves and topped National League outfielders in putouts four times. He also transformed himself into a legitimate batting threat, averaging .302 from 1961 through 1969. Gibson won 11 games in the second half of the 1961 season and, from 1962 to 1972, pitched the Cardinals to another 206 victories, establishing a new club record for career wins.

The 1961 Cardinals were only 33–41 under Hemus, but they improved to 47–33 with Keane. In spring training of the next season, the Cardinals became the first major league team to break down the segregated housing policies of Florida. Busch, responding to complaints from Flood, White, Gibson, and other African Americans on the Cardinals, leased the Skyway Motel and the adjoining Outrigger Inn in St. Petersburg for his entire team. Even Musial and Boyer and other white veterans, who were allowed to stay in homes they had rented for their families, opted to move with their families into the team's headquarters. Keane led the Cardinals to an

8. Bing Devine Ends a Pennant Drought

84–78 record, the first manager to put together consecutive winning seasons since Anheuser-Busch purchased the club.

Keane and Devine, both St. Louis natives who honed their organizational skills in the Cardinals' farm system, shared similar backgrounds and philosophies. Collaborating closely to fortify the Cardinals' roster, they swapped shortstops with the Pirates in November 1962, giving up Julio Gotay for veteran three-time All-Star Dick Groat. Groat averaged .289 in three years with the Cardinals, making the All-Star team the first two seasons and leading National League shortstops in 1964 in assists and double plays. In the spring of 1963, 21-year-old Tim McCarver emerged from the farm system and filled a catching void. In seven seasons as the Cardinals' starter behind the plate, he hit .276, was named to two All-Star teams (going 3-for-3 and scoring the winning run in the tenth inning of the 1966 All-Star Game in St. Louis), and topping National League catchers in fielding average twice and in assists once.

The entire infield of Boyer, Groat, Javier, and White started the 1963 All-Star Game and led the Cardinals to 93 wins and a second-place finish, six games behind the Los Angeles Dodgers. The Cardinals still needed outfielders to flank Flood, particularly after Musial retired following the 1963 season, so on June 15, 1964, Devine and Keane traded pitchers Ernie Broglio, a 21-game winner in 1960, and Bobby Shantz, a veteran reliever who was American League Most Valuable Player back in 1952 when he won 24 games for the Philadelphia Athletics, to the Chicago Cubs in exchange for Lou Brock, a speedy 24-year-old outfielder with only modest major league credentials. Brock immediately took over in left field and displayed a surprising combination of speed and power that took him to the Hall of Fame. Over the final 103 games of the season, Brock hit .348, slugged 12 homers, and stole 33 bases. He scored 81 runs and served as a sparkplug at the top of the Cardinals' batting order. In 16 seasons with the Cardinals, Brock batted .298, scored over 100 runs six times, and led the league in stolen bases for eight of nine years from 1966 through 1974.

Right field remained a persistent problem until late July, when the Cardinals called up 24-year-old Mike Shannon from their Jacksonville farm club. Shannon, a St. Louis native, had given up a football scholarship at the University of Missouri to sign with the Cardinals. In the second half of the 1964 season, the hometown hero added power and punch to the middle of the lineup, connecting for nine homers and driving in 43 runs. Jacksonville also supplied 37-year-old veteran knuckleballer Barney

Boom and Bust in St. Louis

Schultz, who in the last third of the season appeared in 30 games and saved 14.

These mid-season additions invigorated the Cardinals, who were only 39–40 before the All-Star Game and 54–29 afterwards. Boyer, with 24 homers and a league-leading 119 runs batted in, won the National League's Most Valuable Player Award, while White followed closely behind with 21 homers and 102 runs batted in. Nevertheless, with two weeks left in the season, the Cardinals lagged 6½ games behind the first-place Phillies. Then the Phillies faltered, and the Cincinnati Reds, riding a nine-game winning streak, went to the front of the National League race. With a week to play, the Reds enjoyed a one-game lead over the Phillies and a game and a half advantage over the Cardinals. In the last week of the season, the Cardinals swept a three-game series against the Phillies, prolonging Philadelphia's losing streak to ten. Meanwhile, the Reds lost two of three games to the Pirates, putting the Cardinals into first place as the season entered the final weekend of October 2–4. The Reds trailed the Cardinals by only a half-game, and the Phillies, apparently all but eliminated, were now 2½ games back.

The final weekend brought a bizarre conclusion to one of the strangest stretch drives in baseball history. After winning eight games in a row, the Cardinals appeared hexed by Casey Stengel's last-place New York Mets, losing to them on both Friday and Saturday. The floundering Phillies snapped their losing streak, defeating the Reds on Saturday and Sunday. By late Sunday afternoon, as the Phillies finished a 10–0 pounding of the Reds, the eyes of the baseball world focused on St. Louis and Sportsman's Park. With another Mets win, the National League race would end in an unprecedented three-way tie; if the Cardinals won, they would finish at 93–69, edge the Reds and Phillies by a game, and claim their first pennant in 18 years. The Mets took a 3–2 lead in the top of the fifth inning, forcing Keane to summon Gibson out of the bullpen to relieve Simmons. Brock then instigated a pair of three-run rallies in the fifth and sixth innings, allowing the Cardinals to cruise to an 11–5 victory. Gibson earned his 19th win of the season, pitching into the ninth inning before giving way to Schultz, who recorded the last out when Ed Kranepool popped out to McCarver, as Harry Caray relayed his radio broadcast from the field box of owner Gussie Busch. Caray then ran onto the field and started interviewing any of the Cardinals he could get to talk to him.

As in 1926 and 1942, the Cardinals were underdogs in the World Series to the Yankees, who were making their fifth consecutive World Series

8. Bing Devine Ends a Pennant Drought

appearance. Although televised broadcasts of World Series games dated back to 1947, the 1964 World Series marked the first telecasts of games involving the Cardinals. In the opener, Yankees ace Whitey Ford led, 4–2, until the sixth inning, when Shannon blasted a mammoth two-run homer off the Sportsman's Park scoreboard in left field to tie the game. The Cardinals rallied to win, 9–5, but the Yankees took the next two games and held a 3–0 advantage in the sixth inning of the fourth game. The Cardinals loaded the bases, though, and their captain, Ken Boyer, deposited a grand slam into the left-field stands of Yankee Stadium. Cardinals reliever Ron Taylor, a Canadian native who led the 1964 Cardinals with 63 pitching appearances, entered the game in the bottom of the sixth. Then an electrical engineer and later a medical student and physician, he blanked the Yankees without surrendering a hit over the final four innings, making the 4–3 lead stand up the rest of the way.

After Boyer and Taylor evened the Series at two games apiece, Gibson pitched the Cardinals to the title and received the World Series Most Valuable Player award. In the fifth game, he struck out 13 Yankees in 10 innings, winning 5–2 on a three-run, tenth-inning homer by his batterymate McCarver, who batted .478 for the Series. Gibson worked the decisive seventh game on two days' rest, fanning nine batters and pitching another complete game. The Cardinals prevailed, 7–5, in the last World Series contest at Sportsman's Park. Boyer, involved in every Cardinal rally in the seventh game, singled and scored to start their three-run fourth inning, doubled and scored the second run in their three-run fifth, and hit a solo homer for their final run in the seventh.

In the victorious Cardinals clubhouse, it was suggested to Musial that he had retired one year too soon. Musial modestly replied that the Cardinals would not have been champions in 1964, if Devine had not acquired Brock to replace him. With those words, Musial appropriately passed the torch to a new generation of Cardinals champions.

Devine, the primary architect of the champion Cardinals, did not share in the clubhouse celebration. He had been fired on August 17, when the Cardinals still trailed the Phillies by nine games. Moreover, after a radio interview in which Leo Durocher indicated to Harry Caray that he would be interested in managing the team, the impulsive Busch intended to discard Keane in favor of Durocher after the season. He changed his mind when Keane piloted the Cardinals to the Series title, deciding to reward Keane with a contract extension and a hefty raise. Keane resented Busch's plotting to replace him and also harbored a grudge toward him for

Boom and Bust in St. Louis

firing Devine, his friend and collaborator. Busch arranged a press conference, prepared his announcement of signing Keane to a new contract, and awaited Keane's arrival. Keane showed up late with a letter of resignation. He soon accepted an offer to manage the Yankees, who in turn resented him as the successor to Yogi Berra, who had won the pennant in his only year as manager and been fired after losing a seven-game World Series.

Busch realized that St. Louis fans blamed him for firing Devine and driving out Keane, the local boy and World Series-winning skipper. He tried to repair the damage by hiring the popular Red Schoendienst, a nine-time Cardinals All-Star and future Hall of Famer, as manager. Schoendienst had returned to the Cardinals as a player in 1961 and, two years later, joined Keane's coaching staff. He was similar to Keane as a low-key manager who believed in putting his best performers on the field and then letting them play. Less popular was the new general manager, Bob Howsam, viewed as an intruder who claimed inordinate credit for the 1964 championship.

9

El Birdos

The Cardinals of 1967 and 1968 must have been the most remarkable team in the history of baseball. I speak now of the team's social achievements, without which its pitching, batting and fielding would have been less triumphant than they were. The men of that team were as close to being free of racist poison as a diverse group of twentieth-century Americans could possibly be.
—Curt Flood, co-captain and center fielder for the Cardinals' consecutive pennant-winners of 1967–1968[1]

In San Francisco, the team was split along racist lines; the Cardinals were not. In fact, I remember one time in Atlanta when we got to a motel where we were to have a team party. Mike Shannon and Tim McCarver were told they could stay, but the black players had to go. Shannon and McCarver stuck up for us and said, "If you won't let the black guys in here, we're not going in either."
—Orlando Cepeda, who christened the champion Cardinals of 1967–1968 "El Birdos"[2]

Bob Howsam antagonized the Cardinals players with petty memorandums directing them to keep their hair trimmed short, wear the legs of their pants high, and avoid slouching on the bench. He inherited a world championship club that, under his control, nosedived to seventh place with an 80–81 record. After the season, Howsam unloaded Ken Boyer, Bill White, and Dick Groat, the club's oldest and highest-paid veterans. The absence of Boyer and White, who had led the Cardinals in home runs and runs batted in throughout the early 1960s, forced Howsam to make deals for other proven run producers. In May 1966, Howsam acquired

Boom and Bust in St. Louis

In 1967, Lou Brock led the NL in runs scored and stolen bases, and, in that year's victory over the Boston Red Sox in the World Series, batted .414, scored a Series-high eight runs, and set a Series record with seven steals (National Baseball Hall of Fame).

first baseman Orlando Cepeda from the San Francisco Giants and, in December, added right fielder Roger Maris from the New York Yankees.

The Cardinals had a winning record of 83–79 in 1966, but still finished sixth. They were the type of club that thrived on clubhouse camaraderie, and Howsam's senseless front-office regulations chipped away at their treasured team harmony. After Howsam departed to take over as general manager of the Cincinnati Reds, the 1967–1968 Cardinals claimed consecutive pennants.

The 1967 squad was the first to play a full season at the new downtown ballpark. A coalition of businessmen, the Civic Center Redevelopment Corporation, collected over $50 million and built the new stadium. The Cardinals, who had played at Sportsman's Park on the northwestern outskirts of St. Louis since 1920, made their Busch Stadium debut on May 12, 1966. Along with the nearby Gateway Arch, Busch Stadium became a centerpiece of the revitalized St. Louis riverfront. It was named for Gussie

9. El Birdos

Busch, who got the project rolling by donating $5 million from the coffers of Anheuser-Busch and eventually bought the stadium from the city. In 1966, the Cardinals capitalized on the novelty of the new stadium's appeal and its increased seating capacity to draw over 1.7 million spectators, a club record for attendance.

One year later, led by Most Valuable Player Cepeda with a league-leading 111 runs batted in, Curt Flood with a team-high .335 batting average, and Lou Brock, who led the league with 113 runs scored and 52 stolen bases, the Cardinals captured the pennant with 101 wins and, eclipsing the two million mark in attendance, outdrew all of major league baseball. In the World Series, they faced the Boston Red Sox, led by American League Triple Crown winner Carl Yastrzemski and 22-game winner Jim Lonborg. The Red Sox had clinched the American League pennant on the final day of the regular season, with Yastrzemski going 4-for-4 and Lonborg eliminating the Minnesota Twins, 5–3. They remained home for the World Series opener three days later. Bob Gibson, who had missed nearly two months of the season when a line drive off the bat of Pittsburgh Pirates Hall of Famer Roberto Clemente fractured his leg, won the opener, 2–1. Brock went 4-for-4, stole two bases, and scored both of the Cardinals' tallies on runs batted in by Maris. In Game Two, Lonborg limited the Cardinals to one hit, a double by Julian Javier, and evened the Series with a 6–0 victory.

The teams traveled to St. Louis for the first World Series game at Busch Stadium. In the first two innings, the Cardinals jumped on Red Sox starter Gary Bell for three runs, climaxed by a two-run homer by Mike Shannon, who had moved to third base that season to make room for Maris in right field. Maris singled to drive home Brock in the sixth inning and, after beating out an infield hit in the eighth, scored on Cepeda's double off the wall in right-center. Nelson Briles, a reliever who had moved into the starting rotation when Gibson was injured and won nine successive starts, went all the way and won another in a 5–2 victory. A day later, the Cardinals again shelled Red Sox pitching in the first two innings, scoring six runs with every starter except Gibson reaching base safely. Gibson pitched a five-hit shutout, and the Cardinals coasted to a commanding three games to one lead, 6–0. Lonborg won a 3–1 pitching duel over the Cardinals' Steve Carlton in Game Five, though, and the World Series returned to Boston.

In Game Six, the Red Sox won again, 8–4, forcing a seventh and decisive game. Lonborg, on only two days' rest, matched up with Gibson. The

Boom and Bust in St. Louis

Cardinals turned the dream pitching match-up into a mismatch with two runs off Lonborg in the third inning, two more in the fifth, and three in the sixth. Dal Maxvill, who had been a utility infielder in 1964 and started at second base for an injured Javier in the World Series, had replaced Groat as the starting shortstop. He excelled defensively, but hit only .227. However, in Game Seven of the World Series, Maxvill opened the floodgates in the third inning with a triple off the center-field wall, and he subsequently scored the game's first run on a single by Flood. Gibson, allowing only three hits and striking out ten, even hit a home run and cruised to his third win of the Series, 7–2. Maris drove in another run, finishing the World Series with a .385 batting average and a Series-high seven runs batted in. Julian Javier drove a three-run homer over the left-field wall, Fenway's fabled "Green Monster," and wrapped up the Series with a .360 average. Brock, who hit .414 for the Series, scored his Series-high eighth run and stole three bases in the seventh game to set a record with seven stolen bases in a single World Series (his career average was .391 in three World Series and .375 in six All-Star Games).

The Cardinals repeated as National League champions the next year with 97 wins, again attracted over two million fans, and led the National League in attendance. In a season dominated by pitching, Gibson won 22 games and the Most Valuable Player Award with 268 strikeouts and a scintillating 1.12 ERA. The Cardinals batted just .249, fourth in the league, and only Flood, at .301, topped the .300 mark. In the World Series, the Cardinals, backed by two wins by Gibson, led the Detroit Tigers three games to one. The Tigers roared back, however, to win the next three games and take the championship.

In both 1967 and 1968, the Cardinals far outdistanced the second-place San Francisco Giants who might have had better talent but were divided along racial and ethnic lines, barriers that the Cardinals had torn down. The Cardinals' co-captains were Flood, an African American who had grown up in the poverty of an Oakland ghetto, and Tim McCarver, a white Southerner and son of a Memphis policeman. They both credited Gibson for prodding the Cardinals toward a heightened awareness of racial cooperation. Cepeda, a future Hall of Famer and son of a Puerto Rican baseball legend, emerged as another team leader and dubbed the team "El Birdos."

This unity extended to the relationship between the players and the Cardinals' front-office. When Howsam headed for Cincinnati, Busch selected local icon Stan Musial as general manager. Musial did not make any major personnel moves, but was a vast improvement in terms of

9. El Birdos

personnel management. Many of the 1967 Cardinals remembered Musial as an affable teammate and valued his friendship. Musial treated players with respect and, unlike Howsam, did not deluge the Cardinals with memorandums on appropriate behavior.

Following the examples of Musial and Schoendienst, even Gussie Busch developed a paternalistic bond with his players. After winning the 1967 World Series, the Cardinals received relatively prodigious salaries by the standards of the time. The payroll of their starting nine, including ace pitcher Gibson, exceeded $550,000. In addition, the Cardinals gained perks that other clubs lacked. All starters had the option of private rooms on road trips, and, unlike other teams of the era, the Cardinals flew exclusively on a charter jet. Musial resigned as general manager after the 1967 World Series to devote more time to his business interests, and, in another goodwill gesture, Busch brought back Bing Devine to replace him. The players believed they worked for the most benevolent of baseball organizations.

Busch destroyed this harmony in spring training of 1969, his disposition soured by off-season negotiations with the Major League Baseball Players Association. The owners had tried to reduce the percentage of television and radio revenue allocated to the players' pension fund, and the Players Association responded by having players refuse to sign contracts until a compromise resolved this bitter dispute. Once negotiations commenced, several of the pennant-winning Cardinals demanded raises. Busch reluctantly complied, but he now viewed ballplayers as ingrates. On March 22, at the Cardinals' St. Petersburg training site, Busch gathered together the Cardinals, sportswriters, and Anheuser-Busch executives and lashed out at the team, accusing them of being more concerned with money than about their fans or the image of the game.

Busch had crossed a line of no return, and his team could not recover from their public humiliation. In 1967 and 1968, "El Birdos" had drawn strength from their pride in the organization. However, once the players felt the front office no longer appreciated them, they played like other talented teams that fell short of their potential. The Cardinals dropped from 97 wins in 1968 to 87 in 1969, finishing fourth in the new six-team division of the National League East.

Over the next three years, all of the champion Cardinals either retired or were traded away, except for Brock and Gibson. Devine worked side by side with Busch in dismantling the championship club that he had once helped to build. In March 1969, they dealt Cepeda and, seven months

Boom and Bust in St. Louis

later, traded co-captains Flood and McCarver. Flood was despondent over leaving St. Louis and refused to report to Philadelphia, which had a racist reputation. He sued major-league baseball for the freedom to negotiate with a team of his own choosing, and, although the U.S. Supreme Court narrowly ruled against him in 1972, the Flood case was the first step toward attaining free agency four years later.

In 1970, the Cardinals dipped to a record of 76–86, but Schoendienst rallied them the next year to 90 wins and a second-place finish. Brock led the league with 126 runs scored and 64 stolen bases, while Joe Torre, acquired from the Atlanta Braves for Cepeda, topped the league with 137 runs batted in, won the batting championship with a .363 average, and was the National League Most Valuable Player. The three top pitchers were an aging Gibson at 19–11 and a pair of young left-handed farm products, Steve Carlton and Jerry Reuss. Carlton had joined the Cardinals as a 20-year-old in 1965 and, after being rarely used for two seasons, blossomed with a 14–9 record in 1967. For the following four seasons, he averaged 15 wins per year, capped with 20 in 1971. Reuss, a 22-year-old hometown product, won 14 games that year.

The two young hurlers requested raises and, according to Bob Broeg of the *St. Louis Post-Dispatch*, Busch proved "as immovable as a Clydesdale with a mule's disposition."[3] After negotiations broke down, Busch ordered Devine to trade both pitchers. In the next dozen years, Carlton compiled 223 more victories, pitched the Philadelphia Phillies to five divisional titles, and became a 300-game winner and Hall of Fame pitcher. Reuss won over 200 games and pitched for five divisional champions with the Pittsburgh Pirates and the Los Angeles Dodgers. From 1974 to 1978, the best pitcher on the National League East champions was either Reuss or Carlton.

Busch's stubbornness forced the Cardinals to pay a heavy price. After another losing record in 1972, Schoendienst and the Cardinals ended a game and a half short of the divisional crowns in 1973 and 1974. Their runner-up finish in 1974, when Brock stole a record 118 bases at the age of 35, seemed especially poignant because Reuss was the star pitcher for the victorious Pirates. Thereafter, the Cardinals slipped to the status of also-rans, finishing a distant third in 1975 with an 82–80 record. In 1976, they lost 90 games and finished fifth, prompting Busch to make Schoendienst the fall guy for his own mistakes.

10

Vern Rapp, Ken Boyer and Whitey Herzog

> Maybe it was the smile. Maybe it was those crazy back flips he did to open our World Series games, which not only were punctuation marks for the way the Cards played baseball, but gave the fans an image of the joy at the heart of our game.
> —Cardinals manager Whitey Herzog, describing his shortstop, Ozzie Smith, in *You're Missin' a Great Game* (1999)[1]

The Cardinals' new manager, Vern Rapp, raised a ruckus trying to reinstate Bob Howsam's rules and regulations. He made center fielder Bake McBride shave his beard and top reliever Al Hrabosky get a haircut and shave his facial hair. McBride, the NL Rookie of the Year in 1974, had hit .300 or better every year since joining the Cardinals in late July of 1973 and entered the 1977 season with a career average of .319. By mid–June, his average had dipped to .262, and Rapp traded him to Philadelphia, where he helped the Phillies win their first-ever World Series in 1980. Hrabosky protested that his shaggy looks, combined with his "Mad Hungarian" routine on the mound, intimidated opposing batters. After his locks were shorn and his facial hair shaven, Hrabosky saw his earned run average balloon to 4.40, making him appear like a modern-day Samson to fans of the Cardinals. Rapp petulantly traded Hrabosky in December and infuriated fans further. Rapp somehow managed an 83–79 record and a distant third-place finish in 1977. In 1978, with the Cardinals in last place and his players in open rebellion, Rapp was dismissed after a 6–11 start.

Ken Boyer, the Cardinals' former All-Star third baseman, replaced Rapp as manager and returned to the relaxed managerial style of Red Schoendienst, whom he even brought back as a coach. The Cardinals, with

Boom and Bust in St. Louis

their individual freedom restored, nosed out of the cellar to finish fifth. In 1979, they improved to 86–78 and another distant third-place finish. Lou Brock, playing his final season at the age of 40, went out in a blaze of glory, batting .304 and collecting his 3000th hit on a line shot off Cubs pitcher Dennis Lamp that flattened Lamp one pitch after he had thrown at Brock. Keith Hernandez, a 25-year-old farm product and superb defensive first baseman, won the batting championship with a .344 average and tied for the National League Most Valuable Player award with Willie Stargell of the world champion Pittsburgh Pirates. In 1980, though, the Cardinals stumbled to an 18–33 start and, back in last place once again, Gussie Busch reassigned the popular Boyer to the team's scouting and player development program.

Fortunately, Busch provided one last positive legacy for St. Louis baseball. In June 1980, he replaced Boyer as manager with Whitey Herzog and, within three months, hired Herzog as general manager as well. Herzog had a proven track record, having guided the 1976–1978 Kansas City Royals to three straight division titles in the American League. Unlike Rapp, he did not impose rules on hair length, facial hair, or uniform attire. Herzog however, believing the players had taken advantage of the easy-going nature of Boyer, demanded all-out effort. After his arrival, the Cardinals played over the .500 mark, escaped the National League East cellar, and finished in fourth place.

Ozzie Smith joined the Cardinals in 1982 and, as arguably the greatest defensive shortstop in baseball history, helped lead them to three NL pennants and a World Series championship in the next six seasons (National Baseball Hall of Fame).

10. Vern Rapp, Ken Boyer and Whitey Herzog

The 1980 Cardinals had some obvious deficiencies, particularly a weak bullpen. Herzog also realized that the Cardinals were ill-suited for spacious Busch Stadium and its artificial turf because of a lack of speed and inability to stop the opponents' running game. For two years, Herzog used every means of player development, wheeling and dealing like a whirlwind. He promoted farmhands like second baseman Tommy Herr and starting pitcher John Stuper, signed his former Royals catcher, Darrell Porter, as a free agent, and made multiple trades (even sending away popular catcher Ted Simmons, whom Herzog regarded as a defensive liability). In nine different deals, the Cardinals acquired shortstop Ozzie Smith, left fielder Lonnie Smith, center fielder Willie McGee, three-fifths of their starting rotation (Joaquin Andujar, Dave LaPoint, and Steve Mura), and three of their top four relievers (Bruce Sutter, Doug Bair, and Jeff Lahti).

By 1982, only seven holdovers remained from the team that Herzog had inherited, including Hernandez at first base, George Hendrick in right field, and Ken Oberkfell, who moved from second base to third base. Herzog relied on a recipe of speed, defense, and a strong bullpen. His "Runnin' Redbirds" hit fewer home runs in 1982 than any National League team, but stole the most bases. Lonnie Smith led the league with 120 runs scored, stole 68 bases, and finished second in balloting for National League Most Valuable Player. Ozzie Smith, arguably the greatest defensive shortstop ever, anchored one of the slickest-fielding infields in the history of baseball, and the speedy outfielders ranged far and wide to chase down fly balls or prevent extra-base hits. Herzog had braced up the entire bullpen, and future Hall of Famer Sutter topped all major league relievers with 36 saves, earning the Rolaids Relief Award.

The Cardinals, with a 12-game winning streak in April, went quickly to the front of the National League East. They set the pace nearly all season, but the Philadelphia Phillies edged ahead by a half-game on September 13. A day later, Stuper and Sutter combined to shut out the Phillies, 2–0, and the Cardinals reclaimed first place. That crucial victory launched the Cardinals on a eight-game winning streak, and, with a final record of 92–70, they outpaced their Philadelphia pursuers by three games for the Eastern Division title. In the best-of-five National League Championship Series, the Cardinals swept the Western Division champion Atlanta Braves.

The World Series offered a study in contrasts, with Herzog's "Runnin' Redbirds" facing Harvey Kuenn's Milwaukee Brewers. "Harvey's Wallbangers" had topped the major leagues with 216 home runs, while

Boom and Bust in St. Louis

Herzog's speedsters had stolen 200 bases. The so-called "Suds Series," waged between the two biggest beer-producing cities in the country, opened in St. Louis with Harvey's Wallbangers smashing 17 hits in a 10–0 rout. The next night, though, the resilient Runnin' Redbirds struck back, using their speed to steal three bases and repeatedly take an extra base in erasing a 3–0 deficit. Relievers Jim Kaat, Bair, and Sutter shut down the Brewers for five innings, enabling the Cardinals to rally for a 5–4 win.

Up in Milwaukee, Andujar pitched a shutout into the seventh inning, when a line drive caromed off his knee and knocked him out of the game. He won, 6–2, with McGee hitting two home runs and making a pair of spectacular catches. However, the Brewers took the last two Milwaukee contests and, as the World Series returned to St. Louis, the Cardinals faced elimination. For Game Six, Herzog handed the ball to rookie John Stuper, who faced future Hall of Famer and 17-year veteran Don Sutton. The Cardinals shelled Sutton in the fifth inning and clobbered the Brewers, 13–1, while Stuper pitched a complete game.

Andujar, despite his injured knee, started the seventh game. He trailed, 3–1, until the Cardinals staged a sixth-inning comeback. With the bases loaded, Hernandez lined a single to center, scoring Ozzie and Lonnie Smith to tie the game. Hendrick then grounded a single to right, driving home pinch-runner Mike Ramsey and giving the Cardinals a 4–3 advantage. Andujar and Sutter clamped down the Brewers the rest of the way, allowing the Cardinals to salt away a 6–3 triumph and the World Series championship. Sutter struck out Brewers slugger Gorman Thomas for the final out, and Jack Buck, who had joined the Cardinals' radio network in 1954 and succeeded Harry Caray as the primary play-by-play broadcaster, exulted: "A swing and a miss and that's a winner, that's a winner, a World Series winner for the Cardinals!"[2]

The Cardinals fell to fourth and third place in the following two years, but regained the National League East crown in 1985 with 101 wins. Their offense led the National League in runs scored (747), stolen bases (314), and batting average (.264). McGee, who batted .353 to lead the league, was voted Most Valuable Player; new left fielder Vince Coleman, who stole 110 bases, was Rookie of the Year; and Herzog was Manager of the Year. The Cardinals lost the first two games of the National League Championship Series to the Los Angeles Dodgers, but swept the next four games to take the pennant. In the last two contests, the Cardinals prevailed on game-winning homers, a rare walk-off shot from Ozzie Smith in Game Five and a three-run blast from Jack Clark, the team's top slugger, that

10. Vern Rapp, Ken Boyer and Whitey Herzog

erased a Dodgers lead in the top of the ninth inning of Game Six. However, in a controversial seven-game affair, they lost the World Series to the Kansas City Royals.

Two years later, the Cardinals won 95 games and the championship of the National League East once again. Coleman scored 121 runs and stole 109 bases, while McGee and Clark both drove in over 100 runs. The team entered the post-season without an injured Clark and, in an acrimonious National League Championship Series, trailed the San Francisco Giants three games to two. However, returning to St. Louis, the Cardinals shut out the Giants in consecutive games, winning 1–0 in Game Six behind the pitching of John Tudor and relievers Todd Worrell and Ken Dayley and, on the strength of a three-run homer by Jose Oquendo, coasting to a 6–0 victory in Game Seven on a shutout by Danny Cox. Unfortunately, third baseman Terry Pendleton, injured in the seventh game against the Giants, was unavailable for most of the World Series. Often taking the field without two of their top three run producers in Clark and Pendleton, who had driven in 96 runs in the regular season, the Cardinals again lost the World Series in seven games, this time to the Minnesota Twins.

Herzog consistently preserved the Cardinals' emphasis on speed, defense, and a superior bullpen, but often changed personnel. Only Ozzie Smith, Herr, McGee, and pitcher Bob Forsch played on all three pennant winners. During the 1980s, the Runnin' Redbirds topped the National League in steals seven successive seasons and aroused St. Louis with an exciting brand of baseball. The Cardinals broke their season attendance record five times in the decade and, in 1987 and 1989, drew over three million and exceeded every National League team in attendance (leading all of major league baseball in 1987).

The relationship between Herzog and Anheuser-Busch executives frayed over time. August Busch III, the eldest son of Gussie Busch, had forced his father out as the head of the company in 1975, and, although Gussie remained president of the Cardinals, the brewery owned the ballclub. Herzog had a close friendship with Gussie and originally answered only to him. However, after the Cardinals won the 1982 World Series, the brewery insisted on governing the Cardinals with a three-man executive committee, comprised of Gussie Busch and two company attorneys.

Herzog, a model of efficiency, resented needless bureaucracy. He had taken over a last-place team with the second-highest payroll in the league, slashed payroll 30 percent, and won the World Series. Company attorneys on the new executive committee merely delayed and complicated contract

Boom and Bust in St. Louis

negotiations, and Herzog blamed them for sabotaging salary discussions that resulted in the loss of Sutter and Clark to free agency after the 1984 and 1987 seasons.

As long as Gussie Busch lived, Herzog had leverage with the Cardinals' front office, but the president passed away on September 29, 1989, at the age of 90, leaving Herzog without power at corporate headquarters. Fred Kuhlman, one of the Anheuser-Busch attorneys with whom Herzog feuded, became president of the Cardinals.

The 1990 Cardinals, unlike their recent predecessors, were a demoralized club. Ten players were in their option year, and Kuhlman refused to negotiate. Team spirit dissolved, and, in July, Herzog resigned as manager. Ironically, he left the Cardinals in last place, where they had been when he took over. Joe Torre, who had first joined the Cardinals in March 1969 with team morale at low ebb, now became manager under similar circumstances. He could not lift the gloom surrounding the Cardinals, who finished last for the first time since 1918.

11

Exit Anheuser-Busch, Enter Tony La Russa

> You appreciate it more the older you get because you realize then how tough it is to win a World Series.
> —Red Schoendienst, at the Cardinals' Winter Warmup in January 2011, on winning world championship rings with the Cardinals as a player (1946), manager (1967), and coach (1964, 1982, and 2006), quoted in James Rygelski and Robert Tiemann, *Ten Rings* (2011)[1]

> If there's a lesson to be taken away from our 2011 season, one in which we continued to come back over and over, it's this: Just because you're down to your last strike, you're not out yet. You can always do more. You'll always have more at-bats to take.
> —Tony La Russa, in *One Last Strike* (2012)[2]

From 1991 to 1993, the Cardinals' farm system produced a trio of talented outfielders (Ray Lankford, Bernard Gilkey, and Brian Jordan), and manager Joe Torre put together winning teams that finished either second or third in the National League East. Attendance in St. Louis declined from 1990 to 1992, but rebounded beyond 2.8 million in 1993.

The 1994 season looked like a potential breakthrough year. Divisional realignment and expanded playoffs had transferred the Cardinals into the newly created National League Central. Of all the teams in this new division, the Cardinals had sported the best record in the preceding season, so they were considered pre-season favorites. But the pitching staff fell apart, recording an exorbitant earned run average of 5.14, next-to-last in the league and the worst pitching performance for the franchise since 1897. By August 12, when the players went on a strike

Boom and Bust in St. Louis

that ultimately cancelled the rest of the season and the playoffs, the Cardinals were floundering at 53–61.

Skyrocketing salaries caused the clash between players and owners. In 1969, when the Cardinals traded Curt Flood and unwittingly started the game down the path of a salary revolution, major league players had earned an average of $24,909. A quarter-century later, the average major leaguer made nearly $1.2 million, and the minimum salary slightly exceeded $100,000, previously considered the threshold of the most elite players. Horrified owners called for a salary cap while players refused to accept restraints on their marketplace freedom and argued that the owners bore responsibility for the parameters of the salary structure.

Tony La Russa, in 16 years as Cardinals manager from 1996 through 2011, guided them to nine playoff appearances, three NL pennants, and two World Series championships (National Baseball Hall of Fame).

The dispute lingered into spring training, and owners planned to start the 1995 season with replacement players. Two days before the season opened, U.S. District Judge Sonia Sotomayor intervened and ruled that, until a new collective bargaining agreement could be reached, major league baseball would operate under the old collective bargaining agreement. Many embittered fans avoided big-league ballparks in 1995, and crowds decreased 20 percent from the preceding year.

Attendance plunged precipitously at Busch Stadium. Torre had improved the pitching staff, but the Cardinals had the least productive offense in the league and finished 62–81. Torre was dismissed after 47 games and replaced by Mike Jorgensen. August A. Busch III, who had never shown interest in baseball even at the height of Runnin' Redbirds mania, was irate at the lack of post-strike fan support. In December 1995, Anheuser-Busch sold the Cardinals for $150 million to a group of investors, including local

11. Exit Anheuser-Busch, Enter Tony La Russa

banker Andrew Baur and William DeWitt Jr. (whose father and uncle had once co-owned the St. Louis Browns and Sportsman's Park).

These new owners adopted "Baseball like It Oughta Be" as the Cardinals' slogan for the 1996 season. They replaced the artificial turf, which had carpeted Busch Stadium since 1970, with natural grass. The blue backdrop of Busch Stadium was repainted green to match the hue of the grass, and upper-level outfield seats were eliminated to add an old-time scoreboard and flags commemorating Cardinals championships and players' retired numbers. Tony La Russa, who had won three consecutive American League pennants with the Oakland Athletics from 1988 to 1990, was brought in as manager, and he got more financial support than Torre had received. Salaries that year rose from $31 million to $38 million.

La Russa guided the 1996 Cardinals to 88 wins and victory in the National League Central by six games over the Houston Astros. Yet he did not initially endear himself to St. Louis fans because of his treatment of local hero Ozzie Smith, a 15-time All-Star, future Hall of Fame shortstop, and the holder of 13 Gold Gloves and numerous fielding records. La Russa had acquired 26-year-old shortstop Royce Clayton from the San Francisco Giants and turned the 41-year-old Smith into a part-time player. Smith announced that he would retire following the season, his 19th in the majors and 15th with the Cardinals. Fans resented La Russa, whom they blamed for forcing Smith into retirement. Clayton started more than two-thirds of the games, even though Smith outhit him, .282 to .277, and, more importantly, the Cardinals' winning percentage was barely above .500 in Clayton's starts and over .600 in Smith's. La Russa maintained that the presence of Clayton had kept Smith rested and allowed him to enjoy a glorious farewell season. Fans questioned why the well-rested Smith only started three of ten playoff games, especially since the Cardinals were far better with him in the lineup. Matters were made even worse when the Cardinals, after sweeping the San Diego Padres in the first round of the playoffs, lost the National League Championship Series to the Atlanta Braves in seven games and fell a game short of the World Series in Ozzie's last season.

Although the Cardinals failed to make the playoffs in the next three seasons, La Russa actually improved his relationship with local fans by bringing Mark McGwire to St. Louis. Attendance had partially recovered in the divisional championship year of 1996, surpassing 2.6 million, but was still seven percent behind the last pre-strike season of 1993 and then dipped again in a losing 1997 season. On July 31, though,

Boom and Bust in St. Louis

the Cardinals acquired McGwire, the Oakland first baseman who had played for La Russa from 1986 to 1995. McGwire, scheduled to become a free agent after the 1997 season, wanted to sign with a team from his native southern California. The Athletics, reconciled to losing McGwire to free agency, were willing to trade him for established players. The Cardinals gambled on the trade, banking that La Russa could sell McGwire on the virtues of St. Louis.

The strategy paid off. Energetic Busch Stadium crowds inspired McGwire, who hit 24 home runs in the final two months of the season, and he signed with the Cardinals. His late-season heroics fueled speculation that McGwire might break Roger Maris' single-season home run record of 61, especially after McGwire opened the 1998 season with four home runs in four games. He reached 27 by the end of May. The Cardinals began allowing crowds inside the gates two hours before game time just to watch McGwire's batting practice. When the season ended, the club had drawn nearly 3.2 million fans, breaking the attendance record of the 1989 Cardinals.

McGwire clubbed 10 more homers in June, but Sammy Sosa of the Cubs slammed 20 and emerged as a challenger. Heading into July, McGwire held a 37–33 edge, and the Great (and friendly) Home Run Chase was on. On Labor Day, September 7, the Cubs arrived in St. Louis for a pair of games, with McGwire up, 60–58. That afternoon, McGwire tied Maris' record, and he surpassed it the next night. Within a week, Sosa also passed Maris and, on September 25, briefly went ahead of McGwire. Just 46 minutes later, McGwire knotted the count at 66. He snapped the deadlock on the last two days of the season with four more homers, finishing with a flurry of five home runs in his final 11 at bats and the major league record over Sosa, 70–66. Attendance for major league baseball exceeded the pre-strike season of 1993 for the first time, and many fans credited the Great Home Run Chase of 1998 with saving the game.

Three years later, Barry Bonds broke McGwire's record, and McGwire, hobbled with a knee injury, retired. Bonds, McGwire, and Sosa all subsequently faced allegations of using steroids, a substance not tested for by major league baseball until 2002, the year when former National League Most Valuable Player Ken Caminiti admitted his own steroid use and estimated that at least half of major league players were also users. Bonds and Sosa have continued to deny using steroids, but, upon returning to the Cardinals as hitting coach in 2011, McGwire admitted his use and expressed remorse for it.

11. Exit Anheuser-Busch, Enter Tony La Russa

Beyond his on-field presence and box-office appeal, McGwire rejuvenated the Cardinals' front office. The successful courting of McGwire emboldened general manager Walt Jocketty to continue the strategy that had attracted McGwire to St. Louis. By 2004, when the Cardinals won the National League pennant, their lineup included seven starters added by trades or free agency. The entire team's payroll of $83.2 million reached in the upper third of major league baseball.

The only homegrown regular on the 2004 Cardinals, Albert Pujols, succeeded McGwire as the symbolic face of the ball club. After Pujols homered in his Busch Stadium debut on April 9, 2001, Jack Buck, in his 48th and last year of Cardinals radio broadcasts, prophetically anointed the 21-year-old rookie as a new hero in town. A unanimous choice as the league's Rookie of the Year, Pujols pounded 114 homers from 2001 to 2003, tying Hall of Famer Ralph Kiner's record for the most home runs in a player's initial three major league seasons. He won the 2003 batting championship with a .359 average, and in 2004 joined immortals Ted Williams and Joe DiMaggio as the only players to drive in over 500 runs in their first four major league seasons. Pujols played a variety of positions until 2004, when he became established at first base.

By that point, La Russa had calmed local critics with consistent success, although some still grumbled over the team's post-season problems. He took the Cardinals to the playoffs each year from 2000 to 2002. In 2000, his Cardinals swept the Braves in the Division Series, but lost in five games to the New York Mets in the League Championship Series. The eventual World Series champion Arizona Diamondbacks dealt the Cardinals an agonizing five-game setback in the opening round of the 2001 playoffs, and in 2002, after Darryl Kile pitched the Cardinals into first place in his last game before his death from a heart attack, the Cardinals avenged themselves by sweeping the Diamondbacks in the Division Series, but again fell short in the League Championship Series, losing in five games to the Giants.

In 2004, after making a shambles of the Central Division with 105 wins and a 13-game margin over the Houston Astros, the Cardinals dispatched the Los Angeles Dodgers in the Division Series and finally surmounted the obstacle of the League Championship Series. Facing the divisional rival Astros, who had won the wild-card playoff spot, the Cardinals won in seven games, with Pujols hitting .500 and winning the Most Valuable Player Award of the series (from 2001 to 2011, in 74 post-season games with the Cardinals, Pujols hit 18 home runs, drove in 52 runs, and

Boom and Bust in St. Louis

batted .329). Giddiness over their 16th National League pennant and first World Series appearance in 17 years evaporated quickly, though, when the Boston Red Sox swept them.

The Cardinals won 100 games for the second straight year in 2005, taking the Central Division title over the Astros again by 11 games. Pujols hit .330 with 41 homers and 117 runs batted in and was elected National League Most Valuable Player. Chris Carpenter posted a sterling 21–5 win-loss record and received the Cy Young Award as the league's best pitcher. The Cardinals swept the Padres in the first round of the playoffs and moved on to the National League Championship Series against divisional foe Houston, who had again won the league's wild-card spot. In the fifth game, with the Cardinals one out from elimination, Pujols hit a dramatic three-run homer to prolong the series. However, the Cardinals lost the next game, and, for the fourth time under La Russa, the Cardinals' season ended in the League Championship Series.

On Opening Day of 2006, the Cardinals moved into a new, $344.8 million, 46,000-seat Busch Stadium, adjacent to and somewhat overlapping the old Busch Stadium. They had planned on sharing construction costs with the state, county, and city governments, but many politicians and taxpayers opposed public funding. Eventually, a compromise was crafted with the state and local governments that required the Cardinals to shoulder more of the financial burden than originally envisioned. The Cardinals turned to private investors as a source of revenue to alleviate their obligations, selling naming rights to the new park to Anheuser-Busch.

The year 2006 would also be the year when La Russa achieved his goal of managing the Cardinals to a World Series championship. The 2006 Cardinals might have been the most unlikely of all their World Series champions. In the two preceding seasons, the Cardinals had posted the best regular season record in baseball, and in 2006, with a record of 83–78, they became the team with the worst regular season record ever to win a World Series. The Cardinals quickly climbed to the top of the Central Division on May 12 and stayed there for the rest of their injury-riddled year, but a pair of eight-game losing streaks prevented them from pulling away from their pursuers. Nevertheless, on September 19, they held a comfortable seven-game lead over the Cincinnati Reds. The Cardinals staggered down the stretch, however, losing seven straight games. Meanwhile, the defending National League champion Astros, winning nine games in a row, surged past the Reds, and set their sights on the Cardinals. On Wednesday, September 27, trailing 2–1 in the bottom of the eighth

11. Exit Anheuser-Busch, Enter Tony La Russa

to the Padres, the Cardinals rallied and took the lead. With two runners aboard, Pujols blasted his 47th home run of the season, and rookie reliever Adam Wainwright, recently elevated to bullpen closer due to Jason Isringhausen's season-ending hip injury, slammed the door on the Padres in the ninth.

Although the losing streak was finally over, the Cardinals lost the opener of a four-game series against the Milwaukee Brewers the next day, and the Astros defeated the Pittsburgh Pirates to move within a half-game of the lead. The Astros headed from Pittsburgh to Atlanta for the final weekend of the season, and the Braves snapped their winning streak on Friday night. In St. Louis, the Cardinals battered the Brewers, 10–5. Pujols slugged another three-run homer, and third baseman Scott Rolen, recovering from a persistent shoulder injury, had three hits and scored three runs. Pitcher Jeff Weaver, acquired in a midseason trade with the Los Angeles Angels of Anaheim, improved his record with the Cardinals to 5–4 (after struggling to a 3–10 record and a 6.29 earned-run-average with the Angels). On Saturday, trailing 2–0 in the eighth inning, pinch-hitter Scott Spezio cleared the bases with a two-out triple. Wainwright protected the 3–2 lead in the ninth, but the Astros stayed alive with a win over the Braves.

La Russa pondered an intriguing decision as the regular season entered its final day. The Cardinals led by a game and a half. If the Cardinals lost and the Astros won, the Cardinals would be forced to play a make-up game on Monday against the Giants, stemming from a rain-out earlier in the month. Then if the Cardinals should lose to the Giants, they would be required to play the Astros on Tuesday in a playoff game for the Central Division title. Even if the Cardinals survived these extra games, their injury-depleted pitching rotation would be thrown completely out of whack for the playoffs. On the other hand, La Russa preferred to save his best starter, Chris Carpenter, for a Wednesday playoff opener in San Diego. He decided to withhold Carpenter from Sunday's start against the Brewers and use rookie Anthony Reyes, only 5–7 on the season. If Reyes could not defeat the Brewers, La Russa was still gambling that Braves veteran pitcher John Smoltz could eliminate the Astros. He intended to use Carpenter if the make-up game on Monday became necessary, despite the problems that would create for his playoff pitching plans. Reyes gave up four runs in the first inning, and the Cardinals lost to the Brewers, 5–3. Smoltz, fortunately, pitched six shutout innings, and the Braves staved off the Astros, 3–1.

Boom and Bust in St. Louis

The Cardinals had won their third straight Central Division title, but their 83–78 record was the worst of any of the 2006 playoff participants. Nevertheless, as they beat the Padres three games to one in the opening round of the playoffs, numerous factors indicated that the Cardinals were ready for a post-season run. Center fielder Jim Edmonds, slowed by a concussion and injuries to his foot and shoulder, returned to form. He would lead the Cardinals with ten post-season runs batted in and, inserted along with a healthier Rolen into the middle of the batting order again, ensured that opponents paid a price for pitching around Pujols. Rolen, whose ailing shoulder had held him to a .227 average in September, bounced back to bat .275 in the post-season, and Pujols topped the Cardinals with three post-season home runs. The Cardinals' starting rotation, although lacking depth, pitched effectively. A trio of pitchers (Carpenter, Weaver, and Jeff Suppan) recorded an earned run average of 2.38 against the Padres and, starting 14 of the Cardinals' 16 post-season games, posted a record of 7–4 with a 2.58 earned run average. The young bullpen corps, nicknamed the "Baby Birds," blanked the Padres for 13⅓ innings, and they finished the postseason with a 3–1 record and an earned run average of 2.81 in 41⅔ innings of work. Wainwright anchored the "Baby Birds" with a record of 1–0, four saves, and 9⅔ scoreless innings pitched.

The toughest post-season struggle for the 2006 Cardinals took place against the New York Mets in the National League Championship Series. It came down to a deciding seventh game at Shea Stadium. Suppan, who had homered and pitched eight shutout innings in a 5–0 victory in Game Three, took the mound for the Cardinals. He allowed a run in the first inning and then shut the Mets down until the eighth inning, when he gave way to the "Baby Birds" of the bullpen. Edmonds scored the tying run in the second inning on a safety squeeze bunt by Ronnie Belliard, and neither team scored again until the top of the ninth. Rolen, robbed of a home run on a leaping catch by Mets left fielder Endy Chavez in his previous at-bat, grounded a single into left field with one out, and Yadier Molina, who had averaged only .216 in his second season as the Cardinals' regular catcher but batted .358 in the post-season, drove a two-run homer far over the left-field fence. (A .282 career hitter through the 2019 season, Molina has averaged .328 in four World Series and .556 in seven All-Star Games.) In the bottom of the ninth, with the bases loaded and two out, Wainwright's wicked curve struck out Mets slugger Carlos Beltran looking to win the National League pennant.

The Cardinals had made it to the 2006 World Series, but they were

11. Exit Anheuser-Busch, Enter Tony La Russa

underdogs to the Detroit Tigers, who *USA Today* sarcastically suggested might win in three games. La Russa, due to the lengthy series against the Mets, was forced to turn to Reyes to start the World Series in Detroit. Reyes, whose five regular season wins were the fewest ever for a starting pitcher in the first game of a World Series, pitched the game of his life. He gave up a run to the Tigers in the first inning and shut them out for the next seven frames. Meanwhile, Rolen and Pujols homered, and the Cardinals hammered the Tigers' more-heralded rookie Justin Verlander, a 17-game winner, for seven runs in five innings. The opening game resulted in a surprisingly easy 7–2 victory for the Cardinals, and, although Weaver lost a hard-luck decision in Game Two to the Tigers' Kenny Rogers, 3–1, the Cardinals headed home for the first three World Series games at the new Busch Stadium with their three best pitchers set to tame the Tigers.

Carpenter had won the opening playoff game at San Diego and the decisive fourth game against the Padres, but had struggled in two starts against the Mets. He was sensational in Game Three of the World Series, shutting the Tigers out on three hits for eight innings. In the fourth inning, Edmonds drove in two runs with a double down the right-field line, providing Carpenter with all the support that he needed. A throwing error by Tigers reliever Joel Zumaya added a pair of insurance runs in the seventh, and the Cardinals rolled to a 5–0 triumph.

The fielding errors of Tigers pitchers proved pivotal in the next two games. Suppan, the Most Valuable Player of the National League Championship Series, was not nearly as sharp against the Tigers. However, he battled through six innings, allowing three runs. The Cardinals closed the gap to 3–2 on run-scoring doubles by their shortstop, David Eckstein, in the third inning and Molina in the fourth. In the seventh inning, after Eckstein led off with a double to center, So Taguchi sacrificed him to third with a bunt to Tigers reliever Fernando Rodney. When Rodney's throw sailed over first base, Eckstein scored the tying run. Taguchi advanced to second and scored on a two-out single to left by outfielder Preston Wilson. The Tigers managed to tie the game at four-all in the top of the eighth, only to see Eckstein line a double off the glove of Tigers left fielder Craig Monroe for his fourth hit to send home the winning run in the bottom of the eighth. Wainwright retired the Tigers in order in the ninth, and the Cardinals were only one win away from their first world championship in 24 years.

Weaver started Game Five and prevented the Cardinals from being forced to return to Detroit, where weather forecasts called for snow.

Boom and Bust in St. Louis

Trailing 2–1 in the fourth inning, with Molina and Taguchi on second and first, Weaver laid down a bunt. Verlander fielded the ball and threw wildly past third baseman Brandon Inge, allowing Molina to score the tying run and Taguchi to move to third. Eckstein drove in his second run of the night with a grounder that enabled Taguchi to score the go-ahead run, and Eckstein later scored an insurance run in the seventh on Rolen's two-out single to right. His .364 batting average, along with three runs scored and four runs batted in, earned Eckstein the World Series Most Valuable Player Award. Weaver pitched eight innings, turning over a 4–2 lead to Wainwright in the ninth. With two on and two out, Wainwright struck out Inge swinging to wrap up the World Series title.

The 2006 World Series championship culminated a seven-year span in which La Russa guided the Cardinals to the playoffs six times. Over the next four years, though, the Cardinals only made the playoffs once, and their 2009 Central Division title was marred by the Los Angeles Dodgers sweeping them in three games in the opening round of the playoffs. Jocketty had been replaced as general manager at the end of the 2007 season by John Mozeliak, who placed more of an emphasis on developing players from the farm system than on acquiring high-priced veterans.

Nobody expected much from the 2011 Cardinals in spring training, particularly after Wainwright (who had moved to the starting rotation in 2007 and won 20 games in 2010) underwent season-ending elbow surgery before the season ever started. The Cardinals were a pleasant surprise in the early portion of the season, leading the Central Division as late as July 26. However by August 24, when they lost the last game in a three-game sweep by the Dodgers at Busch Stadium, the Cardinals had fallen to a record of 67–63. They trailed the Milwaukee Brewers by 10 games in the Central Division and the Atlanta Braves by 10½ games in the wild-card race.

Despite winning nine of the next 13 games, the Cardinals still trailed Atlanta by 7½ games and Milwaukee by 8½ games, when the Braves arrived in St. Louis on September 9 for a three-game series. In the opener, the Cardinals trailed, 3–1, and were down to their last out in the ninth, when Pujols tied the game with a two-run single off Braves bullpen closer Craig Kimbrel. Jason Motte, the fifth Cardinals reliever to try the role of closer over the course of the season, retired the heart of the Braves order in the top of the tenth. After Cardinals outfielders Matt Holliday and Lance Berkman opened the bottom of the tenth with base hits, pinch-hitter Daniel Descalso advanced the runners with a sacrifice bunt,

11. Exit Anheuser-Busch, Enter Tony La Russa

and second baseman Nick Punto drove Holliday home with the winning run on a sacrifice fly. The Cardinals went on to sweep the Braves, reducing their deficit in the wild-card race to 4½ games and setting up a memorable September stretch drive.

While the Braves lost nine of their next 14 games after leaving St. Louis, the Cardinals won 10 of their next 15, and on September 27, the next-to-last day of the regular season, when the Cardinals pounded the Astros, 13–6, in Houston and the Braves fell, 6–1, at home to the Philadelphia Phillies, the Cardinals finally caught the Braves. On the following night, the Cardinals batted around in the top of the first inning, striking for five runs. Carpenter struck out 11 Astros and pitched a two-hit shutout, winning 8–0. Although the Cardinals game started *later* than the Braves game, it was over an hour *before* the Braves game. The Phillies rallied in the ninth inning off Kimbrel to tie the game at three-all and finally eliminated the Braves in 13 innings, 4–3.

The Cardinals won 23 of their last 32 games and finished with a record of 90–72. Still, they were heavy underdogs to the Phillies, whose 102 regular season wins were the best in baseball. The Cardinals led the opener, 3–1, until the sixth inning, when the Phillies exploded for five runs off Kyle Lohse and went on to an 11–6 win. They turned the tables the following night, though, overcoming a 4–0 deficit against Cliff Lee (previously 7–2 in post-season play). Cardinals center fielder Jon Jay, a left-handed hitter, connected for his second run-scoring hit off the left-handed Lee to tie the game at four-all in the top of the sixth. After Allen Craig tripled to start the seventh, Pujols lined a single to left that gave the Cardinals a 5–4 lead. Six Cardinals relievers shut out the Phillies for six innings, with Motte anchoring the bullpen for the last inning and a third and earning the save. The Phillies took the series lead again in St. Louis, when Cole Hamels outdueled Jaime Garcia 3–2, but the Cardinals evened the series again, 5–3, behind four runs batted in on a two-run double and two-run homer by a St. Louis hometown hero, third baseman David Freese. Edwin Jackson, acquired in a July trade, allowed two runs in the first inning and shut out the Phillies for the next five innings. Five Cardinals relievers, anchored once again by Motte, preserved the win for him. In the fifth and final game, Carpenter pitched a three-hit shutout, edging Phillies ace Roy Halladay. The Cardinals scored the only run of the game with their first two hitters. Shortstop Rafael Furcal, another mid-season acquisition, led off the game with a triple to right-center, and Skip Schumaker, after fouling off five two-strike pitches, lined a run-scoring double down the right-field line.

Boom and Bust in St. Louis

In the National League Championship Series, the Cardinals faced the favored Milwaukee Brewers, their Central Division rival who had won the division by six games over the Cardinals. Garcia took a 5–2 lead into the fifth inning in the opener, but the Brewers exploded for six runs and went on to a 9–6 win. The similarity of the opening-game losses to the Phillies and Brewers convinced La Russa to go quicker to his suddenly deep bullpen, bolstered by the mid-season acquisitions of right-hander Octavio Dotel and left-handers Marc Rzepczynski and Arthur Rhodes. By the time that the Cardinals finished beating the Brewers, four games to two, La Russa's relievers had pitched more innings than his starters, 28⅔ to 24⅓, with a much better earned run average, 1.88 to 7.03. Freese, named Most Valuable Player of the National League Championship Series for hitting .545 with three homers and nine runs batted in, pointed to his newly-won trophy and told reporters: "If I could chop that thing up and give it to the bullpen, I would."[3] His comment was a nice acknowledgment of the bullpen's vital contribution, but Freese and the Cardinals' hitters had made their own contribution by bludgeoning Brewers pitchers, hitting .310 as a team and averaging over seven runs a game.

Freese would also win Most Valuable Player honors in the World Series, batting .348 with a homer and seven runs batted in. He essentially won the award with three dramatic swings of the bat at the end of Game Six and the start of Game Seven. In Game Six, with the Cardinals behind three games to two to the favored Texas Rangers and trailing, 7–5, in the bottom of the ninth inning, two on and two out, Freese was down to his last strike when he drove a game-tying triple to the right-field wall over the head of Rangers right fielder Nelson Cruz. After the Rangers scored twice in the top of the tenth inning, the Cardinals countered with two of their own in the bottom of the tenth, tying the game on a two-out, two-strike hit by Berkman. Jake Westbrook retired the Rangers without incident in the top of the 11th, and Freese led off the bottom half with a game-ending home run to center field.

Carpenter, who had won the opening game of the World Series and was undefeated in three decisions in the post-season, pitched Game Seven. It was only the second time in Carpenter's career that he had pitched on three days of rest, and he struggled in the first inning, giving up two runs. The Rangers starter, Matt Harrison, who had lost Game Three, 16–7 when Pujols tied a World Series record shared by Babe Ruth and Reggie Jackson with three homers in a single game, retired the opening two batters. He pitched cautiously to Pujols and Berkman, who topped all

11. Exit Anheuser-Busch, Enter Tony La Russa

Cardinals starters with a .423 batting average in the World Series. After walking both of them, Harrison faced Freese, who lined a two-run double into the gap in left-center and established a new post-season record with 21 runs batted in. From there, Carpenter shut out the Rangers for the next five innings, and Craig, who had a game-winning pinch-hit in the opener and home runs in Games Three and Six, gave the Cardinals a 3–2 lead in the third when he smashed his third homer of the Series into the Cardinals' bullpen in right field. In the fifth, the Cardinals added to their lead without the benefit of a hit, parlaying three walks and two hit batsmen into a pair of insurance runs. Molina, who had led the Cardinals with a .305 batting average in the regular season, singled home Berkman in the seventh for his team-high ninth run batted in of the World Series. Four Cardinals relievers, anchored yet again by Motte, held the Rangers hitless and scoreless for the final three innings, preserving a 6–2 victory and the World Series championship.

Winning another World Series allowed La Russa, who retired after the World Series, and Pujols, who later signed a free-agent contract with the Los Angeles Angels of Anaheim, to close their Cardinals careers on top. La Russa, who had won a World Series with Oakland in 1989, became only the second major league manager (along with Sparky Anderson) to win a World Series with a team from both leagues. Pujols became the first player in major league history to string together ten consecutive years with over 30 home runs, more than 100 runs batted in, and a batting average of at least .300. In his last season in St. Louis, despite missing slightly over two weeks with a fractured left wrist, he barely fell short of making it 11 consecutive years—homering 37 times, driving in 99 runs, and batting .299. Overall, throughout his tenure with the Cardinals, Pujols won three NL MVP Awards (2005, 2008, and 2009), batted .328, and averaged 40 home runs and 121 runs batted in per year.

Although La Russa managed Cardinal clubs who waltzed to the Central Division crown by ten games or more in 2000, 2002, 2004, and 2005, none of them won a World Series title. It took the 2006 and 2011 Cardinals, who both clinched their playoff spots on the last day of the regular season, to provide La Russa with his World Series championships in St. Louis. La Russa's "Last Day Wonders" joined the remarkable tradition of the "Gas House Gang" of 1934, the "St. Louis Swifties" of 1942, and the "Miracle Cardinals" of 1964. Every Cardinals club which clinched the National League pennant or a playoff spot on the last day of the regular season has gone on to win the World Series. Five Cardinals clubs, spanning

Boom and Bust in St. Louis

77 years and four different managers, and each of them won the World Series over a favored opponent. How does one explain such a phenomenon? Maybe achieving their season-long goal at the last moment imbued them with a sense of being a "team of destiny." Perhaps playing so many pressure-packed games throughout September prepared them better for the post-season than teams who had sewn up their spots with more ease earlier in September. Whatever the cause, the Cardinals' five "Last Day Wonders" compose a sizeable percentage of their 11 World Series victories over the American League.

Epilogue
St. Louis Cardinals Baseball, 2012–2019

The Cardinals entered 2012 with a new manager, Mike Matheny, who had been their starting catcher from 2000 to 2005 and had tutored his successor, Yadier Molina. Matheny initially enjoyed considerable success, leading the Cardinals to four successive playoff appearances from 2012 to 2015 and three consecutive divisional crowns from 2013 to 2015. In 2013, his second season at the helm, he captured the Cardinals' 19th National League pennant by defeating the Los Angeles Dodgers in six games in the National League Championship Series, before losing the World Series in six games to the Boston Red Sox. Actually Matheny never had a losing record as Cardinals manager, although after missing the playoffs in 2016–2017 and barely hovering over the .500 mark at 47–46 in mid-July of 2018, the Cardinals replaced him with Mike Shildt, a coach on his staff and longtime minor league manager. Under Schildt, the Cardinals improved to a record of 41–28, including a major league best record of 22–6 in August, but faded in the September stretch drive and missed the playoffs for a third straight season. However, after acquiring All-Star first baseman Paul Goldschmidt in a trade with the Arizona Diamondbacks, the Cardinals entered spring training and the 2019 season with dreams of not only returning to the playoffs, but of winning another World Series championship. Goldschmidt led the Cardinals with 34 home runs and 97 runs batted in, and his Gold Glove-caliber play in the field allowed their defense to improve from the worst in the NL in 2018 to the best in 2019. The Cardinals, in their 25th season in the NL Central excluding the strike year of 1994, captured their 11th Central crown with a record of 91–71 (compared to only three divisional titles in 25 years in the NL East from 1969 through 1993). They clinched at least a wild-card spot in the playoffs

Epilogue

on the next-to-last Sunday of the season by completing a four-game sweep of the Chicago Cubs at Wrigley Field, all by one run, but did not clinch the NL Central title over the defending champion Milwaukee Brewers until the last day of the regular season with a convincing 9–0 triumph over the Cubs at Busch Stadium. In the playoffs, the Cardinals defeated the NL East champion Atlanta Braves, three games to two, and advanced to the National League Championship Series for the first time since 2014, another season in which they clinched the NL Central title on the last day of the season after ensuring themselves of at least a wild-card earlier. However, the streaking wild card Washington Nationals, who had finished behind the Braves in the regular season, entered the NLCS with twelve wins in their last 14 games and remained hot in a four-game sweep of the Cardinals and in upsetting the favored Houston Astros in seven games in the World Series. Hope for the Cardinals' 20th National League pennant will have to wait for the 2020 season, one consisting of the retired number of Cardinal Hall of Famer Lou Brock.

Appendix A
St. Louis Cardinals Baseball Franchise Records, 1882–2019

Year	Name	League	W–L	Win Pct.	Finish	Manager	Attend.	Post-season
1882	Brown Stockings	AA	37–43	.463	5 of 6	N. Cuthbert	135,000	
1883	Browns	AA	65–33	.663	2 of 8	T. Sullivan (53–26) C. Comiskey (12–7)	243,000	
1884	Browns	AA	67–40	.626	4 of 13	J. Williams (51–33) C. Comiskey (16–7)	212,000	
1885	Browns	AA	79–33	.705	1 of 8	C. Comiskey	129,000	W, WS 3-2-2*
1886	Browns	AA	93–46	.669	1 of 8	C. Comiskey	205,000	W, WS 4–2
1887	Browns	AA	95–40	.704	1 of 8	C. Comiskey	243,000	L, WS 5–10
1888	Browns	AA	92–43	.681	1 of 8	C. Comiskey	166,000	L, WS 4–6
1889	Browns	AA	90–45	.667	2 of 8	C. Comiskey	175,000	
1890	Browns	AA	78–58	.574	3 of 9	T. McCarthy (15–12) C. Roseman (7–8) C. Campau (27–14) J. Gerhardt (20–16) J. Kerins (9–8)	105,000	

Appendix A

Year	Name	League	W-L	Win Pct.	Finish	Manager	Attend.	Post-season
1891	Browns	AA	86–52	.623	2 of 9	C. Comiskey	220,000	
1892	Browns	NL	56–94	.373	11 of 12	J. Glasscock (1–3) C. Stricker (6–17) J. Crooks (27–33) G. Gore (6–9) B. Caruthers (16–32)	192, 442	
1893	Browns	NL	57–75	432	10 of 12	B. Watkins	195,000	
1894	Browns	NL	56–76	.424	9 of 12	G. Miller	155,000	
1895	Browns	NL	39–92	.298	11 of 12	A. Buckenberger (16–34) C. Von der Ahe (1–0) J. Quinn (11–28) L. Phelan (11–30)	170,000	
1896	Browns	NL	40–90	.308	11 of 12	H. Diddlebock (7–10) A. Latham (0–3) C. Von der Ahe (0–2) R. Connor (8–37) T. Dowd (25–38)	184,000	
1897	Browns	NL	29–102	.221	12 of 12	T. Dowd (6–22) H. Nicol (8–32) B. Hallman (13–36) C. Von der Ahe (2–12)	136,400	
1898	Browns	NL	39–111	.260	12 of 12	T. Hurst	151,700	
1899	Perfectos Cardinals**	NL	84–67	.556	5 of 12	P, Tebeau	373,909	
1900	Cardinals	NL	65–75	.464	5 of 8	P. Tebeau (42–50) L Heilbroner (23–25)	255,000	
1901	Cardinals	NL	76–64	.543	4 of 8	P. Donovan	379,988	
1902	Cardinals	NL	56–78	.418	6 of 8	P. Donovan	226,417	
1903	Cardinals	NL	43–94	.314	8 of 8	P. Donovan	226,538	
1904	Cardinals	NL	75–79	.487	5 of 8	K. Nichols	386,750	

St. Louis Cardinals Baseball Franchise Records, 1882–2019

Year	Name	League	W-L	Win Pct.	Finish	Manager	Attend.	Post-season
1905	Cardinals	NL	58–96	.377	6 of 8	K. Nichols (5–9) J. Burke (34–56) S. Robison (19–31)	292,800	
1906	Cardinals	NL	52–98	.347	7 of 8	J. McCloskey	283,770	
1907	Cardinals	NL	52–101	.340	8 of 8	J. McCloskey	185,377	
1908	Cardinals	NL	49–105	.318	8 of 8	J. McCloskey	205,129	
1909	Cardinals	NL	54–98	.355	7 of 8	R. Bresnahan	299,982	
1910	Cardinals	NL	63–90	.412	7 of 8	R. Bresnahan	355,668	
1911	Cardinals	NL	75–74	.503	5 of 8	R. Bresnahan	447,768	
1912	Cardinals	NL	63–90	.412	6 of 8	R. Bresnahan	241,759	
1913	Cardinals	NL	51–99	.340	8 of 8	M. Huggins	203,531	
1914	Cardinals	NL	81–72	.529	3 of 8	M. Huggins	256,099	
1915	Cardinals	NL	72–81	.471	6 of 8	M. Huggins	252,666	
1916	Cardinals	NL	60–93	.392	7 of 8	M. Huggins	224,308	
1917	Cardinals	NL	82–70	.539	3 of 8	M. Huggins	288,491	
1918	Cardinals	NL	51–78	.395	8 of 8	J. Hendricks	110,599	
1919	Cardinals	NL	54–83	.394	7 of 8	B. Rickey	169,059	
1920	Cardinals	NL	75–79	.487	5 of 8	B. Rickey	326,836	
1921	Cardinals	NL	87–66	.569	3 of 8	B. Rickey	384,773	
1922	Cardinals	NL	85–69	.552	3 of 8	B. Rickey	536,998	
1923	Cardinals	NL	79–74	.516	5 of 8	B. Rickey	338,551	
1924	Cardinals	NL	65–89	.422	6 of 8	B. Rickey	272,885	
1925	Cardinals	NL	77–76	.503	4 of 8	B. Rickey (13–25) R. Hornsby (64–51)	404,959	
1926	Cardinals	NL	89–65	.578	1 of 8	R. Hornsby	668,428	W, WS 4–3
1927	Cardinals	NL	92–61	.601	2 of 8	B. O'Farrell	749,340	
1928	Cardinals	NL	95–59	.617	1 of 8	B. McKechnie	761,574	L, WS 0–4
1929	Cardinals	NL	78–74	.513	4 of 8	B. Southworth (43–45) G. Street (1–0) B. McKechnie (34–29)	399,887	
1930	Cardinals	NL	92–62	.597	1 of 8	G. Street	508,501	L, WS 2–4
1931	Cardinals	NL	101–53	.656	1 of 8	G. Street	608,535	W, WS 4–3

Appendix A

Year	Name	League	W-L	Win Pct.	Finish	Manager	Attend.	Post-season
1932	Cardinals	NL	72–82	.468	6 of 8	G. Street	279,219	
1933	Cardinals	NL	82–71	.536	5 of 8	G. Street (46–45) F. Frisch (36–26)	256,171	
1934	Cardinals	NL	95–58	.621	1 of 8	F. Frisch	325,056	W, WS 4–3
1935	Cardinals	NL	96–58	.623	2 of 8	F. Frisch	506,084	
1936	Cardinals	NL	87–67	.565	2 of 8	F. Frisch	448,078	
1937	Cardinals	NL	81–73	.526	4 of 8	F. Frisch	430,811	
1938	Cardinals	NL	71–80	.470	6 of 8	F. Frisch (63–72) M. Gonzalez (8–8)	291.418	
1939	Cardinals	NL	92–61	.601	2 of 8	R. Blades	400,245	
1940	Cardinals	NL	84–69	.549	3 of 8	R. Blades (14–24) M. Gonzalez (1–5) B. Southworth (69–40)	324,078	
1941	Cardinals	NL	97–65	.634	2 of 8	B. Southworth	633,645	
1942	Cardinals	NL	106–48	.688	1 of 8	B. Southworth	553,552	W, WS 4–1
1943	Cardinals	NL	105–49	.682	1 of 8	B. Southworth	517,135	L, WS 1–4
1944	Cardinals	NL	105–49	.682	1 of 8	B. Southworth	461,768	W, WS 4–2
1945	Cardinals	NL	95–59	.617	2 of 8	B. Southworth	594,630	
1946	Cardinals	NL	98–58	.628	1 of 8***	E. Dyer	1,061,807	W, WS 4–3
1947	Cardinals	NL	89–65	.598	2 of 8	E. Dyer	1,247,913	
1948	Cardinals	NL	85–69	.562	2 of 8	E. Dyer	1,111,440	
1949	Cardinals	NL	96–58	.623	2 of 8	E. Dyer	1,430,676	
1950	Cardinals	NL	78–75	.510	5 of 8	E. Dyer	1,093,411	
1951	Cardinals	NL	81–73	.526	3 of 8	M. Marion	1,013,429	
1952	Cardinals	NL	88–66	.571	3 of 8	E. Stanky	913,113	
1953	Cardinals	NL	83–71	.539	3 of 8	E. Stanky	880,242	
1954	Cardinals	NL	72–82	.468	6 of 8	E. Stanky	1,039,698	
1955	Cardinals	NL	68–86	.442	7 of 8	E. Stanky (17–19) H. Walker (51–67)	849,130	

St. Louis Cardinals Baseball Franchise Records, 1882–2019

Year	Name	League	W-L	Win Pct.	Finish	Manager	Attend.	Post-season
1956	Cardinals	NL	76–78	.494	4 of 8	F. Hutchinson	1,029,773	
1957	Cardinals	NL	87–67	.565	2 of 8	F. Hutchinson	1,183,575	
1958	Cardinals	NL	72–82	.468	5 of 8	F. Hutchinson (69–75) S. Hack (3–7)	1,063,730	
1959	Cardinals	NL	71–83	.461	7 of 8	S. Hemus	929,953	
1960	Cardinals	NL	86–68	.558	3 of 8	S. Hemus	1,096,632	
1961	Cardinals	NL	80–74	.519	5 of 8	S. Hemus (33–41) J. Keane (47–33)	855,305	
1962	Cardinals	NL	84–78	.519	6 of 10	J. Keane	953,895	
1963	Cardinals	NL	93–69	.574	2 of 10	J. Keane	1,170,546	
1964	Cardinals	NL	93–69	.574	1 of 10	J. Keane	1,143,294	W, WS 4–3
1965	Cardinals	NL	80–81	.497	7 of 10	R. Schoendienst	1,241,201	
1966	Cardinals	NL	83–79	.512	6 of 10	R. Schoendienst	1,712,980	
1967	Cardinals	NL	101–60	.627	1 of 10	R. Schoendienst	2,090,145	W, WS 4–3
1968	Cardinals	NL	97–65	.599	1 of 10	R. Schoendienst	2,011,167	L, WS 3–4
1969	Cardinals	NL East	87–75	.537	4 of 6	R. Schoendienst	1,682,783	
1970	Cardinals	NL East	76–86	.469	4 of 6	R. Schoendienst	1,629,736	
1971	Cardinals	NL East	90–72	.556	2 of 6	R. Schoendienst	1,604,671	
1972	Cardinals	NL East	75–81	.481	4 of 6	R. Schoendienst	1,196,894	
1973	Cardinals	NL East	81–81	.500	2 of 6	R. Schoendienst	1,574,046	
1974	Cardinals	NL East	86–75	.534	2 of 6	R. Schoendiens	1,838,413	
1975	Cardinals	NL East	82–80	.506	3 of 6	R. Schoendienst	1,695,270	
1976	Cardinals	NL East	72–90	.444	5 of 6	R. Schoendienst	1,207,079	
1977	Cardinals	NL East	83–79	.512	3 of 6	V. Rapp	1,659,287	
1978	Cardinals	NL East	69–93	.426	5 of 6	V. Rapp (6–11) J. Krol (1–1) K. Boyer (62–81)	1,278,215	
1979	Cardinals	NL East	86–76	.531	3 of 6	K. Boyer	1,627,256	
1980	Cardinals	NL East	74–88	.457	4 of 6	K. Boyer (18–33) J. Krol (0–1) W. Herzog (38–35) R. Schoendienst (18–19)	1,385,147	
1981	Cardinals	NL East	59–43	.578	1 of 6****	W, Herzog	1,010,247	

Appendix A

Year	Name	League	W-L	Win Pct.	Finish	Manager	Attend.	Post-season
1982	Cardinals	NL East	92–70	.568	1 of 6	W. Herzog	2,111,906	W, WS 4–3
1983	Cardinals	NL East	79–83	.488	4 of 6	W. Herzog	2,317.914	
1984	Cardinals	NL East	84–78	.519	3 of 6	W. Herzog	2,037,448	
1985	Cardinals	NL East	101–61	.623	1 of 6	W. Herzog	2,637,563	L, WS 3–4
1986	Cardinals	NL East	79–82	.491	3 of 6	W. Herzog	2,471,974	
1987	Cardinals	NL East	95–67	.586	1 of 6	W. Herzog	3,072,122	L, WS 3–4
1988	Cardinals	NL East	76–86	.469	5 of 6	W. Herzog	2,892,799	
1989	Cardinals	NL East	86–76	.531	3 of 6	W. Herzog	3,080,980	
1990	Cardinals	NL East	70–92	.432	6 of 6	W. Herzog (33–47) R. Schoendienst (13–11) J. Torre (24–34)	2,573,225	
1991	Cardinals	NL East	84–78	.519	2 of 6	J. Torre	2,448,699	
1992	Cardinals	NL East	83–79	.512	3 of 6	J. Torre	2,418,483	
1993	Cardinals	NL East	87–75	.537	3 of 7	J. Torre	2,844,328	
1994	Cardinals	NL Cent	53–61	.465	3 of 5	J. Torre	1,866,544	
1995	Cardinals	NL Cent	62–81	.434	4 of 5	J. Torre (20–27) M. Jorgenson (42–54)	1,756,727	
1996	Cardinals	NL Cent	88–74	.543	1 of 5	T. La Russa	2,654,718	L, LCS 3–4
1997	Cardinals	NL Cent	73–89	.451	4 of 5	T. La Russa	2,634,014	
1998	Cardinals	NL Cent	83–79	.512	3 of 6	T. La Russa	3,195,691	
1999	Cardinals	NL Cent	75–86	.466	4 of 6	T. La Russa	3,225,334	
2000	Cardinals	NL Cent	95–67	.586	1 of 6	T. La Russa	3,336,493	L, LCS 1–4
2001	Cardinals	NL Cent	93–69	.574	2 of 6*****	T. La Russa	3,109,578	L, LDS 2–3
2002	Cardinals	NL Cent	97–65	.599	1 of 6	T. La Russa	3,011,756	L, LCS 1–4
2003	Cardinals	NL Cent	93–69	.574	3 of 6	T. La Russa	2,910,386	
2004	Cardinals	NL Cent	105–57	.648	1 of 6	T. La Russa	3,048,427	L, WS 0–4
2005	Cardinals	NL Cent	100–62	.617	1 of 6	T. La Russa	3,538,988	L, LCS 2–4
2006	Cardinals	NL Cent	83–78	.516	1 of 6	T. La Russa	3,407,104	W, WS 4–1

St. Louis Cardinals Baseball Franchise Records, 1882–2019

Year	Name	League	W-L	Win Pct.	Finish	Manager	Attend.	Post-season
2007	Cardinals	NL Cent	78–84	.481	3 of 6	T. La Russa	3,552,180	
2008	Cardinals	NL Cent	86–76	.531	4 of 6	T. La Russa	3,432,917	
2009	Cardinals	NL Cent	91–71	.562	1 of 6	T. La Russa	3,343,252	L, LDS 0–3
2010	Cardinals	NL Cent	86–76	.531	2 of 6	T. La Russa	3,301,218	
2011	Cardinals	NL Cent	90–72	.556	2 of 6	T. La Russa	3,093,954	W, WS 4–3
2012	Cardinals	NL Cent	88–74	.543	2 of 6	M. Matheny	3,262,109	L, LCS 3–4
2013	Cardinals	NL Cent	97–65	.599	1 of 5	M. Matheny	3,369,769	L, WS 2–4
2014	Cardinals	NL Cent	90–72	.556	1 of 5	M. Matheny	3,540,649	L, LCS, 1–4
2015	Cardinals	NL Cent	100–62	.617	1 of 5	M. Matheny	3,520,889	L, LDS, 1–3
2016	Cardinals	NL Cent	86–76	.531	2 of 5	M. Matheny	3,444,490	
2017	Cardinals	NL Cent	83–79	.512	3 of 5	M. Matheny	3,448,337	
2018	Cardinals	NL Cent	88–74	.543	3 of 5	M. Matheny (47–46) M. Shildt (41–28)	3,403,587	
2019	Cardinals	NL Cent	91-71	.562	1 of 5	M. Shildt	3,480,393	L, LCS, 0-4

*Prior to the seventh game, umpire "Honest John" Kelly announced that both teams had agreed that the forfeit awarded to Chicago under questionable circumstances by umpire Dave Sullivan in the second game no longer counted (being relegated to an undecided game like the opening tie) and, therefore, the winner of the upcoming game would win the Series. After St. Louis decisively defeated Chicago 13–4, Chicago changed its mind, reclaimed the forfeit, and declared the Series a tie (3–3-1). Contemporary opinion bitterly divided along league lines. Only the lingering influence of the NL accounts for the Chicago version of a tie appearing in "official" results reported in Total Baseball and baseball-reference.com. The outcome cited here restores the original agreement between the two teams as announced before the seventh and deciding game.

**The new owners of the franchise, the Robison brothers, introduced brand-new bright red uniforms. Although an early winning streak of seven games lent some support to a new nickname of "Perfectos," the name soon sounded pretentious as reality set in and the team slipped in the standings. By midseason, "Cardinals" had won out over "Red Caps" in popular usage.

***The Cardinals and Brooklyn Dodgers ended the regular season in a first-place tie with records of 96–58. In a best-two-of-three playoff series, the Cardinals defeated the Dodgers, two games to none.

****In 1981, the players went on strike on June 12. When the strike was settled on August 6, major league baseball instituted a split season, one before the strike and one after the strike. An extra round of playoffs was scheduled between the winners of the first and second

Appendix A

halves (or a wild card club if the same team won both halves). In the National League, however, neither the Cardinals nor the Cincinnati Reds, who posted the best records for the season in the NL East and NL West respectively, were allowed to claim a divisional title or participate in the expanded playoffs because they had not finished first in either of the artificially-contrived "halves" of the season.

*****The Cardinals and Houston Astros ended the regular season in a first-place tie with records of 93–69. Since both teams had qualified for the playoffs, Houston was awarded the divisional title on the basis of winning the season series against the Cardinals, and the Cardinals entered the playoffs as the NL wild card team.

World Series Champions (13): 1885–1886, 1926, 1931, 1934, 1942, 1944, 1946, 1964, 1967, 1982, 2006, 2011

AA Pennants (4): 1885–1888

NL Pennants (19): 1926, 1928, 1930–1931, 1934, 1942–1944, 1946, 1964, 1967–1968, 1982, 1985, 1987, 2004, 2006, 2011, 2013

NL East Division Titles (3): 1982, 1985, 1987

NL Central Division Titles (11): 1996, 2000, 2002, 2004–2006, 2009, 2013–2015, 2019

NL Wild Card Playoff Appearances (3): 2001, 2011–2012

Years leading either all of MLB or their league in attendance (9): 1882 (MLB), 1884 (MLB), 1886 (MLB), 1891 (MLB), 1901 (MLB), 1967 (MLB), 1968 (NL), 1987 (MLB), 1989 (NL)

Appendix B
Single-Season and Career Leaders for Cardinal Franchise, 1882–2019

Batting Leaders

	Single Season	Career
Batting Average	Tip O'Neill .435, 1887	Jesse Burkett .378, 1899–1901 (1,931 AB)
Runs	Tip O'Neill 167, 1887	Stan Musial 1,949, 1941–1963
Hits	Rogers Hornsby 250, 1922	Stan Musial 3,630, 1941–1963
Doubles	Ducky Medwick, 64, 1936	Stan Musial 725, 1941–1963
Triples	Perry Werden 29, 1893	Stan Musial 177, 1941–1963
Home Runs	Mark McGwire 70, 1998	Stan Musial 475, 1941–1963
Runs Batted In	Ducky Medwick 154, 1937	Stan Musial 1,951, 1941–1963
Stolen Bases	Arlie Latham, 129, 1887* Lou Brock 118, 1974	Lou Brock 888, 1964–1979

*Nineteenth-century stolen base totals are misleading because in most years, including 1887, baserunners were credited with a stolen base whenever they took an extra base. Therefore, under modern-day stolen base rules, the single-season franchise record is 118 by Lou Brock in 1974.

Pitching Leaders

	Single Season	Career
Earned Run Average	Bob Gibson 1.12, 1968	Ed Karger 2.46, 1906–1908 (647 IP)
Wins	Silver King, 45, 1888	Bob Gibson 251, 1959–1975
Win-Loss Percentage	Howie Krist 1.000, (10–0), 1941	Ice Box Chamberlain .719, 1888–1890
Strikeouts	Jack Stivetts 289, 1890	Bob Gibson 3,117, 1959–1975
Games	Steve Kline 89, 2001	Jesse Haines 554, 1920–1937
Saves	Trevor Rosenthal 48, 2015	Jason Isringhausen 217, 2002–2008
Innings Pitched	Silver King 584⅔, 1888	Bob Gibson 3,884, 1959–1975
Complete Games	Silver King 64, 1888	Bob Gibson 255, 1959–1975
Shutouts	Bob Gibson 13, 1968	Bob Gibson 56, 1959–1975

Appendix C
Noteworthy Achievements

Most Valuable Players

Year	Player	Position
1925	Rogers Hornsby	2B
1926	Bob O'Farrell	C
1928	"Sunny Jim" Bottomley	1B
1931	Frank Frisch	2B
1934	"Dizzy" Dean	P
1937	Joe "Ducky" Medwick	OF
1942	Mort Cooper	P
1943	Stan Musial	OF
1944	Marty Marion	SS
1946	Stan Musial	1B
1948	Stan Musial	OF
1964	Ken Boyer	3B
1967	Orlando Cepeda	1B
1971	Joe Torre	3B
1979	Keith Hernandez	1B
1985	Willie McGee	OF
2005	Albert Pujols	1B
2008	Albert Pujols	1B
2009	Albert Pujols	1B

Triple Crown Winners

Year	LG	Player
1887	AA	Tip O'Neill
1922	NL	Rogers Hornsby
1925	NL	Rogers Hornsby
1937	NL	Joe "Ducky" Medwick

Noteworthy Achievements

Rookies of the Year

Year	LG	Player	Position
1954	NL	Wally Moon	OF
1955	NL	Bill Virdon	OF
1974	NL	Bake McBride	OF
1985	NL	Vince Coleman	OF
1986	NL	Todd Worrell	P
2001	NL	Albert Pujols	1B–3B–OF

Cy Young Award Winners

Year	LG	Pitcher
1968	NL	Bob Gibson
1970	NL	Bob Gibson
2005	NL	Chris Carpenter

Batting Champions

Year	LG	Player	AVG
1887	AA	"Tip" O'Neill	.435
1888	AA	"Tip" O'Neill	.335
1901	NL	Jesse Burkett	.376
1920	NL	Rogers Hornsby	.370
1921	NL	Rogers Hornsby	.397
1922	NL	Rogers Hornsby	.401
1923	NL	Rogers Hornsby	.384
1924	NL	Rogers Hornsby	.424
1925	NL	Rogers Hornsby	.403
1931	NL	Chick Hafey	.349
1937	NL	Joe "Ducky" Medwick	.374
1939	NL	Johnny Mize	.349
1943	NL	Stan Musial	.357
1946	NL	Stan Musial	.365
1948	NL	Stan Musial	.376
1950	NL	Stan Musial	.346
1951	NL	Stan Musial	.355
1952	NL	Stan Musial	.336
1957	NL	Stan Musial	.351
1971	NL	Joe Torre	.363
1979	NL	Keith Hernandez	.344

Appendix C

Year	LG	Player	AVG
1985	NL	Willie McGee	.353
1990	NL	Willie McGee	.335
2003	NL	Albert Pujols	.359

Home Run Champions

Year	LG	Player	HR
1882	AA	Oscar Walker	7
1887	AA	"Tip" O'Neill	14
1890	AA	"Count" Campau	9
1922	NL	Rogers Hornsby	42
1925	NL	Rogers Hornsby	39
1928	NL	"Sunny Jim" Bottomley	31
1934	NL	"Ripper" Collins	35
1937	NL	Joe "Ducky" Medwick	31
1939	NL	Johnny Mize	28
1940	NL	Johnny Mize	43
1998	NL	Mark McGwire	70
1999	NL	Mark McGwire	65
2009	NL	Albert Pujols	47
2010	NL	Albert Pujols	42

Runs Batted in Champions

Year	LG	Player	RBI
1886	AA	"Tip" O'Neill	107
1887	AA	"Tip" O'Neill	123
1920	NL	Rogers Hornsby	94
1921	NL	Rogers Hornsby	126
1922	NL	Rogers Hornsby	152
1925	NL	Rogers Hornsby	143
1926	NL	"Sunny Jim" Bottomley	120
1928	NL	"Sunny Jim" Bottomley	136
1936	NL	Joe "Ducky" Medwick	138
1937	NL	Joe "Ducky" Medwick	154
1938	NL	Joe "Ducky" Medwick	122
1940	NL	Johnny Mize	137
1946	NL	Enos Slaughter	130
1948	NL	Stan Musial	131

Noteworthy Achievements

Year	LG	Player	RBI
1956	NL	Stan Musial	109
1964	NL	Ken Boyer	119
1967	NL	Orlando Cepeda	111
1971	NL	Joe Torre	137
1999	NL	Mark McGwire	147
2010	NL	Albert Pujols	118

Stolen Base Champions

Year	LG	Player	SB
1888	AA	Arlie Latham	109
1890	AA	Tommy McCarthy	83
1900	NL	"Patsy" Donovan	45
1927	NL	Frank Frisch	48
1931	NL	Frank Frisch	28
1933	NL	"Pepper" Martin	26
1934	NL	"Pepper" Martin	23
1936	NL	"Pepper" Martin	23
1945	NL	Red Schoendienst	28
1966	NL	Lou Brock	74
1967	NL	Lou Brock	52
1968	NL	Lou Brock	62
1969	NL	Lou Brock	53
1971	NL	Lou Brock	64
1972	NL	Lou Brock	63
1973	NL	Lou Brock	70
1974	NL	Lou Brock	118
1985	NL	Vince Coleman	110
1986	NL	Vince Coleman	109
1987	NL	Vince Coleman	107
1988	NL	Vince Coleman	81
1989	NL	Vince Coleman	65
1990	NL	Vince Coleman	77

Earned Run Average Champions

Year	LG	Pitcher	ERA
1885	AA	Bob Caruthers	2.07
1886	AA	Dave Foutz	2.11
1888	AA	Silver King	1.63

Appendix C

Year	LG	Pitcher	ERA
1889	AA	Jack Stivetts	2.25
1893	AA	Ted Breitenstein	3.18
1914	NL	Bill Doak	1.72
1921	NL	Bill Doak	2.59
1922	NL	Phil Douglas	2.63
1942	NL	Mort Cooper	1.78
1943	NL	Max Lanier	1.90
1948	NL	Harry Brecheen	2.24
1968	NL	Bob Gibson	1.12
1976	NL	John Denny	2.52
1988	NL	Joe Magrane	2.18
2009	NL	Chris Carpenter	2.24

Strikeout Champions

Year	LG	Pitcher	SO
1891	AA	Jack Stivetts	259
1930	NL	"Wild Bill" Hallahan	177
1931	NL	"Wild Bill" Hallahan	159
1932	NL	"Dizzy" Dean	191
1933	NL	"Dizzy" Dean	199
1934	NL	"Dizzy" Dean	195
1935	NL	"Dizzy" Dean	190
1948	NL	Harry Brecheen	149
1958	NL	Sam Jones	225
1968	NL	Bob Gibson	268
1989	NL	Jose DeLeon	201

Chapter Notes

Foreword

1. Auguste Choteau, *Narrative of the Settlement of St. Louis* (St. Louis: Knapp, 1858), 3.
2. Shirley Christian, *Before Lewis and Clark: The Story of the Choteaus, the French Dynasty That Ruled America's Frontier* (New York: Farrar, Straus and Giroux, 2004), 54.
3. *Ibid.*, 35.
4. James Neal Primm, *Lion of the Valley: St. Louis, Missouri, 1764–1980* (St. Louis: Missouri Historical Society Press, 1998), 3d ed., 8–9.
5. Choteau, *Narrative of the Settlement of St. Louis*, 3.
6. *Ibid.*, 4.
7. *Ibid.*
8. *Ibid.*
9. Carl J. Ekberg and William E. Foley, "Nicolas de Finiels," in Lawrence O. Christensen, William E. Foley, Gary R. Kremer, and Kenneth H. Winn, eds., *Dictionary of Missouri Biography* (Columbia: University of Missouri Press, 1999), 300.
10. Nicolas de Finiels, *An Account of Upper Louisiana* (Columbia: University of Missouri Press, 1989), edited by Carl J. Ekberg and William E. Foley; translated by Carl J. Ekberg, 75.
11. Louis Houck, *A History of Missouri: From the Earliest Explorations and Settlements until the Admission of the State into the Union* (Chicago: R. R. Donnelley & Sons, 1908), Vol. II, 50.
12. Primm, *Lion of the Valley*, 58.
13. Charles Peterson, *Colonial St. Louis: Building a Creole Capital* (Tuscon, AZ.: Patrice Press, 1992), 27.
14. Houck, *History of Missoui*, Vol. II, 29.
15. Peterson, *Colonial St. Louis*, 27.
16. Houck, *History of Missouri*, Vol. II, 54.
17. Peterson, *Colonial Sr. Louis*, 27.
18. Houck, *History of Missouri*, Vol. II, 29.
19. Carl Ekberg, *French Roots in the Illinois Country: The Mississippi Frontier in Colonial Times* (Urbana: University of Illinois Press, 2000), 110.
20. Description of the Wilson Price Hunt and the Hunt family papers in the archive of the Missouri Historical Society (http://collections.mohistory.org/archive/ARC: A0735).
21. Hunt's Minutes; 1:199; archive of the Missouri Historical Society (source originally found in Ekberg, *French Roots in the Illinois Country*, 269).
22. Houck, *History of Missouri*, Vol. II, 56.
23. Paul Beckwith, *Creoles of St. Louis* (St. Louis: Nixon-Jones, 1893), 70–71.
24. John Reynolds, *Pioneer History of Illinois: Containing the Discovery in 1673, and the History of the Country to the Year 1818, when the State Government was Organized* (Chicago: Fergus Printing Company, 1887), 2d ed., 256–57.
25. E. B. Washburne, *Henry Gratiot: A Pioneer of Wisconsin* (Chicago: Fergus Printing Company, 1884), 12.
26. *Ibid.*, 12.
27. David Block, *Baseball Before We Knew It: A Search for the Roots of the Game* (Lincoln, NE.: Bison Books, 2006), 101.
28. William Bradford, *History of the*

Chapter Notes

Plymouth Plantation (Boston: Little, Brown, 1856), 112.
29. Clarence Walworth Alvord, *Laws of the Territory of Illinois. 1809–1811* (Springfield, IL: Illinois State Journal Co. State Printers, 1906), xi.
30. *Ibid.*, 18.
31. Robert Henderson, *Ball, Bat and Bishop: The Origins of Ball Games* (New York: Rockport Press, 1947), 47–48.
32. *Ibid.*, 121–22.
33. Block, *Baseball Before We Knew It*, 279.
34. Henderson, *Ball, Bat and Bishop*, 140–41.
35. Block, *Baseball Before We Knew It*, 151; Henderson, *Ball, Bat and Bishop*, 141.
36. Block, *Baseball Before We Knew It*, 148.
37. Guillaume Louis Gustave Belleze, *Jeux des Adoolescents* (1856; reprint, Charleston, SC: Nabu Press, 2010), 48–49.

Introduction

1. *St. Louis Dispatch*, May 6, 1875; *St. Louis Republican*, May 7, 1875.
2. *Worcester Spy* quoted in the *Chicago Tribune*, July 18, 1880; *Cincinnati Enquirer* quoted in Harold Seymour and Dorothy Seymour Mills, *Baseball: Early Years* (New York: Oxford University Press, 1989), 92, and Robert Harris Walker, *Cincinnati and the Big Red Machine* (Bloomington: Indiana University Press, 1988), 14.
3. *Chicago Tribune*, October 1, 15, 1880.
4. Frederick Jackson Turner, "The Middle West," in Turner, *Frontier in American History* (New York: Henry Holt, 1920), 146.
5. Spink quoted in David Pietrusza, *Major Leagues: The Formation, Sometimes Absorption, and Mostly Inevitable Demise of Eighteen Professional Organizations, 1871 to Present* (Jefferson, NC: McFarland, 1991), 67.
6. *St. Louis Globe-Democrat*, September 3, November 4, 1881; Lee Allen, *100 Years of Baseball* (New York: Bartholomew House, 1950), 67.
7. Richard Jensen, *Winning of the Midwest: Social and Political Conflict, 1886–1896* (Chicago: University of Chicago Press, 1971), 70.
8. *Chicago Tribune*, November 6, 1881; Allen, *100 Years of Baseball*, 66–67; David Nemec, *Beer and Whisky League: The Illustrated History of the American Association—Baseball's Renegade Major League* (New York: Lyons and Burford, 1994).
9. Hulbert quoted in Pietrusza, *Major Leagues*, 72.
10. Albert G. Spalding, *America's National Game* (New York: American Sports Publishing Company, 1911), 241.
11. Lee Allen, *The World Series* (New York: G. P. Putnam's Sons, 1969), 19; Glenn Dickey, *The History of the World Series* (New York: Stein and Day, 1984), 16.
12. *St. Louis Post-Dispatch*, July 12, 14, 1886; *Missouri Republican*, September 26, Oct. 1–2, 1886; *St. Louis Globe-Democrat*, October 2, 1886. The *Missouri Republican* praised the Browns for attracting fans from the rural hinterlands and female spectators, whom they credited for a "softening and refining effect" that resulted in a "more civil and respectful" audience. The *St. Louis Globe-Democrat* lauded the ball club for uniting all ages and classes within the city: "Men and boys, silk hats and common ones, mingled together, yelled together, and, in fact, went crazy together." The *Missouri Republican* quoted from October 23, 1886; *St. Louis Globe-Democrat* quoted from October 24, 1886,
13. *Chicago News*, reprinted in *Missouri Republican*, October 20, 26, 1886,
14. Nemec, *Beer and Whisky League*, 110–11; Seymour and Mills, *Baseball: Early Years*, 218; *Sporting News*, November 20, Dec. 4, 1886.
15. *Sporting News*, November 13, 20, 1886,
16. *Sporting News*, September 21, 1889.
17. *Sporting News*, October 26, 1889.
18. *Sporting News*, November 24, 1888; Seymour and Mills, *Baseball: Early Years*, 129.
19. *Sporting News*, February 1, 1890.
20. Nemec, *Beer and Whisky League*, 235; David Nemec, *Great Encyclopedia of 19th Century Major League Baseball* (New York: Donald I. Fine Books, 1997), 467–68. In reality, three charter members of the American Association (the St. Louis Car-

Chapter Notes

dinals, Cincinnati Reds, and the Pittsburgh Pirates) still exist in major league baseball today as part of an unbroken chain beginning with its November 1881 formation. In contrast, only one charter member of the National League (the Chicago Cubs) is still playing professional baseball in the same city that they started in with its February 1876 formation.

21. There was no World Series in 1904 because the NL champion New York Giants refused to participate. In 1994, the Major League Baseball Players Association went on strike in August, and, when management and labor failed to resolve their differences, the remainder of the season was cancelled. The dispute lingered into spring training, and the owners planned to proceed with replacement players until Judge Sonia Sotomayor, then an U.S. District Judge and later a U.S. Supreme Court Justice, ruled just two days before the scheduled start of the season that Major League Baseball would operate under the old collective bargaining agreement until a new one could be reached. Her decision perhaps saved baseball as we know it and, after eight work stoppages since 1972, ushered in an unusual harmonious relationship between the owners and the players' union. Charles Alexander, *John McGraw* (New York: Penguin Books, 1989), 108–109; John Thorn, Pete Palmer, Michael Gershman, and David Pietrusza, eds., *Total Baseball*, 6th ed. (New York: Total Sports, 1999), 322, 2002, 2366.

Chapter 1

1. Brian McKenna, "Helene Britton versus Roger Bresnahan," www.baseball-fever.com.

Chapter 2

1. Paul Dickson, *Baseball's Greatest Quotations* (New York: Harper Perennial, 1991), 357.
2. Red Smith, *To Absent Friends from Red Smith* (New York: Atheneum, 1982). 435.
3. J. Roy Stockton, *Gashouse Gang and a Couple of Other Guys* (New York: A. S. Barnes, 1945), 5.
4. Donald Honig, *October Heroes: Great World Series Games Remembered by the Men Who Played them* (New York: Simon and Schuster, 1979), 91.

Chapter 3

1. Anthony J. Connor, *Voices from Cooperstown: Baseball's Hall of Famers Tell It Like It Was* (New York: Collier Books, 1984), 286.
2. Honig, *October Heroes*, 86, 91.
3. Paul E. Doutrich, *Cardinals and the Yankees, 1926: A Classic Season and St. Louis in Seven* (Jefferson, NC: McFarland, 2010), 2.
4. Richard Peterson, ed., *St. Louis Baseball Reader* (Columbia: University of Missouri Press, 2006), 132–33.
5. J. Roy Stockton, "St. Louis Cardinals," in Ed Fitzgerald, ed., *National League* (New York: Grosset and Dunlap, 1959), 183.
6. Lawrence S. Ritter, *The Glory of Their Times: Story of the Early Days of Baseball Told by the Men Who Played It* (New York: Macmillan, 1966), 238–239.

Chapter 4

1. Ritter, *Glory of Their Times*, 238.
2. Bob Broeg, *Bob Broeg's Redbirds: Century of Cardinals Baseball* (St. Louis: River City, 1981), 43.
3. Alexander, *John McGraw*, 286.
4. Response of Philadelphia crowd quoted in Red Smith, "Pepper Martin vs. Philadelphia, 1931," in Daniel Okrent and Harris Lewine, eds., *Ultimate Baseball Book* (Boston: Houghton Mifflin, 1991), 163.
5. B. A. Bridgewater, "Telling the World of Sports," *Tulsa World*, February 8, 1949.
6. *St. Louis Post-Dispatch*, October 11, 1931.

Chapter 5

1. *Sporting News*, October 18, 1934.
2. G. H. Fleming, *The Dizziest Sea-*

Chapter Notes

son: *Gashouse Gang Chases the Pennant* (New York: William Morrow and Company, 1984), 100, and Peterson, *St. Louis Baseball Reader*, 291; Frisch quoted in Peterson, *St. Louis Baseball Reader*, 183; Dean quoted in Robert Gregory, *Diz: The Story of Dizzy Dean and Baseball during the Great Depression* (New York: Viking Penguin, 1992), 80.
   3. Leo Durocher with Ed Linn, *Nice Guys Finish Last* (New York: Pocket Books, 1976), 25–26.
   4. Author's Correspondence with Burgess Whitehead.
   5. Fleming, *The Dizziest Season*, 32, 93.
   6. *St. Louis Post-Dispatch*, October 10, 1934.
   7. McNamee quoted from YouTube video, Classic Baseball on the Radio, 1934 World Series Game 1; Author's Correspondence with Pat Crawford; Williams quoted in Gregory, *Diz*, 213.
   8. Author's Correspondence with Pat Crawford.
   9. Gregory, *Diz*, 237.

Chapter 6

1. Enos Slaughter with Kevin Reid, *Country Hardball: The Autobiography of Enos "Country" Slaughter* (Greensboro, NC: Tudor Publishers, 1991), 61.
   2. James N. Giglio, *Musial: Stash to Stan the Man* (Columbia: University of Missouri Press, 2001), 7.
   3. E. D. Fischer, "Billy Southworth's St. Louis Swifties," in Peterson, *St. Louis Baseball Reader*, 237.
   4. Stan Musial as told to Bob Broeg, *The Man's Own Story* (Garden City, NY: Doubleday, 1964), 29.
   5. Jerome M. Mileur, *High-Flying Birds: 1942 St. Louis Cardinals* (Columbia: University of Missouri Press, 2009), 205, 236.
   6. Okrent and Lewine, *Ultimate Baseball Book*, 238.
   7. *New York Times*, October 6, 1942; Mileur, *High-Flying Birds*, 224.
   8. William B. Mead, *Baseball Goes to War* (Washington, DC: Broadcast of Interview Source, 1998), 187.

Chapter 7

1. Okrent and Lewine, *Ultimate Baseball Book*, 237.
   2. Mead, *Baseball Goes to War*, 16.
   3. Donald Honig, *Baseball When the Grass Was Real: Baseball from the Twenties to the Forties Told by the Men Who Played It* (Lincoln: University of Nebraska Press, 1993), 219.
   4. Slaughter with Reid, *Country Hardball*, 88.
   5. Associated Press and *New York Times* quoted in Bruce Lowitt, "Country's Mad Dash Wins It for St. Louis," *St. Petersburg Times*, October 4, 1999.
   6. Giglio, *Musial*, 145.

Chapter 8

1. Bob Gibson with Phil Pepe, *Ghetto to Glory: Story of Bob Gibson* (New York: Popular Library, 1968), 126.
   2. Musial quoted in Connor, *Voices from Cooperstown*, 181–82; Slaughter from Slaughter with Reid, *Country Hardball*, 81.
   3. Jules Tygiel, *Baseball's Great Experiment: Jackie Robinson and His Legacy* (New York: Vintage Books, 1984), 286.
   4. Red Smith, "Tomorrow in Brooklyn," *New York Herald-Tribune*, September 26, 1950, included in *Red Smith on Baseball: The Game's Greatest Writer on the Game's Greatest Years* (Chicago: Ivan R. Dee, 2000), 101–103.
   5. Dickson, *Baseball's Greatest Quotations*, 357.
   6. Interview with Gene Kirby, producer of the "Game of the Week," by Paul MacFarlane of the *Sporting News*.
   7. On the "force-feeding" plan, see Broeg from *Bob Broeg's Redbirds*, 150.
   8. *Ibid.*, 151.
   9. Giglio, *Musial*, 185.

Chapter 9

1. Curt Flood with Richard Carter, *The Way It Is* (New York: Pocket Books, 1972), 68.

Chapter Notes

2. Orlando Cepeda with Bob Markus, *High & Inside: Orlando Cepeda's Story* (South Bend, IN: Icarus Press, 1983), 57–58.

3. Broeg from *Bob Broeg's Redbirds*, 201.

Chapter 10

1. Whitey Herzog and Jonathan Pitts, *You're Missin' a Great Game: From Casey to Ozzie, the Magic of Baseball and How to Get It Back* (New York: Simon and Schuster, 1999), 98.

2. Buck quoted from YouTube video, MLB, "Cardinals win the 1982 World Series."

Chapter 11

1. James Rygelski and Robert Tiemann, *Ten Rings: Stories of the St. Louis Cardinals World Championships* (St. Louis: Reedy Press, 2011), x.

2. Tony La Russa with Rick Hummel, *One Last Strike: Fifty Years in Baseball, Ten and a Half Games Back, and One Final Championship Season* (New York: William Morrow, 2013), 400.

3. *Sports Illustrated, Special Collector's Edition: Sr. Louis Cardinals World Champions 2011*, 33.

Bibliography

Newspapers

Chicago News
Chicago Tribune
Cincinnati Enquirer
Missouri Republican (St. Louis)
New York Daily News
New York Herald-Tribune
New York Sun
New York Times
New York World-Telegram
Pittsburgh Press
St. Louis Dispatch
St. Louis Globe-Democrat
St. Louis Post-Dispatch
St. Louis Republic
St. Louis Republican
St. Louis Star
St. Louis Star-Times
The Sporting News
Tulsa World
Worcester (MA) Spy

Baseball Guides

Reach's Official American Association Baseball Guide. 1886; reprint, St. Louis: Horton Publishing Company, 1989.
Reach's Official American Association Baseball Guide. 1887; reprint, St. Louis: Horton Publishing Company, 1989.
Reach's Official American Association Baseball Guide. 1890; reprint, St. Louis: Horton Publishing Company, 1989.
Reach's Official Baseball Guide. 1892; reprint, St. Louis: Horton Publishing Company, 1989.
Spalding's Official Baseball Guide. 1881; reprint, St. Louis: Horton Publishing Company, 1988.
Spalding's Official Baseball Guide. 1886; reprint, St. Louis: Horton Publishing Company, 1987.
Spalding's Official Baseball Guide. 1887; reprint, St. Louis: Horton Publishing Company, 1988.
Spalding's Official Baseball Guide. 1892; reprint, St. Louis: Horton Publishing Company, 1987.

Censuses

Compendium of the Ninth Census, 1870. New York: Arno Press, 1976.
Compendium of the Tenth Census, 1880. New York: Arno Press, 1976.
Abstract of the Eleventh Census, 1890. New York: Arno Press, 1976.

Bibliography

Books

Alexander, Charles C. *Breaking the Slump: Baseball in the Depression Era* (New York: Columbia University Press, 2002).
_____. *John McGraw* (New York: Penguin Books, 1989).
_____. *Our Game: An American Baseball History* (New York: MJF Books, 1991).
_____. *Rogers Hornsby: A Biography* (New York: Henry Holt, 1996).
Allen, Lee. *100 Years of Baseball* (New York: Bartholomew House, 1950).
_____. *The World Series* (New York: G. P. Putnam's Sons, 1969).
Allen, Maury. *Roger Maris: A Man for All Seasons* (New York: D. I. Fine, 1986).
Alvord, Clarence Walworth. *Laws of the Territory of Illinois, 1809–1811* (Springfield, IL: Illinois State Journal Co. State Printers, 1906).
Axelson, Gustav W. *"Commy": The Life Story of Charles A. Comiskey* (Chicago: Reilly and Lee, 1919).
Bakker, Pamela A. *Eyes on the Sporting Scene, 1870–1930: Will and June Rankin, New York's Sportswriting Brothers* (Jefferson, NC: McFarland, 2013).
Barthel, Thomas. *The Fierce Fun of Ducky Medwick* (Lanham, MD: Scarecrow Press, 2003).
_____. *Pepper Martin: A Baseball Biography* (Jefferson, NC: McFarland, 2003).
Bartlett, Arthur. *Baseball and Mr. Spalding: The History and Romance of Baseball* (New York: Farrar, Straus, and Young, 1951).
Beckwith, Paul. *Creoles of St. Louis* (St. Louis: Nixon-Jones, 1893).
Belleze, Guillaume Louis Gustave. *Jeux des Adolescents* (1856; reprint, Charleston, SC: Nabu Press, 2010)
Bjarkman, Peter C., ed. *Encyclopedia of Major League Baseball Teams: National League* (Westport, CT: Meckler, 1991).
Block, David. *Baseball Before We Knew It: A Search for the Roots of the Game* (Lincoln, NE: Bison Books, 2006).
Borst, Bill. *Baseball Through a Knothole: A St. Louis History* (St. Louis: Krank Press, 1980).
Bowman, John, and Joel Zoss. *Diamonds in the Rough: The Untold History of Baseball* (New York: Macmillan, 1989).
Bradford, William. *History of the Plymouth Plantation* (Boston: Little, Brown, 1856).
Broeg, Bob. *Bob Broeg's Redbirds: A Century of Cardinals Baseball* (St. Louis: River City Publishers, 1981).
_____. *Memories of a Hall of Fame Sportswriter* (Champagne, IL: Sagamore, 2012).
_____. *My Baseball Scrapbook* (St. Louis: River City Publishers, 1983).
_____. *The Pilot Light and the Gas House Gang.* (St. Louis: Bethany Press, 1980).
_____. *Super Stars of Baseball: Their Lives, Their Loves, Their Laughs, Their Laments* (St. Louis: Sporting News, 1971).
Buck, Jack. *That's a Winner* (Champagne, IL: Sagamore, 1997).
Carmichael, John. *My Greatest Day in Baseball: 47 Dramatic Stories Told by 47 Famous Stars* (New York: Grosset and Dunlap, 1945).
Carter, Craig, ed. *Daguerreotypes: Complete Major and Minor League Records of Baseball's Greats*, 8th ed. (St. Louis: Sporting News, 1990).
Cash, Jon David. *Before They Were Cardinals: Major League Baseball in Nineteenth-Century St. Louis* (Columbia: University of Missouri Press, 2002).
Cepeda, Orlando, with Bob Markus. *High & Inside: Orlando Cepeda's Story* (South Bend, IN: Icarus Press, 1983).
Chapman, Bruce, and David M. Spindel. *St. Louis Cardinals: Over 100 Years of Baseball Memories and Memorabilia* (New York: Abbeville Press, 1995).
Choteau, Auguste. *Narrative of the Settlement of St. Louis* (St. Louis: Knapp, 1856).
Christensen, Lawrence O., William E. Foley, Gary R. Kremer, and Kenneth H. Winn, eds. *Dictionary of Missouri Biography* (Columbia: University of Missouri Press, 1999).

Bibliography

Christian, Shirley. *Before Lewis and Clark: The Story of the Choteaus, the French Dynasty That Ruled America's Frontier* (New York: Farrar, Straus and Giroux, 2004).
Church, Seymour R.,. *Baseball: The History, Statistics, and Romance of the American National Game* (1902; reprint, Princeton, NJ: Pyne Press, 1974).
Coffin, Tristram Potter. *Old Ball Game: Baseball in Folklore and Fiction* (New York: Herder and Herder, 1971).
Conklin, Carroll. *Cardinal Pride: The Story of the St. Louis Cardinals in the 1960s* (Lewis Center, OH: Bright Stone Press, 2018).
Connor, Anthony J. *Voices from Cooperstown: Baseball's Hall of Famers Tell It Like It Was* (New York: Collier Books, 1984).
Crepeau, Richard C. *Baseball: America's Diamond Mind, 1919–1941* (Orlando: University Press of Florida, 1980).
Curran, William. *Mitts: A Celebration of the Art of Fielding* (New York: William Morrow, 1985).
Davis, Mac. *Lore and Legends of Baseball* (New York: Lantern Press, 1953).
Deutsch, Jordan A., Richard M. Cohen, Roland T. Johnson, and David S. Neft, eds. *Scrapbook History of Baseball* (Indianapolis: Bobbs-Merrill, 1975).
Devine, Bing, with Tom Wheatley. *Memoirs of Bing Devine: Stealing Lou Brock and Other Winning Moves by a Master GM* (Champagne, IL: Sports Publishing, 2004).
Dickey, Glenn. *History of the World Series* (New York: Stein and Day, 1984).
Dickson, Paul. *Baseball Dictionary* (New York: Facts on File, 1989).
_____. *Baseball's Greatest Quotations* (New York: Harper Perennial, 1991).
Doutrich, Paul E. *Cardinals and the Yankees, 1926: A Classic Season and St. Louis in Seven* (Jefferson, NC: McFarland, 2010).
Durocher, Leo, with Ed Linn. *Nice Guys Finish Last* (New York: Pocket Books, 1976).
Edison, Charles, ed. *Fireside Book of Baseball* (New York: Simon & Schuster, 1956).
_____. *New Baseball Reader* (New York: Viking Penguin, 1991).
Ekberg, Carl. *French Roots in the Illinois Country: The Mississippi Frontier in Colonial Times* (Urbana: University of Illinois Press, 2000).
Falkner, David. *Nine Sides of the Diamond: Baseball's Great Glove Men on the Fine Art of Defense* (New York: Times Books, 1990).
Feldmann, Doug. *Dizzy and the Gas House Gang: The 1934 St. Louis Cardinals and Depression-Era Baseball* (Jefferson, NC: McFarland, 2000).
_____. *El Birdos: The 1967 and 1968 St. Louis Cardinals* (Jefferson, NC: McFarland, 2007).
_____. *Fleeter Than Birds: 1985 St. Louis Cardinals and Small Ball's Last Hurrah* (Jefferson, NC: McFarland, 2002).
_____. *Gibson's Last Stand: Rise, Fall, and Near Misses of the St. Louis Cardinals, 1969–1975* (Columbia: University of Missouri Press, 2011).
_____. *St. Louis Cardinals Past & Present* (Minneapolis: MVP Books, 2009).
_____. *Whitey Herzog Builds a Winner, 1979–1982* ((Jefferson, NC: McFarland, 2018).
Finch, David. *For the Good of the Country: World War II Baseball in the Major and Minor Leagues* (Jefferson, NC: McFarland, 2002).
Finiels, Nicolas de. *An Account of Upper Louisiana* (Columbia: University of Missouri Press, 1989), edited by Carl J. Ekberg and William E. Foley, translated by Carl J. Ekberg.
Fischler, Stan. *Showdown: Baseball's Ultimate Confrontations* (New York: Tempo Books, 1978).
Fitzgerald, Ed, ed. *National League* (New York: Grosset and Dunlap, 1959).
Fleming, G. H. *Dizziest Season: The Gashouse Gang Chases the Pennant* (New York: William Morrow, 1984).
Flood, Curt, with Richard Carter. *The Way It Is* (New York: Pocket Books, 1972).
Freese, Mel R. *St. Louis Cardinals in the 1940s* (Jefferson, NC: McFarland, 2007).
Gallen, David, ed. *Baseball Chronicles* (New York: Carroll & Graf, 1991).
Garagiola, Joe. *Baseball Is a Funny Game* (New York: Bantam Books, 1960).

Bibliography

Gershman, Michael. *Diamonds: Evolution of the Ballpark* (Boston: Houghton Mifflin, 1993).

Gibson, Bob, with Phil Pepe. *From Ghetto to Glory: The Story of Bob Gibson* (New York: Popular Library, 1968).

____, with Lonnie Wheeler. *Stranger to the Game: The Autobiography of Bob Gibson* (New York: Penguin Books, 1996).

Gies, Joseph, and Robert Shoemaker. *Stars of the Series: A Complete History of the World Series* (New York: Thomas Y. Crowell, 1965).

Giglio, James N. *Musial: From Stash to Stan the Man* (Columbia: University of Missouri Press, 2001).

Gilbert, Bill. *They Also Served: Baseball and the Home Front, 1941–1945* (New York: Crown Publishers, 1992).

Goldstein, Warren. *Playing for Keeps: A History of Early Baseball* (Ithaca, NY: Cornell University Press, 1989).

Grayson, Harry. *They Played the Game: The Story of Baseball Greats* (New York: A. S. Barnes, 1944).

Gregory, Robert. *Diz: The Story of Dizzy Dean and Baseball During the Great Depression* (New York: Viking Penguin, 1992).

Gutman, Dan. *Baseball Babylon* (New York: Penguin Books, 1992).

Hagen, Harry. *This Is Our St. Louis* (St. Louis: Knight Publishing, 1970).

Halberstam, David. *October 1964* (New York: Fawcett Columbine, 1995).

Hall, Alvin L., ed. *Cooperstown Symposium on Baseball and the American Culture* (1989) (Westport, CT: Meckler, 1991).

Hart, Jim Allee. *History of the St. Louis Globe-Democrat* (Columbia: University of Missouri Press, 1961).

Heidenry, John, and Brett Topol. *The Boys Who Were Left Behind: The 1944 World Series Between the Hapless St. Louis Browns and the Legendary St. Louis Cardinals* (Lincoln: University of Nebraska Press, 2006).

____. *The Gashouse Gang: How Dizzy Dean, Leo Durocher, Branch Rickey, Pepper Martin, & Their Colorful, Come-from-Behind Ball Club Won the World Series and America's Heart During the Great Depression* (New York: Public Affairs, 2007).

Henderson, Robert W. *Ball, Bat and Bishop: The Origins of Ball Games* (New York: Rockport Press, 1947).

Hernandez, Keith. *I'm Keith Hernandez: A Memoir* (New York: Little, Brown, 2018).

Herzog, Whitey, and Kevin Horrigan. *White Rat: A Life in Baseball* (New York: Harper & Row, 1987).

____, and Jonathan Pitts. *You're Missin' a Great Game: From Casey to Ozzie, the Magic of Baseball and How to Get It Back* (New York: Simon & Schuster, 1999).

Hetrick, J. Thomas. *Chris Von der Ahe and the St. Louis Browns* (Lanham, MD: Scarecrow Press, 1999).

Honig, Donald. *Baseball America: The Heroes of the Game and the Times of Their Glory* (New York: Macmillan, 1985).

____. *Baseball Between the Lines: Baseball in the 40s and 50s as Told by the Men Who Played It* (New York: Coward, McCann, & Geoghegan, 1976).

____. *Baseball When the Grass Was Real: Baseball from the Twenties to the Forties Told by the Men Who Played It* (Lincoln: University of Nebraska Press, 1993).

____. *Baseball's 10 Greatest Teams* (New York: Macmillan, 1982).

____. *The October Heroes: Great World Series Games Remembered by the Men Who Played Them* (New York: Simon & Schuster, 1979).

Hood, Robert. *Gashouse Gang* (New York: Morrow, 1976).

Hornsby, Rogers, and William Surface. *My War with Baseball* (New York: Coward-McCann, 1962).

Houck, Louis. *A History of Missouri: From the Earliest Explorations and Settlements until the Admission of the State into the Union* (Chicago: R. R. Donnelley, 1908).

Bibliography

Humber, William. *Cheering for the Home Team: The Story of Baseball in Canada* (Erin, Ontario: Boston Mills Press, 1983).
James, Bill. *Historical Baseball Abstract* (New York: Villard Books, 1988).
_____. *The New Bill James Historical Baseball Abstract* (New York: Free Press, 2003).
Jensen, Richard. *The Winning of the Midwest: Social and Political Conflict, 1886–1896* (Chicago: University of Chicago Press, 1971).
Karst, Gene, and Martin J. Jones. *Who's Who in Professional Baseball* (New Rochelle, NY: Arlington House, 1973).
Kirby, Gene. *Dizzy: Dean of Baseball & My Podnah* (San Antonio: Cool Cat Communications, 2016).
Lanasche, Jerry. *Forgotten Championships: Postseason Baseball, 1882–1981* (Jefferson, NC: McFarland, 1989).
La Russa, Tony, with Rick Hummel. *One Last Strike: Fifty Years in Baseball, Ten and a Half Games Back, and One Final Championship Season* (New York: William Morrow, 2013).
Leprince, Xavier. *Les Jeux des Jeunes Garcons*, 4th ed. (Paris: Chez Nepveu, 1815).
Levine, Peter. *A. G. Spalding and the Rise of Baseball: The Promise of American Sport* (New York: Oxford University Press, 1985).
Lieb, Frederick. *The St. Louis Cardinals: Story of a Great Baseball Club* (New York: G. P. Putnam's Sons, 1944).
_____. *The Story of the World Series: An Informal History* (New York: G. P. Putnam's Sons, 1949).
Lipsitz, George. *Sidewalks of St. Louis: Places, People, and Politics in an American City* (Columbia: University of Missouri Press, 1991).
Lowenfish, Lee. *Branch Rickey: Baseball's Ferocious Gentleman* (Lincoln: University of Nebraska Press, 2009).
Lowry, Philip J. *Green Cathedrals: The Ultimate Celebration of All 271 Major League and Negro League Ballparks Past and Present* (Reading, MA: Addison-Wesley, 1992).
McCann, Kevin D. *Ken Boyer: All-Star, MVP, Captain* (Dickson, TN: BrayBree, 2015).
McCarver, Tim, and Phil Pepe. *Few and Chosen: Defining Cardinal Greatness Across the Eras* (Chicago: Triumph Books, 2005).
_____, and Ray Robinson. *Oh, Baby, I Love It* (New York: Dell, 1988).
Mead, William B. *Baseball Goes to War* (Washington, D.C.: Broadcast Interview Source, 1998).
_____. *Even the Browns: The Zany, True Story of Baseball in the Early Forties* (Chicago: Contemporary Books, 1978).
Meany, Tom. *Baseball's Greatest Players* (New York: Grosset and Dunlap, 1953).
Megdal, Howard. *The Cardinals Way: How One Team Embraced Tradition and Moneyball at the Same Time* (New York: Thomas Dunne Books/St. Martin's Press, 2016).
Mileur, Jerome M. *High-Flying Birds: The 1942 St. Louis Cardinals* (Columbia: University of Missouri Press, 2009).
_____. *The Stars Are Back: The St. Louis Cardinals, Boston Red Sox and Player Unrest in 1946* (Carbondale: Southern Illinois University Press, 2013).
Molina, Bengie, with Joan Ryan. *Molina: The Story of the Father Who Raised an Unlikely Baseball Dynasty* (New York: Simon & Schuster, 2016).
Morris, Peter, William J. Ryczek, Jan Finkel, and Richard Malatzky, eds. *Base Ball Pioneers, 1850–1870: The Clubs and Players Who Spread the Sport Nationwide* (Jefferson, NC: McFarland, 2012).
Musial, Stan, as told to Bob Broeg. *The Man's Own Story* (Garden City, NY: Doubleday, 1964).
Neft, David S. and Richard Cohen. *World Series: Complete Play-by-Play of Every Game, 1903–1989* (New York: St. Martin's Press, 1990).
Nelson, Daniel. *Managers and Workers: Origins of the New Factory System in the United States, 1880–1920* (Madison: University of Wisconsin Press, 1975).

Bibliography

Nemec, David. *The Beer and Whisky League: The Illustrated History of the American Association—Baseball's Renegade League* (New York: Lyons and Burford, 1994).
_____. *Great Encyclopedia of 19th Century Major League Baseball* (New York: Donald I. Fine, 1997).
_____. *Rank and File of 19th Century Major League Baseball* (Jefferson, NC: McFarland, 2012).
_____, ed. *Major League Baseball Profiles, 1871–1890*, vols. 1 and 2 (Lincoln: University of Nebraska Press, 2011).
_____, and Saul Wisnia. *Baseball: More Than 150 Years* (Lincolnwood, IL: Publications International, 1997).
Nowlin, Bill, and John Harry Stahl, eds. *Drama and Pride in the Gateway City: The 1964 St. Louis Cardinals* (Lincoln: University of Nebraska Press, 2013).
Okkonen, Marc. *Baseball Memories, 1930–1939* (New York: Sterling, 1994).
Okrent, Daniel, and Harris Lewine, eds. *Ultimate Baseball Book* (Boston: Houghton Mifflin, 1991).
Olson, Audrey L. *St. Louis Germans, 1850–1920* (New York: Arno Press, 1980).
Pearson, Daniel. *Baseball in 1889: Players versus Owners* (Bowling Green, OH: Bowling Green State University Popular Press, 1993).
Peterson, Charles. *Colonial St. Louis: Building a Creole Capital* (Tuscon, AZ: Patrice Press, 1992).
Peterson, Richard, ed. *St. Louis Baseball Reader* (Columbia: University of Missouri Press, 2006).
Pietrusza, David. *Judge and Jury: The Life and Times of Judge Kenesaw Mountain Landis* (South Bend, IN: Diamond Communications, Inc., 1998).
_____. *Major Leagues: The Formation, Sometimes Absorption, and Mostly Inevitable Demise of Eighteen Professional Organizations, 1871 to Present* (Jefferson, NC: McFarland, 1991).
Pona, Steve. ed. *Chris Von der Ahe: Case for Hall of Fame Consideration* (St. Louis: Saint Louis Baseball Historical Society, 2015).
Porter, David L., ed. *Biographical Dictionary of American Sports: Baseball* (New York: Greenwood Press, 1987).
Powers, Jimmy. *Baseball Personalities: The Most Colorful Figures of All Time* (New York: Rudolph Field, 1949).
Primm, James Neal. *Lion of the Valley: St. Louis, Missouri, 1764–1980*, 3d ed (St. Louis: Missouri Historical Society Press, 1998).
Quirk, Charles E., ed. *Sports and the Law: Major Legal Cases* (New York: Garland, 1996).
Rader, Benjamin C. *Baseball: A History of America's Game* (Urbana: University of Illinois Press, 1992).
Rains, Rob. *Taking Flight: St. Louis Cardinals and the Building of America's Best Franchise* (Chicago: Triumph Books, 2016).
_____, and Alvin Reid. *Whitey's Boys: A Celebration of the '82 Cards World Championship* (Chicago: Triumph Books, 2002).
Rammelkamp, Julian S. *Pulitzer's Post-Dispatch, 1878–1883* (Princeton, NJ: Princeton University Press, 1967).
Reidenbaugh, Lowell. *Baseball's Hall of Fame: Cooperstown, Where the Legends Live Forever* (New York: Gramercy Books, 1999).
_____, ed. *The Sporting News' First Hundred Years* (St. Louis: Sporting News, 1985).
_____. *The Sporting News Selects Baseball's 25 Greatest Pennant Races* (St. Louis: Sporting News, 1987).
_____. *The Sporting News Selects Baseball's 25 Greatest Teams* (St. Louis: Sporting News, 1988).
_____. *The Sporting News' Take Me Out to the Ballpark* (St. Louis: Sporting News, 1982).
Reynolds, John. *Pioneer History of Illlinois: Containing the Discovery in 1673, and the*

Bibliography

History of the Country to 1818, When the State Government was Organized (Chicago: Fergus Printing Company, 1887).
Riess, Steven A. *Touching Base: Professional Baseball and American Culture in the Progressive Era* (Westport, CT: Greenwood Press, 1980).
_____, ed. *Encyclopedia of Major League Baseball Clubs*, 2 vols. (Westport, CT: Greenwood Press, 2006).
Ritter, Lawrence S. *The Glory of Their Times: The Story of the Early Days of Baseball Told by the Men Who Played It* (New York: Macmillan, 1966).
Rodgers, Daniel T. *Work Ethic in Industrial America: 1850–1920* (Chicago: University of Chicago Press, 1971).
Ryczek, William J. *Blackguards and Red Stockings: A History of Baseball's National Association, 1871–1875* (Jefferson, NC: McFarland, 1992).
Rygelski, James, and Robert L. Tiemann. *10 Rings: Stories of the St. Louis Cardinals World Championships* (St. Louis: Reedy Press, 2011).
Schoendienst, Red, with Rob Rains. *Red: A Baseball Life* (Champagne, IL: Sports Publishing, 1998).
Seymour, Harold, and Dorothy Seymour Mills. *Baseball: The Early Years* (New York: Oxford University Press, 1989).
_____, and _____. *Baseball: The Golden Age* (New York: Oxford University Press, 1971).
Shapiro, Milton. *Dizzy Dean Story* (New York: J. Messner, 1963).
Simon, Tom, ed. *Deadball Stars of the National League* (Washington, D.C.: Brassey's, 2004).
Slaughter, Enos, with Kevin Reid. *Country Hardball: The Autobiography of Enos "Country" Slaughter* (Greensboro, NC: Tudor, 1991).
Smith, Curt. *America's Dizzy Dean* (St. Louis: Bethany Press, 1978).
_____. *Voices of the Game: The First Full-Scale Overview of Baseball Broadcasting, 1921 to the Present* (South Bend, IN: Diamond Communications, 1987).
Smith, Don. *Glory Years of Baseball* (New York: Stadia Sports Publishing, 1972).
Smith, Ozzie, with Rob Rains. *Wizard* (Chicago: Contemporary Books, 1988).
Smith, Red. *Red Smith on Baseball: The Game's Greatest Writer on the Game's Greatest Years* (Chicago: Ivan R. Dee, 2000).
_____. *The Red Smith Reader* (New York: Vintage Books, 1982).
_____. *Strawberries in Winter Time: The Sporting World of Red Smith* (New York: Quadrangle/New York Times, 1974).
_____. *To Absent Friends from Red Smith* (New York: Atheneum, 1982).
Smith, Robert. *Baseball* (New York: Simon & Schuster, 1947).
_____. *Baseball in America* (New York: Holt, Rinehart, and Winston, 1963).
_____. *Baseball in the Afternoon: Tales from a Bygone Era* (New York: Simon & Schuster, 1993).
_____. *An Illustrated History of Baseball* (New York: Grossett and Dunlap, 1973).
Smith, Ron. *The Sporting News Selects Baseball's 100 Greatest Players* (St. Louis: Sporting News, 1998).
Snyder, Brad. *A Well-Paid Slave: Curt Flood's Fight for Free Agency in Professional Sports* (New York: Viking Penguin, 2000).
Spalding, Albert G. *America's National Game* (New York: American Sports, 1911).
Spink, Alfred H. *National Game* (St. Louis: National Game, 1910).
Spink, J. G. Taylor. *Judge Landis and Twenty-five Years of Baseball* (New York: Thomas Y. Crowell, 1947).
Sports Illustrated, Special Collector's Edition: St. Louis Cardinals World Champions 2011 (New York: Time, 2011).
Staten, Vince. *Ol' Diz: A Biography of Dizzy Dean* (New York: HarperCollins, 1992).
Steinberg, Steve. *Baseball in St. Louis, 1900–1925* (Chicago: Arcadia Publishing, 2004).
Stockton, J. Roy. *Gas House Gang and a Couple of Other Guys* (New York: A. S. Barnes, 1945).

Bibliography

Suehsdorf, A.D. *Great American Baseball Scrapbook* (New York: Rutledge, 1978).
Thorn, John. *A Century of Baseball Lore* (New York: Galahad, 1980).
_____. *The National Pastime* (New York: Warner, 1987).
_____, and John Holway. *The Pitcher* (New York: Prentice Hall, 1987).
_____, and Pete Palmer, eds. *Total Baseball*, 2d ed. (New York: Warner, 1991).
_____, and _____, eds. *Total Baseball*, 3d ed. (New York: Harper Perennial, 1993).
_____, _____, Michael Gershman, and David Pietrusza, eds. *Total Baseball*, 6th ed. (New York: Total Sports, 1999).
Tiemann, Robert L. *Cardinal Classics: Outstanding Games from Each of the St. Louis Baseball Club's 100 Seasons, 1882–1981* (St. Louis: Baseball Histories, 1982).
_____, ed. *St. Louis's Favorite Sport: Convention Brochure of the 22nd National SABR Convention* (Cleveland: Society for American Baseball Research, 1992).
Turner, Frederick Jackson. *Frontier in American History* (New York: Henry Holt, 1920).
Tygiel, Jules. *Baseball's Great Experiment: Jackie Robinson and His Legacy* (New York: Vintage Books, 1984).
Van Ravensway, Charles. *St. Louis: An Informal History of the City and Its People, 1764–1865* (St. Louis: Missouri Historical Society Press, 1991).
Voigt, David Q. *America Through Baseball* (Chicago: Nelson-Hall, 1976).
_____. *American Baseball*, 3 vols. (University Park: Pennsylvania State University Press, 1983).
_____. *Baseball: An Illustrated History* (University Park: Pennsylvania State University Press, 1987).
Wade, Richard C. *Urban Frontier: The Rise of Western Cities, 1790–1830* (Cambridge, MA: Harvard University Press, 1959).
Walker, James. *Crack of the Bat: A History of Baseball on the Radio* (Lincoln: University of Nebraska Press, 2015).
Walker, Robert Harris. *Cincinnati and the Big Red Machine* (Bloomington: Indiana University Press, 1988).
Wallop, Douglas. *Baseball: An Informal History* (New York: W. W. Norton, 1969).
Ward, Geoffry C., and Ken Burns. *Baseball: An Illustrated History* (New York: Alfred A. Knopf, 1994).
Washburne, E. B. *Henry Gratiot: A Pioneer of Wisconsin* (Chicago: Fergus Printing Company, 1884).
Weiss, Stuart L. *Curt Flood Story: The Man Behind the Myth* (Columbia: University of Missouri Press, 2007).
Wolff, Rick, ed. *Baseball Encyclopedia*, 8th ed. (New York: Macmillan, 1990).

Articles

Anderson, David W. "Don Gutteridge," https://sabr.org/bioproject.
Armour, Mark. "Chief Wilson," https://sabr.org/bioproject.
_____. "Orlando Cepeda," https://sabr.org/bioproject.
_____."Sam Breadon,' https://sabr.org/bioproject.
Ayers, Thomas. "Bill DeLancey," https://sabr.org/bioproject.
Baldassaro, Lawrence,. "Ernie Orsatti," https://sabr.org/bioproject.
_____. "Tony La Russa," https://sabr.org/bioproject.
Berger, Ralph. "Paul Derringer," www.bioproj.sabr.org.
Boxerman, Burton. "Ken Boyer," https://sabr.org/bioproject.
_____. "Kenton Lloyd Boyer," in Lawrence O. Christensen et al., eds. *Dictionary of Missouri Biography*.
Bridgewater, B. A. "Telling the World of Sports," *Tulsa World*, February 8, 1949.
Broeg, Bob. "The Mystery of Stan Musial," *Saturday Evening Post*, May 1, 1954.

Bibliography

Buck, Jack. "A Changing World" and "Whitey and the 1980s," in Buck. *That's a Winner.*
Carlson, Stan N. "St. Louis Cardinals: Baseball's Perennial Gas House Gang," in Peter C. Bjarkman, ed. *Encyclopedia of Major League Baseball Teams: National League.*
Carrello, Tommy. "Dots Miller," https://sabr.org/bioproject.
Carter, Gregg Lee. "Baseball in St. Louis, 1867–1875: An Historical Case Study in Civic Pride," *Bulletin of the Missouri Historical Society* (July 1975).
Cash, J.D. "Origins—The Spirit of St. Louis in the History of Professional Baseball: May 4–8, 1875," *Gateway Heritage: Quarterly Magazine of the Missouri Historical Society* (Spring 1995).
Cash, Jon David. "Chris Von der Ahe, the American Association versus National League Cultural War, and the Rise of Major League Baseball," *Missouri Historical Review* (October 2014).
_____. "Christian Frederick Wilhelm Von der Ahe," in Lawrence O. Christensen et al., eds. *Dictionary of Missouri Biography.*
_____. "St. Louis Cardinals," in Steven A. Riess, ed. *Encyclopedia of Major League Baseball Clubs: National League.*
Christensen, Lawrence O. "August A. Busch, Jr.," in Christensen et al., eds. *Dictionary of Missouri Biography.*
Corbett, Warren. "Bill McKechnie," https://sabr.org/bioproject.
_____. "Bill White," https://sabr.org/bioproject.
_____. "Eddie Dyer," www.bioproj.sabr.org.
_____. "Harry Walker," https://sabr.org/bioproject.
_____. "Howie Pollet," https://sabr.org/bioproject.
_____. "Jimmy Brown," https://sabr.org/bioproject.
_____. "Joe Garagiola," https://sabr.org/bioproject.
_____. "Marty Marion," https://sabr.org/bioproject.
_____. "Terry Moore," https://sabr.org/bioproject.
_____. "Tommy Thevenow," https://sabr.org/bioproject.
Costello, Rory. "John Tudor," https://sabr.org/bioproject.
Daley, Jon. "Billy Southworth." www.bioproj.sabr.org.
Devine, Bing, with Tom Wheatley. "1964: Bittersweet Season,' in Devine. *Memoirs of Bing Devine: Stealing Lou Brock and Other Winning Moves by a Master GM.*
Donovan, Loretta, "Dal Maxvill," https://sabr.org/bioproject.
Ekberg, Carl J. and William E. Foley. "Nicolas de Finiels," in Christensen et al., eds. *Dictionary of Missouri Biography.*
Erion, Greg. "Chick Hafey." www.bioproj.sabr.org.
_____. Dick Sisler," https://sabr.org/bioproject.
Faber, Charles F. "Allen Sothoron." www.bioproj.sabr.org.
_____. "Burleigh Grimes." www.bioproj.sabr.org.
_____. "Joe Medwick." https://sabr.org/bioproject.
_____. "Ozzie Smith," https://sabr.org/bioproject.
Findling, J. E. "The Louisville Grays' Scandal of 1877," *Journal of Sport History* (Summer 1976).
Finkel, Jan. "Pete Alexander." www.bioproj.sabr.org.
_____. "Stan Musial." www.bioproj.sabr.org.
Fischer, E. G. "Billy Southworth's St. Louis Swifties," in Robert L. Tiemann, ed. *St. Louis's Favorite Sport: Convention Brochure of the 22nd National SABR Convention.*
Fleitz, David. "Jake Beckley," https://sabr.org/bioproject.
Frisch, Frank, and J. Roy Stockton. "The Gas House Gang." *Saturday Evening Post,* July 4, 1936.
_____, and Charles Dexter. "The Gas House Gang and II," *Saturday Evening Post,* July 18, 1959.
Fuqua, John. "Johnny Beazley." www.bioproj.sabr.org.
Geisler, Paul, Jr. "Julian Javier," https://sabr.org/bioproject.

Bibliography

_____. "Paul Dean," https://sabr.org/bioproject.
Gillespie, Ray. "Ray Blades to Set Up 'Honor System,' Bar All Drinking in Carrying Out Rickey Policies as Cardinal Manager," St. Louis Star-Times, 1938, www.carolyar.com.
Goldfarb, Irv. "Charles Comiskey," https://sabr.org/bioproject.
Gordon, Peter M. "Mike Mowrey," https://sabr.org/bioproject.
Green, John. "Andy High." www.bioproj.sabr.org.
Greene, Bob. "Where Has Baseball Gone Wrong? Ask Bill and Enos," *Chicago Tribune*, April 8, 1996.
Griffith, Nancy Snell. "Flint Rhem," https://sabr.org/bioproject.
Grillo, Jerry. "Johnny Mize." www.bioproj.sabr.org.
Halper, Donna L. "Chris Carpenter," https://sabr.org/bioproject.
Hannon, Robert E. "A Century of Baseball," *St. Louis Commerce* (May, 1966).
Honig, Donald. "Les Bell," in Honig. *The October Heroes.*
Johnson, Bill. "Jim Bottomley," https://sabr.org/bioproject.
Jones, David. "Jesse Burkett," https://sabr.org/bioproject.
Karst, Gene. "The Cardinals' First Publicity Man," in Robert L. Tiemann, ed. *St. Louis's Favorite Sport: Convention Brochure of the 22nd National SABR Convention.*
Kates, Maxwell. "Ron Taylor," https://sabr.org/bioproject.
Katz, Fred. "Life with the Cardinals," *Sport,* July 1968.
Kermisch, Al. "The First World Series," In John Thorn. *The National Pastime.*
King, Norm. "Bruce Sutter," https://sabr.org/bioproject.
_____. "Pepper Martin," https://sabr.org/bioproject.
Lampe, Anthony B. "Background of Professional Baseball in St. Louis," *Bulletin of the Missouri Historical Society* (October 1950).
Lethart, Patrick. "Jim Kaat," https://sabr.org/bioproject.
Leydon, Dick. "Rabbit Maranville," https://sabr.org/bioproject.
Livacari, Gary. "Jimmie Wilson," https://sabr.org/bioproject.
Lokemoen, Kristin. "Red Schoendienst," https://sabr.org/bioproject.
Lynch, Mike. "Austin McHenry," https://sabr.org/bioproject.
MacGregor, David. "Doug Bair," https://sabr.org/bioproject.
Marlett, Jeffrey. "Leo Durocher," https://sabr.org/bioproject.
Martell, Michael. "Keith Hernandez," https://sabr.org/bioproject.
Martin, Robert F. "Sports versus the Sabbath: Professional Baseball and Blue Laws," in Charles E. Quirk, ed. *Sports and the Law: Major Legal Cases.*
McCann, Kevin. "Mike Shannon," https://sabr.org/bioproject.
McClure, Arthur F. and Vivian Richardson. "Wesley Branch Rickey," in Lawrence O. Christensen et al., eds. *Dictionary of Missouri Biography.*
McCue, Andy. "Branch Rickey," https://sabr.org/bioproject.
McKenna, Brian. "Helene Britton versus Roger Bresnahan." www.baseball-fever.com.
Melton, John E. "James Leroy Bottomley," in Lawrence O. Christensen et al., eds. *Dictionary of Missouri Biography.*
Murphy, Justin. "Ray Sadecki," https://sabr.org/bioproject.
Nowlin, Bill. "Charley Gelbert," https://sabr.org/bioproject.
_____. "Jack Rothrock." https://sabr.org/bioproject.
O'Brien, Dan. "Rube Waddell," https://sabr.org/bioproject.
O'Connor, W. J. "Miller Huggins Wins Recognition as Great Pilot," *Pittsburgh Press,* August 22, 1914.
Pereira, Paul. "Ray Sanders." www.bioproj.sabr.org.
Rice, Stepehn V. "George Harper," https://sabr.org/bioproject.
Richard, Mike. "Ernie White." www.bioproj.sabr.org.
Rogers III, C Paul. "Burgess Whitehead," https://sabr.org/bioproject.
_____ "Rogers Hornsby," https://sabr.org/bioproject.
Rygelski, Jim. "Baseball's 'Boss President': Chris Von der Ahe and the Nineteenth-Century

Bibliography

St. Louis Browns," *Gateway Heritage: Quarterly Magazine of the Missouri Historical Society* (Summer 1992).
Sallee, Eric, and Paul Sallee. "Ed Konetchy," www.bioproj.sabr.org.
_____. "Slim Sallee," https://sabr.org/bioproject.
_____. "Steve Evans," https://sabr.org/bioproject.
Sandweiss, Eric. "Grover Cleveland Alexander," in Lawrence O. Christensen et al., eds. *Dictionary of Missouri Biography*.
Schul, Scott. "Bobby Wallace," https://sabr.org/bioproject.
Seymour, Harold. "St. Louis and the Union Baseball War," *Missouri Historical Review* (April 1957).
Shedden, David. "The First Televised World Series Game," Sept. 30, 2014, https://www.poynter.org/. Accessed 12/21/2018.
Sher, Jack. "Dizzy Dean: The One and Only," *Sport Magazine*, May 1948.
_____. "The Ups and Downs of Old Pete," *Sport Magazine*, April 1950.
Silverman, Al. "Ol' Diz," in Charles Edison, ed. *The Fireside Book of Baseball*.
Sloope, Terry. "Bob Gibson," https://sabr.org/bioproject.
_____. "Curt Flood," https://sabr.org/bioproject.
Smith, Curt. "Dizzy Dean Easily Hall's Best Broadcast Choice," February 15, 2006, http://curtsmith.mlblogs.com/, Accessed 12/21/2018.
Smith, Jeffrey E. "Jay Hanna 'Dizzy' Dean," in Lawrence O. Christensen et al., eds. *Dictionary of Missouri Biography*.
_____. "Rogers Hornsby," in Lawrence O. Christensen et al., eds. *Dictionary of Missouri Biography*.
Smith, Red. "Dizzy Dean's Day," *St. Louis Star*, October 1, 1934, also included in *Red Smith Reader*.
_____. "Pepper Martin vs. Philadelphia, 1931," in Daniel Okrent and Harris Lewine, eds. *Ultimate Baseball Book*.
_____. "Sam Breadon," *New York Herald-Tribune*, April 22, 1949.
_____. "Tomorrow in Brooklyn," *New York Herald-Tribune*, September 26, 1950.
Snodgrass, Michael, R. "Charles James 'Chick' Hafey," in Lawrence O. Christensen et al., eds. *Dictionary of Missouri Biography*.
Spink, Alfred H. "Al Spink, Writing in 1921, Gave Graphic Picture of Comiskey as Player and Manager," *Sporting News*, Oct. 29, 1931.
_____. "Chris Von der Ahe," in Spink. *National Game*.
Spink, J. G. Taylor. "Landis—the Great Emancipator," in Spink, J. G. Taylor. *Judge Landis and Twenty-five Years of Baseball*.
Sporting News. "We Gave 'Em the Goose," October 30, 1886.
Stahl, John. "Barney Schultz," https://sabr.org/bioproject.
_____. "Johnny Keane," https://sabr.org/bioproject.
_____. "Nelson Briles," https://sabr.org/bioproject.
Stein, Fred. "Frankie Frisch," www.bioproj.sabr.org.
Steinberg, Steve. "Bill Doak," https://sabr.org/bioproject.
_____. "Miller Huggins." https://sabr.org/bioproject.
Stockton, J. Roy. "Pepper Martin, World Series Sensation, Tells How He Does It," *St. Louis Post-Dispatch*, October 8, 1931.
_____. "St. Louis Cardinals," In Ed Fitzgerald, ed. *National League*.
Story, Ronald. "The Country of the Young: The Meaning of Baseball in Early American Culture," in Alvin L. Hall, ed. *Cooperstown Symposium on Baseball and the American Culture (1989)*.
Strauss, Joe. "11th Heaven: Wild Cards Win World Series," *St. Louis Post-Dispatch*, October 29, 2011.
Sullivan, Margaret Lo Piccolo. "St. Louis Ethnic Neighborhoods, 1850–1930," *Bulletin of the Missouri Historical Society* 33, no. 2 (January 1977).
Swaine, Rick. "Whitey Kurowski," www.bioproj.sabr.org.

Bibliography

Thomas, Joan M,. "Frank Robison," https://sabr.org/bioproject.
_____. "Helene Britton," https://sabr.org/bioproject.
_____. "Roger Bresnahan," https://sabr.org/bioproject.
_____. "Stanley Robison," https://sabr.org/bioproject.
Time. "The Kids," October 12, 1942.
Tobias, E. H. "Series on Early Baseball in St. Louis," *Sporting News,* October 26, 1895– February 15, 1896.
Turner, Frederick Jackson. "The Middle West," in Turner. *Frontier in American History.*
Vasey, Glen. "Danny Litwhiler," www.bioproj.sabr.org.
Veit, Edward. "Curt Simmons," https://sabr.org/bioproject.
Vitty, Cort. "Ripper Collins," https://sabr.org/bioproject.
Vivance, Corme. "Steve Carlton," www.bioproj.sabr.org.
Walker, James. "The Humble (Ad-Free!) Origins of the First World Series Broadcasts," *The Conversation,* October 27, 2015.
Wancho, Joseph. "Bake McBride," https://sabr.org/bioproject.
_____. "Bob O'Farrell," https://sabr.org/bioproject.
_____. "Dick Groat," https://sabr.org/bioproject.
_____. "Dizzy Dean," https://sabr.org/bioproject.
_____. "Enos Slaughter," www.bioproj.saabr.org.
_____. "Gabby Street," https://sabr.org/bioproject.
_____. "George Hendrick," https://sabr.org/bioproject.
Watkins, John J. "George Watkins," https://sabr.org/bioproject.
Wicker, Tom. "Enos Slaughter, on His Toes," in Daniel Okrent and Harris Lewine, eds. *Ultimate Baseball Book.*
Williams, Dave. "Lou Brock," https://sabr.org/bioproject.
_____. "Tim McCarver," https://sabr.org/bioproject.
_____. "Yogi Berra," https://sabr.org/bioproject.
Williams, Phil. "Rebel Oakes," https://sabr.org/bioproject.
Wolf, Gregory H. "Bill Hallahan," https://sabr.org/bioproject.
_____. "Bill Sherdel," https://sabr.org/bioproject.
_____ "Harry Brecheen," https://sabr.org/bioproject.
_____. "Jesse Haines," https://sabr.org/bioproject.
_____. "Max Lanier," https://sabr.org/bioproject.
_____. "Mort Cooper," https://sabr.org/bioproject.
_____. "Pat Crawford," https://sabr.org/bioproject.
Wolinsky, Russell. "Ray Blades," https://sabr.org/bioproject.

Sporting News Files

Dean, Paul.
Martin, Pepper.

Interviews and/or Correspondence

Crawford, Pat. Correspondence 1987-1989, Interviewed 1987.
Kirby, Gene. Interviewed by Paul MacFarlane of *The Sporting News,* 1986.
Martin, Stu. Interviewed 1991.
Slaughter, Enos "Country." Interviewed 1991.
Whitehead, Burgess "Whitey." Correspondence 1987, Interviewed 1991.

Bibliography

Websites

www.baseball-reference.com.
www.baseball-reference.com/boxes/
www.bioproj.sabr.org.
www.thisgameofgames.com/
www.youtube.com.

Videos

YouTube, Classic Baseball on the Radio, 1934 World Series, Game 1.
YouTube, MLB, 'Cardinals win the 1982 World Series."

Index

Aaron, Hank 97
Abell, Ferdinand 34
Adams, Sparky 73–74, 79, 84
Alexander, Grover Cleveland 63, 64, 66, 67, 74
Alston, Tom 122
American Association (AA): consolidation with National League 37–39; cultural war with National League 29–37; formation 17–28, 29
American League (AL): Agreement with NL 43; formation 40; surpasses attendance of NL in 1901–1902 41–43; National takes over lease of original Sportsman's Park on Grand Avenue 41; St. Louis Browns move to Baltimore and become the Orioles 59, 121; transfers Milwaukee franchise to St. Louis 41
American Tobacco Company 78
Andujar, Joaquin 137, 138
Anheuser-Busch 22, 121, 124, 138, 142–143, 146
Arizona Diamondbacks (NL): in 2002–2002 NLDS with Cardinals 145
Arroyo, Luis 122
Associated Press 116
Atlanta Braves: in 1982 and 1996 NLCS with Cardinals 137, 143; in 2000 and 2019 NLDS with Cardinals 145, 156; in 2011 wild-card race with Cardinals 150–151
Averill, Earl 90

Bair, Doug 137, 138
Baker Bowl (Philadelphia) 64–65, 76
Ball, Phil 19, 50, 52, 58, 72, 121
Baltimore baseball teams: in American League until franchise transfers to New York 40; Baltimore investors buy St. Louis Browns from Bill Veeck and turn them into Baltimore Orioles in 1954, 59, 121; consolidates with National League 38; in formation of American Association 27–28; loses franchise when NL downsizes 40
Barrett, Red 107
"Baseball like It Oughta Be" 143
Bauer, Andrew 22, 142–143
Beaumont High School (St. Louis): 19, 54
Beazley, Johnny 99, 100, 101, 102
Beckley, Jake 45
Bell, Gary 131
Bell, Les 57, 60, 61, 62, 63, 65, 67, 71
Belliard, Ronnie 148
Beltran, Carlos 148
Berkman, Lance 150, 152–153
Berra, Yogi 110
Bishop, C. Orrick 25
Bishop, Max 79
Black Patch War (1904–1908) 78
Blades, Ray 52, 62, 63, 94
Blake, Sherriff 64
Blasingame, Don 122
Block, David (*Baseball Before We Knew It*) 10
Bonds, Barry 144
Book-Cadillac Hotel (Detroit) 88
Boston baseball teams: in American Association 37; in American League 40; Boston Red Sox (AL) in World Series of 1946, 1967, 2004, and 2013 with Cardinals 115–116, 131–132, 146, 155; in consolidation of National League and American Association 38; in formation of National League 25; NL Braves lure Billy Southworth from Cardinals with a lucrative contract to manage them 108; Southworth's Braves defeat Brooklyn Dodgers on last day of 1946 season to help Cardinals ultimately win NL pennant 114–115; Southworth's Braves win 1948 NL pennant over Cardinals 118;

Index

wins 1914 NL pennant and World Series over Philadelphia Athletics 50
Bottomley, Sunny Jim 56, 62, 65, 71, 76, 82, 83, 110
Bowman, Bob 95
Boyer, Ken 122, 123–124, 125, 126, 127, 129, 135, 136
Bradford, William 9
Brazle, Al 115
Breadon, Sam 19, 20, 51, 53–54, 56, 67–68, 69, 70, 77, 86, 87, 89, 94, 103, 107, 108, 109, 114, 116–117, 120
Brecheen, Harry "The Cat" 105, 106, 115, 116
Bresnahan, Roger 19, 48–49
breweries: in Cincinnati 27; in Milwaukee 138; in St. Louis 27, 138
Briles, Nelson 131
Britton, Helene Robison 19, 45, 47, 48, 49, 51, 53
Brock, Lou 21, 125, 126, 127, 130, 131, 132, 133, 134, 136, 156
Broglio, Ernie 125
Brooklyn baseball teams: in consolidation of National League and American Association 38; defeat New York Giants twice on last weekend of 1934 season to help Cardinals win NL pennant 87; joins American Association 30; jumps to National League 34; in National League pennant races of 1930, 1941, 1942, 1946, 1947, and 1949 with Cardinals 75–77, 97, 99–100, 114–115, 118Brotherhood of Professional Baseball Players 35, 37
Brown, Jimmy 93, 96, 99, 102, 109
Brush, John 35, 37
Buck, Jack 138, 145
Burkett, Jesse "The Crab" 41
Busch, August III 139, 142
Busch, Gussie 15, 20, 21, 22, 120, 121, 122, 123, 124, 126, 127, 128, 130–131, 133, 136, 139, 140
Busch Bavarian Beer 121
Busch Memorial Stadium (home of Cardinals, 1966–2005): 1, 2, 13, 130–131, 137, 142, 143, 144, 145
Busch Stadium (current home of Cardinals since 2006): 1, 6, 12, 146, 149, 156
Byrne, Charles 34, 37

Caminiti, Ken 144
Caray, Harry 117, 123–124, 126, 127, 138
Carleton, Tex 88, 89

Carlton, Steve 21, 131, 134
Carpenter, Chris 146, 147, 148, 149, 151, 152, 153
Caylor, O.P. 26, 27, 29
Cepeda, Orlando 129, 130, 131, 132, 133, 134
Chapman, Charles E. 61
Chicago baseball teams: in American League 40; Brock gets 3000th hit vs. Cubs 136; Cardinals clinch at least a wild card in 2019 playoffs with four-game sweep of Cubs at Wrigley Field 155–156; Chicago White Stockings (NL) in World Series of 1885–1886 with St. Louis Browns (AA) 30–32; in consolidation of National League and American Association 38; Cubs lose on last day of 1942 season to Cardinals who clinch NL pennant 100; Cubs trade Lou Brock to Cardinals in 1964 125; in development of baseball 23; in formation of National League 24–25; in National Association 23–24; in National League pennant races of 1930 and 1935 with Cardinals 75–77, 89–90; Stan Musial gets 3000th hit vs. Cubs 123
Chicago News 32
Chicago Tribune 26, 28
Chouteau, Auguste 2, 3–4, 7
Cincinnati baseball teams: in consolidation of National League and American Association 38; in development of baseball 23; expelled from National League 26; in formation of American Association 27–28, 29; in formation of National League 25; jumps to National League 34; in National League pennant races in 1926 and 1964 with Cardinals 63–65, 126
Cincinnati Enquirer 26
Civic Center Redevelopment Corporation 130
Civilian Conservation Corps (CCC) 112
Clark, George Rogers 7
Clark, Jack 22, 138–139, 140
Clayton, Royce 143
Clemente, Roberto 131
Cleveland baseball teams: in consolidation of National League and American Association 38; joins American Association 34; jumps to National League 34; Robison brothers transfer their best players from Cleveland to St. Louis 41
Cochran, Mickey 78, 79

192

Index

Cody, Buffalo Bill 30, 62
Coleman, Vince 138, 139
Collins, Ripper 77, 83, 86, 88, 110
Combs, Earle 67
Comiskey, Charles 30, 31, 36, 37, 38, 39–40, 41
Connery, Bob 57
Cooper, Mort 95, 96, 99–100, 102–103, 104, 106, 107, 108, 109, 115
Cooper, Walker 95, 96, 98, 101, 102–103, 107, 108, 109, 110, 118
Cotard, Francois 6
Cox, Danny 139
Crabtree, Estel 96
Craig, Allen 151, 153
Crawford, Pat x, 88, 100
Crespi, Frank "Creepy" 96, 99
Cruz, Nelson 152
Cunningham, Joe 122
Cupples Station 1

Daniel, Dan 89
Dark, Alvin 122
Davis, Curt 90, 95
Davis, Spud 71, 84
Dawson, James 102
Dayley, Ken 139
Dean, Albert Monroe 86
Dean, Dizzy 15, 76, 82, 83, 86, 87, 88, 89, 90, 93, 100–101, 117, 119
Dean, Paul 82, 85, 86–87, 88, 89, 90
DeLancey, Bill 84, 85, 93–94
Del Greco, Bobby 122
Delker, Eddie 74
Derringer, Paul 77–78, 84
Descalso, Daniel 150
Detroit baseball teams: Tigers (AL) in World Series of 1934, 1968, and 2006 with Cardinals 87–89, 132, 148–150; Wolverines (NL) in 1887 World Series with St. Louis Browns (AA) 20–31
Devine, Bing 20, 21, 123, 125, 127, 128, 133
DeWitt, William, Jr. 22, 142–143
Dickson, Murry 115
DiMaggio, Joe 102, 145
Doak, "Spittin Bill" 49
Doerr, Bobby 116
Dolan, Cozy 49
Dotel, Octavio 152
Douthit, Taylor 57, 61, 62, 64–65, 71, 76, 78
Dreyfuss, Barney 20, 58–59
Duke, James 78

Durocher, Leo 84, 86, 88, 93, 95, 114, 127
Dusak, Erv "Four-Sack" 111, 114
Dyer, Eddie 108, 109

Earnshaw, George 77, 78, 79
Ebbets Field (Brooklyn) 75–76, 95, 99, 114, 115
Eckstein, David 149, 150
Edmonds, Jim 148, 149
Evans, Steve 48, 49

farm system 20, 54–55, 58–59, 81; "force-feeding" plan of 1954–1955 122, 123, 137, 150
Ferris, Boo 115
Finiels, Nicolas de 4, 6
Flood, Curt 124, 129, 131, 132, 134, 142
Ford, Whitey 127
Ford Motor Company 87
Forsch, Bob 139
Fort Smith (Ark.) farm club 20, 55, 61
Fowle, Charles 25
Foxx, Jimmie 77
Freese, David 151, 152, 153
Frick, Ford 1, 102
Frisch, Frank 69, 70, 71, 76, 79, 82, 83, 84, 86, 87, 90, 92, 93, 94
Furcal, Rafael 151

Galehouse, Denny 104, 106
Garagiola, Joe 109, 110, 115
Garcia, Jaime 151, 152
"Gas House Gang" origins of nickname 86, 88, 89; in Cardinals history 153–154
Gehrig, Lou 72
Gelbert, Charley 74, 76, 78, 84
Gibson, Bob 21, 118, 119, 124, 126, 127, 131, 132, 133
Gilkey, Bernard 141
Goldschmidt, Paul 155
"Good Old Mountain Music" 102
Gotay, Julio 125
Gould, Jim 67
Graham, Frank 102
Grand Avenue Park (St. Louis) 23–24, 27
Gratiot, Charles 7
Gratiot, Henry 6, 7–8, 10, 11, 12
Gratiot, Victoire Laclede 7
Grimes, Burleigh 75, 76, 77, 78, 79, 81
Grimm, Charley 93
Groat, Dick 125, 129
Grove, Lefty 77, 78, 79
Gumbert, Harry "Gunboat" 98, 99
Gutteridge, Don 93

193

Index

Hafey, Chick 57, 61, 62, 63, 71, 81, 83
Haines, Jesse 55, 66, 75, 76, 77, 101
Haley, Martin J. 100
Hallahan, "Wild Bill" 75–76, 77, 78, 79, 88
Hannegan, Robert 20, 119
Harmon, Bob 49
Harper, George Washington 71, 72, 74
Harrison, Matt 152
Hartford baseball team: in formation of National League 25; resigns from National League (1877) 25–26
"Harvey's Wallbangers" 137
Hedges, Robert Lee 47, 50, 52
Hemus, Solly 124
Henderson, Robert (*Ball, Bat, and Bishop*) 10
Hendrick, George 137, 138
Hernandez, Keith 136, 137, 138
Herr, Tommy 137, 139
Herzog, Whitey 15, 21, 98, 135, 136, 137, 138, 139, 140
High, Andy 71, 73, 76, 79, 81, 82, 85
Holliday, Matt 150–151
Hoover, Herbert 78
Hopp, Johnny 96, 98, 99, 102–103, 105, 110, 111
Hornsby, Rogers 56–58, 60, 61, 62, 64, 67
Houston (Tex.) farm club 20, 55, 60, 61, 62, 83
Houston Astros: lose on last day of 2011 season to Cardinals who clinch wild-card in playoffs 151; in NL Central Division race of 2006 with Cardinals 146–148; in NLCS of 2004–2005 with Cardinals 145–146
Howsam, Bob 21, 128, 129–130, 132–133, 135
Hrabosky, Al 135
Huggins, Miller 48, 49, 50, 51, 53, 57
Hughson, Tex 115
Hulbert, William 25–26, 28, 29, 34. 39
Hunt, Theodore 6–7
Hutchinson, Fred 122, 124

Illinois Territory 9
Inge, Brandon 150
Isringhausen, Jason 147

Jackson, Edwin 151
Jackson, Larry 122
Jacksonville (Fl.) farm club 125–126
Jakucki, Sig 105

Javier, Julian 124, 125, 132
Jay, Jon 151
Jefferson National Expansion Memorial (Gateway Arch) 1, 3, 130
Jocketty, Walt 145
Johnson, Ban 40, 41, 43
Jones, James 51, 52–53
Jordan, Brian 141
Jorgenson, Mike 142

Kaat, Jim 138
Kansas City baseball teams: in American Association 34; Kansas City Royals (AL) in controversial 1985 World Series with Cardinals 139; in National League 34
Karst, Gene 86
Keane, Johnny 20, 124, 125, 126, 127, 128
Kile, Darryl 145
Kimbrel, Craig 150, 151
Kiner, Ralph 145
Klein, Lou 112
Klinger, Bob 116
Kluttz, Clyde 110
Koenig, Mark 67
Konetchy, Ed 48, 49
Koy, Ernie 96
Kramer, Jack 105
Kranepool, Ed 126
Kremer, Ray 64
Krist, Howie 99
Kuenn, Harvey 137
Kuhlman, Fred 22, 140
Kurowski, George "Whitey" 96, 97, 99, 100, 102–103, 115, 120

Laclede's Landing 1–2, 3
Lahti, Jeff 137
Lamp, Dennis 136
Landis, Kenesaw Mountain 20, 58–59, 89, 95, 102, 103
Lane, Frank "Trader" 112, 122, 123
Lanier, Max 94, 99–100, 101, 102–103, 105, 106, 107, 112, 113. 114
Lankford, Ray 141
LaPoint, Dave 137
La Russa, Tony 22, 141, 142, 143, 145, 146, 147, 150, 152, 153
Lawrence, Brooks 122
Lazzeri, Tony 67
League Park (St. Louis, Vandeventer Avenue and Natural Bridge Road, home of St. Louis Cardinals NL 1899–1910) 46, 47–48

194

Index

Lee, Bill 89
Lee, Cliff 151
Lewis, Lloyd 55
Liquest, Pierre Laclelde 3–4, 7
Litwhiler, Danny 106, 107, 111–112
Lohse, Kyle 151
Lonborg, Jim 131, 132
Los Angeles baseball teams: Dodgers (NL) in NLCS of 1985 and 2013 with Cardinals 138–139, 155; Dodgers (NL) in NLDs of 2004 and 2009 with Cardinals 145, 150; Angels of Anaheim (AL) sign Albert Pujols to free-agent contract 153
Louisville baseball teams: in consolidation of National League and American Association 38; in formation of American Association 27–28, 29; in formation of National League 25; resigns from National League (1877) 25–26
Lucas, Anne 6
Lucas, Jean Baptiste 2, 3, 6–7

Mack, Connie 40, 41, 77
MacPhail, Larry 95, 103
Maranville, Rabbit 70, 71, 74
Marion, Marty 94–95, 102–103, 106, 108, 120
Maris, Roger 130, 131, 132, 144
Martin, Freddie 112–113
Martin, Pepper 70, 78, 79, 86, 90, 91, 92, 93
Martin, Stu x, 93
Matheny, Mike 155
Mathewson, Christy 50, 74
Maxvill, Dal 132
Mays, Willie 97
McBride, Bake 135
McCarthy, Joe 63
McCarver, Tim 118, 125, 126, 127, 132, 134
McCullough, Clyde 100
McGee, Willie 137, 138, 139
McGoogan, W.J. 87
McGraw, John 65, 70, 72
McGwire, Mark 143–144, 145
McHenry, Austin 56
McKechnie, Bill 70, 71, 72, 73, 77
McKnight, Denny 29, 32, 33
McNamee, Graham 88
McQuinn, George 104, 106
Medwick, Joe "Ducky" 82–83, 86, 88–89, 90, 91, 95, 119
Miller, Dots 49–50

Milwaukee (Wis.) farm club 60
Milwaukee baseball teams: Braves (NL) in 1957 NL pennant race with Cardinals 123; Milwaukee Brewers (AL) in 1982 World Series with Cardinals 137–138; Brewers (AL) transfer to St. Louis and become St. Louis Browns for 1902 season 41; Brewers (NL) in 2011 NLCS with Cardinals 152; Brewers (NL) in 2019 NL Central Division race with Cardinals 155–156
Minnesota baseball team: Twins (AL) in 1987 World Series with Cardinals 139
"Miracle Cardinals of 1964" in Cardinals history 153–154
Mize, Johnny "The Big Cat" 84, 92, 97, 98, 104, 110, 118, 119
Molina, Yadier 148, 149, 150, 153, 155
Monroe, Craig 149
Moon, Wally 122
Moore, Terry 92, 96, 98, 100, 102, 107, 113, 120
Motard, Joseph 5–6, 12
Motte, Jason 150, 151, 153
Mowrey, Mike 48, 49
Mozeliak, John 150
Mullin, Willard 98
Munger, George 115
Mura, Steve 137
Murray, Red 48
Musial, Stan 1, 2, 6, 13, 21, 93, 97, 98, 99, 100, 101, 102–103, 105, 107, 110–111, 113, 114, 115, 118, 119–120 123, 124, 125, 127, 132–133

National Association (NA) 23–25
National League (NL): consolidation with American Association 37–38; cultural was with American Association 29–37; formation 24–25
Navin, Frank 20, 58–59
New York baseball teams: in American Association 30, 34; in American League (AL) 40; Cardinals clinch 1926 NL pennant with win over New York Giants 65; in consolidation of National League and American Association 38; in formation of National League 25; loses franchise in National League 25; New York Giants (NL) in 1888 World Series with St. Louis Browns (AA) 30–31; rejoins National League 30; New York Giants in NL pennant races in 1928 and 1934 with Cardinals 72, 87;

195

Index

New York Mets (NL) in NLCS of 2000 and 2006 with Cardinals, 145, 148; New York Yankees (AL) in World Series of 1926, 1928, 1942, 1943, and 1964 with Cardinals 65–67, 72, 101–102, 103, 126–127*New York Sun* 81, 102
New York Times 102, 116
New York World-Telegram 88, 89, 98

Oakes, Rebel 48, 49
Oberkfell, Ken 137
O'Dea 97–98, 104, 109
O'Farrell, Bob 62, 64, 67, 68, 69, 70, 71
Oklahoma Land Rush 78
Old Cathedral (St. Louis) 2, 3
Old Courthouse (St. Louis) 2, 3
Oquendo, Jose 139
Orsatt, Ernie "Showboat" 74, 79, 82, 86, 92
Outrigger Inn (St. Petersburg, Fl.) 124
Owen, Mickey 04, 95, 113

Pasquel, Joege 113
Pendleton, Terry 139
Pesky, Johnny 116
Philadelphia baseball teams: in American League 40–41; Athletics (AL) in World Series of 1930–1931 with Cardinals 77–80; Athletics (AL) upset in 1914 World Series by "Miracle Braves" of Boston 50; in consolidation of National League and American Association 38, 39; in formation of American Association 27–28, 29; in formation of National League 25; loses franchise in National League 25; Phillies (NL) in 1964 pennant race with Cardinals 126; Phillies (NL) in 2011 NLDS with Cardinals 151; rejoins National League 30
Pittsburgh baseball teams: in consolidation of National League and American Association 38; in formation of American Association 27–28; jumps to National League 32–35; in 1926–1927 NL pennant races with Cardinals 63–64, 69, 70
Players League (1890): demise of 37; in 1890 season 36; formation 35
poisoned ball 10
Pollet, Howie 96, 97, 99, 102, 115
Polo Grounds (New York): 65
Porter, Darrell 137
Potter, Nelson 104
Primm, James Neal 13

Pujols, Albert 145, 146, 147, 149, 150, 151, 152–153
Punto, Nick 151

Ramsey, Mike 138
Rapp, Vern 135
Raymond, Bugs 4–8
Reese, Pee Wee 15
Reichler, Joe 74
Reinhart, Art 64
Reiser, Pete 95
Reuss, Jerry 21, 134
Reyes, Anthony 147, 149
Rhem, Flint 64, 66
Rhodes, Arthur 152
Rice, Del 109, 110
Rickey, Branch 19, 51, 52–53, 54, 55, 56, 58, 70, 71, 84, 85, 91, 94, 103, 110, 114, 120
Rickey, Frank 94
Roberts, Robin 123
Robison, Frank 18–19, 41, 46, 47
Robison, Stanley 18–19, 41, 46, 47
Robison Field (St. Louis, Vandeventer Avenue and Natural Bridge Road, home of St. Louis Cardinals NL, 1911–1919) 19, 37–48, 50, 51, 54
Rochester (NY) farm club 72, 74, 77, 78
Rodney, Fernando 149
Rogell, Billy 88
Rolen, Scott 147, 148, 149, 150
Roosevelt, Franklin D. 112
Rothrock, Jack 85
Rowe, Schoolboy 88
"Runnin' Redbirds: origins of nickname 137, 139
Ruth, Babe 66, 67, 72
Rzepczynski, Marc 152

Sadecki, Ray 118, 124
Saigh, Fred 20. 119, 120
St. Joseph (Mo.) farm club 61–62
St. Louis Brown Stockings (1875–1877): in formation of National League 24–25; in National Association (1875) 23–24; resigns from National League (1877) 25–26
St. Louis Browns (1882–1899): as champions of American Association 30–32; in consolidation of National League and American Association 37–39; in formation of American Association 16–17, 27–28, 29; new owners, the Robison brothers, change team colors

196

Index

to bright-red in 1899 leading to name change to Cardinals 41; in World Series of 1885–1888 with NL champions 30–32

St. Louis Browns (AL, 1902–1953): AL Milwaukee franchise moves to St. Louis and become St. Louis Browns in 1902 41; in All-St. Louis World Series of 1944 104–106; competition with NL Cardinals for control of St. Louis 45, 46, 50–51, 58–59; sold by Bill Veeck to Baltimore investors and become Baltimore Orioles in 1954 59, 121; wins only AL pennant on last day of 1944 season 104

St. Louis Cardinals (NL, 1899–2019): 1, 6, 12, 13, 14, 15; Cardinals earned over $4 million in Breadon's 28 years as Cardinal President 117; Cardinals Radio Network formed 116–117; clinch 1926 NL pennant 65; clinch 1928 NL pennant 72; clinch 1930 NL pennant 76; competition with AL Browns for control of St. Louis 45, 46, 50–51, 58–59; defeat Boston Red Sox in 1946 World Series 115–116; defeat Brooklyn Dodgers in playoff for 1946 NL pennant 114–115; defeat New York Yankees in 1926 World Series 65–67; 1926–1931 achievements 79–80; 1930–1931 profits 73; 1932–1933 deficits 86; 1934 profits exceed $100,000 and convince Breadon baseball turned corner to economic recovery 89in 1985 and 1987 World Series 139; in 2004 World Series 146; in 2013 World Series 155; profits of 1928 season 71; repeat as NL champions in 1968 and in World Series 132; win 1931 NL pennant and World Series over Philadelphia Athletics 77–79; win 1934 NL pennant on last day of season and World Series over Detroit Tigers 87–89; win 1942 NL pennant on last day of season and World Series over New York Yankees 100–102; win 1943–1944 NL pennants 103; win 1964 NL pennant on last full year at new Busch Memorial Stadium 130–131; win 1967 World Series over Boston Red Sox 131–132; win 1982 World Series over Milwaukee Brewers 137–138; win 2006 World Series over Detroit Tigers 148–150; win 2011 World Series over Texas Rangers 152–154; in World Series of 1943 and 1944 All-St. Louis World Series 103, 104–106

St. Louis Dispatch: 23
St. Louis Globe-Democrat: 27, 100
St. Louis Post-Dispatch: 67, 68, 87
St. Louis Republican: 24
St. Louis Star: 67
"St. Louis Swifties": in Cardinals history 153–154; origins of nickname 98
St. Paul baseball team: 39
Salary Classification Plan 35
Sallee, Slim 48, 49
San Diego Padres (NL): in 2005–2006 NLDS with Cardinals 146, 148
San Francisco Giants (NL): runner-up to Cardinals in 1967–1968 NL pennant races 129, 132; in 1987 and 2002 NLCS with Cardinals 139, 145
Sanders, Ray 98, 99, 102–103, 106, 110
Schildt, Mike 155
Schoendienst, Red 21, 112, 120, 122, 123, 128, 133, 134, 135, 141
Schuble, Heinie 70
Schultz, Barney 125–126
Schumaker, Skip 151
Scott, Dred 2
Shannon, Mike 125, 127, 131
Shantz, Bobby 125
Shea Stadium (New York): 148
Sherdel, Bill 63, 64, 65, 66, 75
Simmons, Curt 124, 126
Simmons, Lou 29
Simmons, Ted 137
Sisler, Dick 110, 111
Sisler, George 110
Skyway Motel (St. Petersburg, Fl.) 124
Slaughter, Enos "Country" x, 92, 96, 98, 99, 101, 102, 107, 108, 113, 114, 115, 116, 118–119, 120, 122
Smith, Lonnie 137, 138
Smith, Ozzie 135, 136, 137, 138, 139, 143
Smith, Red 53–54, 120
Smoltz, John 147
Sosa, Sammy 144
Sothoron, Allen 63
Sotomayor, Sonia 142
Southworth, Billy 62, 64, 65, 66, 71, 72, 94, 95, 98, 99, 108, 114, 118
Spalding, A.G. 29, 31, 32, 33, 34, 35, 37, 39
Spezio, Scott 147
Spink, Al 27, 30–31
Sportsman's Park (St. Louis, Grand Avenue, home of St. Louis Browns AA

197

Index

1882–1891; St. Louis Browns NL 1892; St. Louis Browns AL 1902–1953; St. Louis Cardinals NL 1920–1966, officially renamed Busch Stadium 1953–1966): 17, 18, 19, 27, 30, 31, 38, 40–41, 46, 47, 54, 63, 66, 72–73, 76, 79, 99, 191, 104, 110, 114, 115, 116, 121, 122, 126, 127, 143

Sportsman's Park (St. Louis, Vandeventer Avenue and Natural Bridge Road, home of St. Louis Browns NL 1893–1898): 17–18, 46

Stainback, Tuck 101
Stengel, Casey 98, 126
Stephens, Vern 106
Stockton, J. Roy 55, 67, 116, 117
Street, Gabby 73, 77, 82, 84, 117
Stuper, John 137, 138
Sutter, Bruce 22, 137, 138, 140
Sutton, Don 138
Syracuse (NY) farm club 56, 57, 60

Taguchi, So 149, 150
Taylor, Ron 127
tennis 10
Terry, Bill 87
Texas Rangers (AL): in 2011 World Series with Cardinals 152–154
Thevenow, Tommy 57, 61, 62, 64, 66, 70, 71, 74
Torre, Joe 134, 140, 141, 142
Triplett, Coaker 96, 98
Truman, Harry 119
Tudor, John 139
Turner, Frederick Jackson 26–27

Veeck, Bill 121
Verban, Emil 106, 109, 112
Virdon, Bill 122
Von der Ahe, Chris 16–18, 24, 27, 28, 29, 30–32, 34, 35, 36, 37, 38–39, 40–41, 46, 50
Von der Ahe, Edward 36

Waddell, Rube 46
Wainwright, Adam 147, 148, 149, 150
Walker, Bill 88
Walker, Harry "The Hat" 111, 116
wall ball 11
Wallace, Bobby 41
Ward, John Montgomery 35
Warneke, Lon 89
Washington baseball teams: in American League 40; in consolidation of National League and American Association 38; loses franchise when NL downsizes 40; Washington Nationals (NL) sweep Cardinals in 2019 NLCS and upset Houston Astros (AL) in World Series 156
Watkins, George 74, 76, 79, 84
Weaver, Jeff 147, 148, 149–150
Westbrook, Jake 152
White, Bill 124, 125, 126, 129
White, Ernie 99, 100, 101
Whitehead, Burgess x, 85
Wicker, Tom 107
Williams, Joe 88, 89
Williams, Ted 145
Wilson, Chief 50
Wilson, Jimmie 71, 82, 84
Wilson, Preston 149
Wood, Wilbur 81
Worrell, Todd 139
Wrigley Field (Chicago): 123, 155–156

Yankee Stadium (New York): 66, 101
Yastrzemski, Carl 131
York, Rudy 115

Zumaya, Joel 149

www.ingramcontent.com/pod-product-compliance
Ingram Content Group UK Ltd.
Pitfield, Milton Keynes, MK11 3LW, UK
UKHW042006140426
5217IPUK00015B/1019